Faith and Fermentation

Exploring Biblical Teachings and Baptist Perspectives on Alcohol

By
Gary E. Risenhoover

Published by Kinetic Digital Publishers

www.kineticdigitalpublishers.com

For permissions, inquiries, or other correspondence, please visit our website.

ISBN eBook: 979-8-90235-126-9

ISBN Paperback: 979-8-90235-127-6

ISBN Hardcover: 979-8-90235-128-3

LCCN: 2026908998

TABLE OF CONTENTS

Preface

In the gentle glow of an autumn twilight, imagine walking through an orchard where the heavy scent of ripened fruit mingles with the crisp whisper of falling leaves. Each tree stands as a sentinel to stories untold, stories of joy and restraint, of celebration and caution, of sacred tradition woven intricately with human frailty. It is in this twilight orchard, where faith and fermentation converge, that I invite you to journey with me. This book, *Faith and Fermentation: Exploring Biblical Teachings and Baptist Perspectives on Alcohol*, is born from a desire to roam these shaded paths with open eyes and a curious heart, seeking to understand the complex interplay between divine guidance and human experience surrounding one of life's most culturally loaded substances: alcohol.

Few topics within Christian discourse stir as much fervor, confusion, or quiet judgment as alcohol. This humble elixir, grape juice transfigured by time and nature into wine, barley fermented into beer, fruit brewed and distilled into spirits, has occupied a peculiar place within biblical narrative and denominational teaching alike. From the joyous wedding at Cana to the stern warnings etched within Proverbs and the sobering calls for temperance echoed in Baptist halls, alcohol symbolizes both blessing and peril, delight and discipline. For many believers, especially within the Baptist tradition, alcohol is a crucible of faith, a test of moral clarity, an emblem of sobriety, and, at times, a source of division. It is a subject ripe with tension, ripe for harvest, yet too often left untouched in meaningful conversation.

This book does not claim to have the final answer. Instead, it seeks to illuminate the shadows where scripture and tradition intersect and sometimes diverge, peeling back layers of historical context, theological reflection, and lived experience to reveal a richer, more nuanced picture. My hope is that this exploration will cultivate a space where believers and seekers alike can approach the subject not with judgment or fear, but with empathy, courage, and thoughtful reflection. The vineyard of faith has many branches, and it is time to savor the fruit of dialogue with reverence and joy.

At the heart of this endeavor lies a compelling tension: the biblical celebration of wine as a symbol of blessing, happiness, and divine provision contrasts sharply with the Baptist tradition's steadfast call to temperance, shaped by centuries of cultural, moral, and spiritual urgency. This tension is neither accidental nor easily resolved. Wine appears repeatedly in scripture as a gift to be enjoyed. Psalm 104 praises God for giving wine that "gladdens the human heart," while Ecclesiastes reminds us of the pleasure found in drinking with wisdom. Yet alongside these affirmations, there runs a steady current of caution and control, from the warnings against drunkenness to the admonitions that call for self-mastery. How do we reconcile these voices? How have Baptists navigated this terrain, often in a world whose attitudes toward alcohol shift with the tides of culture?

Within these pages, you will meet voices from diverse epochs and perspectives: the Biblical Scholar revealing the nuanced shades of ancient texts, the Baptist Theologian guiding us through denominational doctrines forged in fire and conviction, Contemporary Baptist Voices sharing stories from the frontlines of faith and daily living, and the Ecumenical Observer bringing a wider Christian panorama into view. Together, these narratives compose a symphony of insight, challenging us to move beyond simplistic dichotomies of sin and liberty toward a deeper understanding shaped by historical awareness, theological integrity, and pastoral sensitivity.

This book's structure mirrors the complexity of its subject. Chapters vary in length and focus, reflecting the dynamic nature of the conversation itself. Some sections plunge deeply into scripture; others trace the currents of Baptist history and theology; while still others dwell on culture, personal testimony, and ethical reflection. This variation is intentional, a rhythm of thought nudging the reader into moments of both scholarly contemplation and heartfelt engagement. Like wandering through the orchard, some trees invite prolonged study, others brief admiration, yet all contribute to the rich landscape.

You will find within these chapters a series of metaphors and images that gently beckon to our imaginations. The orchard itself is a guiding emblem, its fruit a testament to nature's bounty and the season's call to temperance. The twilight hour, neither fully day nor night, embodies the delicate balance we seek: between joy and restraint, celebration and sobriety, freedom and faithfulness. It is a space where complexities are not obscured but embraced, where tension becomes a catalyst for growth rather than division.

The journey here is not without challenge. Readers may find certain insights unsettling, some traditions questioned, and familiar doctrines reconsidered. This is the nature of honest dialogue, discomfort mingles with discovery. Yet the destination promises richer faith, greater unity, and more profound compassion. In a world too often polarized by extremes, *Faith and Fermentation* offers a pathway to harmony, encouraging us to listen carefully to scripture's whispers and Baptist convictions with equal reverence, and to craft a shared vocabulary that honors both.

In writing this book, I have sought to be a companion and a guide, never a judge nor an arbiter. My own faith journey is ongoing, shaped by encounters with sacred texts, spirited community debates, and the lives of those I have had the privilege to know. I am moved by the potential of this topic to foster empathy, illuminate truth, and nurture covenantal community. May these pages serve as a lantern, a gentle hand, and an open door, inviting you into a dialogue that is as much about grace as about guidance.

So, step into the twilight orchard with me. Let us walk among the vines where history, scripture, and tradition entwine. May we find there not only complexity but clarity; not only conviction but compassion; and not only discipline but delight. For in understanding the dance between faith and fermentation, we glimpse a fuller picture of God's grace, robust, nuanced, and ever inviting us into deeper communion.

Welcome to this exploration. May it enrich your heart, expand your mind, and deepen your spirit.

Introduction: The Intersection of Faith and Fermentation

Setting the Scene

Imagine standing at the edge of an orchard as twilight gently descends, where the fading light filters through boughs heavy with fruit, casting dappled shadows that dance with the subtle movements of the evening breeze. The orchard is a place of quiet mystery, a sanctuary at the borderline between day and night, where the vibrant energy of life slowly reclines into a tranquil pause. It is neither the unyielding brightness of noon nor the impenetrable darkness of midnight, but rather a liminal space infused with a soft glow that invites contemplation and wonder. In this orchard, every fruit is a story, every leaf a whisper of the intertwining of joy and restraint, of blessing and caution, of celebration and sobriety. This orchard at twilight serves as the heart of this exploration, a metaphor that seeks to illuminate the intricate terrain where faith and fermentation meet, where ancient texts and modern convictions converge, and where personal experience intertwines with communal belief.

In inviting you into this metaphorical orchard, the purpose is not to prescribe a single path through its rows or to pronounce a definitive verdict on the nature of alcohol within the Christian journey. Instead, it is to offer a landscape for reflection, one that acknowledges the fullness of biblical teaching and the depth of Baptist tradition while remaining open to the tensions and harmonies that arise from their encounter. The twilight hour, with its ambivalent light, suggests that this journey will not be one of stark binaries or simplistic answers, but rather one characterized by nuance, grace, and a willingness to dwell in complexity. Just as the orchard challenges a visitor to see beyond the surface of ripe fruit to the cycles of growth, harvest, and dormancy that govern life beneath the soil, so too does the topic of alcohol within faith require a pilgrimage beyond surface judgments into historical context, theological insight, and lived realities.

Alcohol, especially as represented by wine, the emblematic fruit of fermentation in Scripture, has long occupied a unique and often contested place within the Christian imagination. It is portrayed both as a divine blessing that brings joy and fellowship, and as a potential snare that leads to folly and destruction. Within the pages of this book, we will embark on a journey through the orchards of biblical narrative, poring over the rich soil of ancient texts that mention wine, strong drink, and their associated metaphors and admonitions. These references invite us to consider alcohol not merely as a social or culinary item, but as a deeply symbolic element embedded in the fabric of spiritual life. They challenge readers to wrestle with the dual reality that wine can be both a gift of God and a temptation to excess.

Equally, the journey necessitates an exploration of the Baptist tradition, a community rooted in a commitment to moral clarity and personal holiness that has often manifested in a cautionary, sometimes prohibitive stance toward alcohol. Baptists have historically championed temperance as a vital expression of faithfulness, grounding this ethic in concerns for health, witness, and social responsibility. Yet this tradition has also faced internal tensions, as well as external criticisms, regarding the interpretation and application of biblical principles on drinking. Here in this twilight orchard, the Baptist voice is both a custodian of deep convictions and a participant in an ongoing dialogue that questions how to harmonize scriptural teaching with cultural realities and personal conscience.

What, then, of the fruit borne in this orchard of faith and fermentation? It is the fruit of discernment, a crop that invites reflective pause rather than rapid consumption; the fruit of humility that appreciates mystery without succumbing to uncertainty; the fruit of joy tempered by reverence; the fruit of unity fostered amid diversity. The questions that gird this examination are many and profound: How do the biblical texts concerning alcohol illuminate or complicate our understanding of temperance and joy? In what ways has Baptist history shaped attitudes toward drinking, and how do contemporary voices challenge or reaffirm those attitudes? What role does cultural context play in shaping religious convictions about alcohol, and how might those convictions evolve without compromising core tenets of faith?

Envisioning these questions against the backdrop of the twilight orchard compels us to recognize that the relationship between faith and alcohol is far from monochrome. It is a palette of intertwined colors and shifting shades, much like the interplay of light and shadow that defines the orchard at dusk. This metaphor encourages us to appreciate the beauty of complexity without seeking to flatten it into easy absolutes. It also invites a posture of patient listening and respectful dialogue, an essential approach in a topic that often engenders sharp division within communities dedicated to love and unity.

Throughout these pages, you will encounter distinctive voices, each contributing unique perspectives to this orchard's rich mosaic. The author/narrator acts as a guiding hand, moving between ancient words and modern reflections, weaving together scholarship and spirituality with a heart attuned to grace. The biblical scholar brings expert illumination to the texts, untangling linguistic nuances, historical settings, and cultural underpinnings that deepen our appreciation for Scripture's references to alcohol and its uses. The Baptist theologian opens the lens onto denominational convictions, exploring the doctrinal frameworks that have long shaped Baptist responses while unpacking recent theological reconsiderations. Contemporary Baptist voices add texture and vitality through personal stories and diverse viewpoints, revealing the lived realities of negotiation between tradition and modernity. Finally, an ecumenical observer offers a broader Christian perspective, enriching the conversation by situating Baptist beliefs within the wider fellowship of the church universal.

This multiplicity of perspectives reflects the orchard itself, a place where different trees grow side by side, sometimes bearing fruit of contrasting flavors, yet woven into the same ecosystem. It is a reminder that within the community of faith, unity does not necessitate uniformity, and truth need not be confined within narrow boundaries. Rather, faith grows healthiest when nurtured by dialogue that respects differences and searches for common ground.

The twilight orchard metaphor also calls us into a spiritual posture akin to that of a contemplative wanderer, one who does not rush to consume the fruit indiscriminately but who savors its textures and tastes, mindful of both sustenance and the potential for indigestion. It is an invitation to heartful engagement that transcends judgment and embraces empathy. Recognizing the cultural weight and personal dimensions that surround alcohol within Christian life, this book encourages readers to explore their own convictions with openness and courage, to confront assumptions, and to discover deeper waters of faith where moral clarity and compassionate understanding intermingle.

In the shifting light of this orchard dusk, the interplay of shadow and radiance becomes a metaphor for the tension and harmony that characterize the discourse on alcohol among believers. Shadows remind us of the risks, addiction, broken relationships, and the erosion of witness that accompany misuse, while the soft illumination, speaking to wine as a symbol of God's provision, joy, and communal blessing, urges us not to dismiss its rightful place in life's celebrations and sacred rituals. Together, these elements craft a landscape of spiritual richness and ethical challenge, demanding wisdom to navigate paths that neither fall into reckless indulgence nor rigid prohibition.

As you embark on this journey, consider the orchard as a sacred laboratory of faith, where Scripture's ancient words meet the evolving story of the Baptist community and where personal testimony intertwines with theological reflection. It is a field ripe for harvest, filled with the aroma of old vines and the promise of new insights. Within its borders, you are invited to ponder who you are as a believer or seeker in relation to these themes, to wrestle honestly with questions that may unsettle or affirm, and to emerge with a more textured grasp of how faith steers moral decisions about alcohol.

This book is, thus, an exploration of both head and heart, of tradition and experience, of the seen and the unseen. It recognizes that the discussion surrounding alcohol in the Baptist faith is not merely an abstract theological exercise but a lived reality, one that touches family dinners, church fellowship halls, moments of celebration, and times of sorrow. It acknowledges the deeply personal nature of these convictions, while also affirming the communal implications of how faith communities counsel one another in love and truth.

To dwell in the orchard at twilight is to reckon with the paradoxes and promises embedded in the intersection of faith and fermentation. It beckons us to a journey marked by listening as much as speaking, humility over certainty, and grace in place of judgment, an invitation to inhabit the mystery with eyes wide open and hearts fully engaged. May this metaphor guide you through a rich terrain of discovery, encouraging both steady footing and open horizons, as together we explore how ancient wisdom and contemporary faith might blend into a harvest of understanding and unity.

So, let us step forward into this orchard, committed to savoring its fruit with reverence and joy, mindful always of the delicate balance between delight and discipline. May this twilight place become, for each reader, a space of reflection and renewal, where faith and fermentation join hands in a dance as old as Scripture, yet ever new in its expression through human hearts. Here begins our journey, not toward simplistic conclusions, but toward a more profound embrace of the complexities that shape our walk with God, our community, and the gifts of creation, including the cup that holds the fruit of the vine.

Why This Conversation Matters

In the quiet hours of evening, as the sun dips gently beyond the horizon and the orchard, laden with ripened fruits, bathes in the soft glow of twilight, a certain kind of contemplation unfolds. It is in this metaphorical orchard that we begin our journey, a place where faith and fermentation intertwine in a dance of complexity, beauty, and caution. This orchard is not just a patch of land but a vivid landscape of human experience, a fertile ground where joy, temptation, restraint, and reverence all find expression and meaning. Why, then, should we concern ourselves with this intersection, faith and alcohol, in a world spinning rapidly under the weight of social change, cultural clashes, and evolving spiritual landscapes? What makes this conversation not only relevant but urgent today?

At first glance, alcohol might appear as merely a cultural or social concern, something relegated to dining tables, celebratory toasts, or moments of personal indulgence. Yet beneath this surface lies a profound spiritual and ethical dimension that calls for thoughtful reflection. For those of us standing within the walls of faith traditions, especially within the Baptist heritage known for its historical stance on temperance, the subject is neither trivial nor tangential. Instead, it is a matter pregnant with significance, woven intricately into the fabric of daily living, personal choices, communal identity, and theological conviction. The metaphorical orchard at twilight reveals itself as a place of paradox, where the sweetness of the fruit tempts, but the shadows warn, and invites us to explore its branches with both reverence and critical eyes.

The relevance of this exploration emerges from several converging realities. First and foremost is the pervasive and undeniable presence of alcohol in human culture. Across centuries and civilizations, wine, beer, and other fermented beverages have held roles that range from sacramental to social, from medicinal to sinful. The Bible itself, a foundational text for Christians and especially Baptist communities, is replete with references to alcohol, and yet these references are complex, sometimes celebratory, sometimes cautionary. This duality mirrors the lived human experience, where alcohol represents joy and fellowship but also risk and ruin. Engaging with these biblical texts, therefore, is not a mere academic exercise but a necessary act of wrestling with the sacred and the profane in our own lives.

Moreover, the contemporary world amplifies the urgency of this dialogue. In an age where alcohol-related issues, whether addiction, health consequences, or moral struggles, frequently surface in public discourse, silence or simplicity fails the depth of the problem. For faith communities, especially those with a legacy shaped by strong temperance teachings, the questions are many: How do we remain faithful to our scriptural heritage without ignoring the nuanced realities of individuals and communities? How do we balance warnings against excess with acknowledgment of moderation's place? What does spiritual maturity look like when applied to ethical decisions about drinking? These questions resist easy answers, demanding a framework of thoughtful engagement rather than divisive absolutism. By situating our discussion within the orchard at twilight, we acknowledge complexity without capitulation, light without losing shadow.

Another aspect underscoring the contemporary relevance is the shifting posture of many within the Baptist tradition concerning alcohol. Historically, Baptist communities often embraced abstinence, associating alcohol consumption with moral peril and social harm. Yet, as society evolves, so do theological interpretations and pastoral practices. Voices rise from within Baptist circles, advocating for renewed perspectives that move beyond prohibition towards responsible stewardship, informed by grace and personal conscience. This internal dynamism challenges not only denominational norms but also invites wider ecumenical conversations. Against this backdrop, the significance of our conversation becomes clearer: it is a crossroads where history, scripture, culture, and personal faith converge, prompting renewal and reflection.

Additionally, this dialogue touches deeply upon broader themes vital for spiritual formation and communal health, faith and morality, joy and discipline, unity and diversity within the body of Christ. These themes transcend any single issue, and, in exploring alcohol through a faith-based lens, we gain insight into how faith shapes not just ritual practice but the very ways believers navigate complex moral terrain. The orchard metaphor elegantly encapsulates these tensions and harmonies: each fruit offers sweetness, yet the orchard as a whole invites vigilance. Wine can be a blessing, signifying God's provision, enriching communal celebration, and even serving sacramental purposes, yet it can also become a snare if misused. Thus, reflecting on alcohol through faith forces us into a richer understanding of our commitments to holiness, love, and neighbor.

The conversation also holds significant pastoral implications. Within local Baptist churches and faith communities scattered across diverse contexts, members come bearing varied experiences and convictions regarding alcohol. Some may wrestle with the consequences of addiction, others may come from cultures where drinking is normalized, and yet others may seek spiritual guidance on how to engage social settings. Confronting these realities with sensitivity and wisdom fosters spaces of healing, acceptance, and accountability rather than judgment or alienation. The book that unfolds here aims to illuminate these experiences, offering voices from the contemporary Baptist landscape whose testimonies breathe life into the conversation beyond theological abstraction. It is precisely because this topic touches so many lives, from personal struggles to communal celebrations, that we must face it openly and thoughtfully.

Furthermore, the conversation holds ecumenical significance that extends beyond Baptist borders. Christian traditions, varying widely in their approaches to alcohol, share Scriptures yet interpret them divergently. By embracing a spirit of dialogue, we open windows into mutual understanding, recognizing that unity does not demand uniformity but a shared commitment to grace and truth. Comparing Baptist perspectives with those of other denominations helps illuminate the assumptions and convictions shaping our beliefs. Our orchard, then, is not fenced but part of a broader vineyard where grapes grow in different soils, producing wines distinct yet interconnected. Awareness of this wider Christian context enriches our exploration, prompting humility and learning.

In contemporary society, the cultural attitudes toward alcohol are also undergoing transformations that bear watching. With changes in laws, social norms, and health-awareness campaigns, the landscape is shifting. Some contexts celebrate craft brewing and wine tasting as art forms; others emphasize sobriety and wellness movements; and still others grapple with public health crises tied to misuse. This vibrant, sometimes volatile milieu demands that faith communities engage with clarity and compassion, navigating a world where the proverbial orchard's fruits may be more accessible, and sometimes more fraught, than ever before. Ignoring or retreating from these realities risks disconnecting faith from lived experience or failing in its call to offer wisdom amid cultural currents.

On a personal level, exploring alcohol through a faith-based lens invites believers and seekers into a deeper spiritual journey. It challenges assumptions, invites self-examination, and encourages reliance on divine guidance amidst ambiguity. Faith is often thought of in terms of doctrines or worship, but it permeates every facet of life, inviting questions about how we honor God in the choices we make, choices about what we consume, how we relate to others, and how we steward our bodies and communities. The metaphor of the orchard at twilight eloquently captures this spiritual tension: the desire to savor sweetness alongside the call to discern shadows. Traversing this terrain requires courage, humility, and openness to transformation.

This journey likewise urges us to reconsider what it means to embody the fruit of the Spirit in our daily lives when it comes to alcohol. Patience, self-control, gentleness, and love are not abstract virtues but lifelines that sustain us amid temptation and complexity. These qualities illuminate a path beyond simplistic verdicts toward a mature faith that honors freedom and responsibility in tandem. By rooting our reflections in Scripture, tradition, and lived reality, this conversation fosters spiritual depth and practical wisdom.

Moreover, in grappling with the ethical dimensions of drinking, we confront broader questions about the role of faith in public witness and social responsibility. How does the church, as a community called to embody Christ's love, respond to issues like addiction, impaired judgment, and social harm connected to alcohol? What prophetic voice can it raise in a world where excess and exploitation often mark alcohol's shadow side? Exploring these questions does not lead us to easy answers but invites a posture of compassionate engagement and justice-seeking. Our faith calls us to be both stewards of grace and advocates for the vulnerable, standing beside those harmed by misuse and celebrating the goodness of God's creation when rightly appreciated.

This conversation also matters because it speaks to the heart of Christian unity and fellowship. Divergent views on alcohol have historically fueled division within churches and denominations, creating fault lines of judgment and separation. Yet the call of the gospel is toward reconciliation and peace, an invitation to dwell in the orchard together despite differing tastes and temperaments. Embracing this conversation with openness and humility models what it means to honor the unity of the Spirit amid theological diversity. It becomes a microcosm of the Christian journey itself: navigating tension without fracturing, loving without condoning harm, and celebrating freedom without abandoning discipline.

In this light, the pages that follow offer more than theology or history; they offer a bridge, a meeting place at the edge of day and night where we can look honestly at faith and fermentation, appreciating their intertwined stories and enduring mystery. They invite readers into a communal reflection where questions are not shunned but welcomed as signs of a living faith wrestling with the realities of this world. Whether one approaches the topic from a place of certainty or curiosity, personal struggle or pastoral care, the invitation is to enter the orchard, heart wide open.

Ultimately, why this conversation matters is because it touches, in profound ways, the daily lives of faith communities and individuals seeking to live faithfully in a complex world. It shapes how we understand scripture, how we relate across differences, how we embody holiness in the mundane, and how we extend grace to others and ourselves. In embracing the nuanced dance of faith and fermentation, we join a timeless tradition of spiritual seekers walking the line between restraint and rejoicing, body and soul, shadow and light. This is not a mere theological sidebar but a central terrain where faith is tested, refined, and deepened.

So, as twilight envelops the orchard and the first rustling of evening breeze whispers through the branches heavy with fruit, we stand invited to pause, listen, and begin this exploration. We do so not to resolve every tension or to silence dissenting voices but to hold them tenderly within a greater narrative of faith, hope, and love. We embark knowing that the questions raised here, about the role of alcohol in life and faith, are as old as the vine and yet forever new, calling us into a journey marked by discovery, respect, and transformation. It is in this spirit that we begin, together, within the orchard at twilight, ready to savor the sweetness, heed the shadows, and walk forward toward a deeper communion with God, self, and community.

Overview of the Book's Approach

As you begin this exploration, imagine stepping through the gates of a sprawling orchard at twilight, where the soft glow of the setting sun casts elongated shadows between rows of fruit-laden trees. This orchard is no ordinary garden; each tree, branch, and fruit represents the layered and often ambivalent relationship between faith and fermentation, particularly within the context of biblical teachings and the Baptist tradition. The fruit hanging heavy from these trees is as varied as the perspectives you will encounter, a nuanced harvest of joy, caution, celebration, and restraint, all intertwined beneath the canopy of divine revelation and human interpretation. This metaphorical orchard invites you, the reader, to wander with attentive eyes and a reflective heart, discovering the richness of this topic without hastening toward simple answers or quick judgments.

This book's approach is rooted in patience and dialogue, refusing to succumb to either rigid prohibitionism or uncritical acceptance. Instead, it seeks a middle ground where complexity is embraced, questions are welcomed, and the diverse seasonal fruits of scripture, tradition, and lived experience are fully tasted and appreciated. From the very start, the intention is not merely to instruct but to nurture a space where faith and scholarship coexist, where reverence for the sacred text meets honest grappling with historical realities and modern challenges. Our journey will thread through ancient vineyards and early Christian fermenting techniques, passages from the Old and New Testaments where wine alternately symbolizes blessing and folly, and centuries of Baptist voices who have wrestled with these same questions amid shifting cultural tides.

This book is constructed as a carefully layered narrative, one that invites you to move through it in stages rather than rushing to a tidy conclusion. The structure has been deliberately varied to mirror the orchard's uneven terrain. Some chapters are expansive, inviting you to linger and absorb the depth of theological reflection and historical detail;

others are more concise, offering fresh perspectives or personal testimonies that punctuate the scholarly dialogue with warmth and immediacy. By alternating chapter lengths and subchapter depths, the reading rhythm itself becomes a pedagogical tool, reflecting the ebb and flow of conviction and doubt, certainty and curiosity that often accompany discussions about faith and alcohol.

Central to this methodology is the triangulation of voices woven throughout the narrative. The author's guiding voice acts as your thoughtful and empathetic companion, grounding the journey in a clear-eyed yet compassionate interpretation of scripture, combined with an openness to diverse viewpoints. Alongside this narrator stands the Baptist theologian, whose insights illuminate the denominational convictions rooted in moral clarity and a centuries-old commitment to temperance. These theological contributions do not merely restate dogma but engage with scripture and history dynamically, revealing both the strengths and limits of traditional Baptist perspectives. Complementing this is the biblical scholar, a voice steeped in the ancient world, who draws back the curtain on cultural, linguistic, and historical contexts often overlooked but vital for understanding the biblical references to wine and other fermented beverages in their original intent and reception.

Then there are the contemporary Baptist voices, whose stories and reflections disrupt any monolithic understanding. These are men and women whose lives are animated by personal struggles and triumphs around faith, alcohol, and community engagement, voices that catch the glittering interplay of grace and discipline as they negotiate real choices in complex social landscapes. Their testimonies provide not only anecdotal richness but also a grounding reality check, reminding us that doctrine and scripture meet flesh-and-blood believers navigating joy, temptation, healing, and reconciliation. Finally, the ecumenical observer broadens our lens to include how other Christian traditions have engaged with alcohol, offering comparative insights that often challenge Baptist assumptions and enrich the dialogue. This multiplicity of perspectives frames the book not as a proclamation of truth but as an invitation to a shared and respectful exploration.

Throughout this journey, the guiding questions remain at the heart of the narrative: How do the biblical texts speak about alcohol, and what do they mean in our contemporary context? How has Baptist theology, rooted in a profound concern for holiness, community well-being, and moral discipline, shaped attitudes toward alcohol, sometimes in ways that seem at odds with scripture's varied portrayals? What tensions exist between faith and cultural practice, between joy and restraint, between individual liberty and communal responsibility? By posing these questions upfront, the book acknowledges the discomfort and diversity of opinion that often accompany discussions of alcohol within Baptist and broader evangelical circles. Yet, it does so without shying away from the difficult edges, embracing tension as fertile soil for spiritual growth rather than a wedge for division.

The methodological emphasis is, therefore, one of balance: between explicit scriptural study and theological interpretation, between historical context and contemporary application, between personal narrative and academic analysis. Every chapter is designed to challenge assumptions, invite reflection, and foster a spirit of reconciliation and understanding. For example, scriptural passages celebrating wine as a divine gift, such as the joyous feast in Ecclesiastes or the miracle at Cana, are given careful exegesis alongside warnings found in Proverbs and the sobering imagery of drunkenness leading to folly and destruction. This duality is preserved rather than resolved simplistically, mirroring the orchard's mixed bounty, where ripe and tantalizing fruit grows alongside leaves that hint at decay if neglected or misused.

When turning to the Baptist tradition, the narrative traces the denomination's historical roots in a culture deeply shaped by calls for temperance as a sign of moral and spiritual integrity. Here, the methodology includes tracing primary documents, sermons, and doctrinal statements, revealing how Baptist leaders over time have articulated concerns about alcohol's capacity to harm both individual souls and the fabric of the community. Yet, it also explores moments of nuance and diversity within Baptist history, sometimes surprising instances where moderate use was tolerated or even celebrated, challenging caricatures of an absolute prohibition stance. The inclusion of contemporary voices within the denomination serves to highlight ongoing debates and evolving perspectives, grounding the historical survey in present-day concerns and lived experience.

In the more reflective chapters, this methodology expands to a cultural and ethical examination, inviting readers to consider how societal shifts, from the temperance movements of the 19th and early 20th centuries to today's multifaceted alcoholic marketplace, have influenced religious attitudes and moral judgments. This approach recognizes that neither scripture nor tradition can be read in isolation but must be interpreted amidst the changing social realities that believers inhabit. It also raises probing ethical questions about sobriety, moderation, personal freedom, and communal well-being that every reader must wrestle with in their own context. This interplay between the personal and corporate, the timeless and the timely, is intentionally highlighted to provoke careful discernment rather than easy answers.

To ensure engagement and accessibility, the writing style throughout balances scholarly rigor with heartfelt reflection, eschewing dense jargon in favor of clear, vivid prose, rich with imagery and metaphor. The orchard at twilight is a recurring motif used to remind readers of the beauty and ambiguity inherent in this topic. The metaphor evokes not only the passage of time but also the coexistence of light and shadow, the recognition that faith journeys often traverse moments of clarity and uncertainty, joy and sobriety, celebration and reflection. This style invites you to linger in the orchard's ambiance, to ask questions freely, and to savor the complexity rather than bypass it.

Moreover, this book's structure encourages reflection and dialogue by varying lengths and formats within chapters. Some sections offer extended theological and exegetical discussions, while others provide brief vignette-style personal narratives or concise summaries. This dynamic pacing is designed to mirror the reader's own thought process as they digest new information, pause for contemplation, and integrate fresh insights. Embedded throughout are occasional reflective questions and prompts, intended as gentle invitations to internal dialogue or group discussion. The aim is not to mandate a particular conclusion but to cultivate a thoughtful and empathetic community of readers grappling with these perennial questions together.

In essence, approaching this book is akin to savoring a fine vintage, allowing the complexities and subtleties to unfold gradually, emerging from layers of historical depth, theological reflection, scriptural nuance, and lived experience. Each chapter contributes a new flavor, a new aroma, further enriching the overall bouquet of understanding. While some may approach the topic cautiously, seeking reassurance or clear moral guidance, others may arrive ready to challenge inherited assumptions. Regardless of initial stance, the hope is that this journey through the twilight orchard of faith and fermentation will deepen your appreciation not only for the subject itself but for the larger spiritual vocation of navigating tension, ambiguity, and grace.

By the end of this book, you will have encountered a spectrum of interpretations and testimonies, seen how the Baptist tradition wrestles with alcohol from both historical and contemporary vantage points, and engaged in a nuanced conversation that honors scripture's multifaceted witness. The narrative will invite you to consider how your own faith informs your views, how community shapes your convictions, and how dialogue can transform polarized debates into opportunities for mutual understanding. In doing so, it will help build bridges where there have long been walls, allowing the human heart and divine wisdom to meet amid the orchard's fading light, where the sweetness of the grape mingles with the sobering shadows of twilight.

Thus, this book's approach is intentional, holistic, and invitational. It is not a manifesto nor a polemic; it is a companion for seekers wishing to navigate the labyrinthine relationship between faith and alcohol with open minds and compassionate spirits. In reading these pages, you step into an orchard vibrant with history and hope, where every fruit is a story, every shadow a lesson, and every moment a chance to learn how faith, with its rich traditions and timeless truths, can gently guide and transform our encounters with the intoxicating mystery of fermentation. Welcome to this journey, may it be as illuminating as it is enriching, as challenging as it is comforting, as complex as it is profoundly human.

Gary E. Risenhoover

Biblical Foundations: Alcohol in Scripture

Old Testament Perspectives

In the vast and intricate tapestry of the Old Testament, wine emerges as a symbol rich with both blessing and warning, woven deeply into the fabric of Israel's spiritual and cultural narrative. The ancient texts reveal a nuanced attitude toward fermentation, reflecting a society intimately familiar with the grape's transformative potential, a metaphorical and practical expression of joy, vitality, and the divine gift of creation, alongside a thoughtful restraint that underscores the human propensity for excess and folly. The Torah and the prophetic writings together present a balanced perspective, illuminating the sacred and the profane dimensions of wine, compelling believers, then and now, to consider its place not simply as a beverage but as a bearer of spiritual significance.

Beginning with the Torah, the Pentateuch, we encounter the earliest reflections on wine in the foundational stories of Israel. The narratives of Genesis, Exodus, Leviticus, Numbers, and Deuteronomy provide a backdrop where wine is more than mere sustenance, it is an emblem of God's benevolent provision and the fertility of the Promised Land. One of the most notable instances appears in the story of Noah, whose vineyard symbolizes a new beginning after the flood, a restoration of human civilization and divine favor. The wine Noah produces is the first recorded in the biblical canon, signaling both the familiar and the mysterious properties of fermented grape juice. Here, wine stands as a testament to the cycle of life and renewal, but also as a prelude to the complexities it introduces, the vulnerability to intoxication and the moral dilemmas it can provoke. The text does not shy away from illustrating the paradox: Noah's subsequent drunkenness and shame serve as an implicit cautionary tale, evoking both the blessing and the risk inherent in wine's allure.

Moving further into the Torah, wine reappears in laws and rituals that formalize its role within Israelite religious life and social customs. The Mosaic legislation in Leviticus and Deuteronomy touches upon wine indirectly, emphasizing sobriety for priests and the sanctity required in worship, as well as reinforcing hospitality customs that often included sharing wine at communal meals and celebrations. Wine was central during the Passover feast and other festivals, symbolizing rejoicing in God's deliverance and providence. Yet, these celebrations also carried an implicit call for moderation, a theme woven subtly across the text and given particular weight in priestly rules that underscore the importance of clear-mindedness and holiness. The Torah thus portrays wine as a blessed gift meant to enhance life and worship, examined alongside the imperative to live in disciplined reverence before God.

The poetic voice of the Old Testament further elevates wine's imagery, especially in the Psalms and Solomon's Song of Songs. While outside the direct scope of the Torah, these writings are deeply connected to Israel's early scriptural heritage and enrich our understanding of wine's spiritual and cultural symbolism. Psalms celebrate wine as a source of gladness and spiritual refreshment, underscoring its role in expressing joy and divine blessing. The Song of Songs, a lyrical love poem imbued with intoxicating imagery, uses the metaphor of wine to express passion and delight, alluding to the sacred pleasure and beauty woven into human relationships. These poetic portrayals, though celebratory, are balanced with sober reminders of wine's potent power, the intoxicant that can ensnare if consumed without wisdom.

The prophetic literature then provides a compelling counterpoint, unveiling a voice of caution that resonates throughout Israel's history, especially during periods of moral decay and societal upheaval. Prophets like Isaiah, Amos, Hosea, and Micah intertwine wine imagery with themes of justice, repentance, and divine judgment, reflecting the complexities of its social and spiritual implications. For example, Isaiah speaks of the "cup of trembling" and the "cup of God's wrath," where wine becomes a metaphor for the coming judgment against unfaithfulness and oppression. This potent symbolism transforms the familiar drink into a harbinger of divine retribution, blending earthly experience with heavenly admonition. The prophetic writings remind Israel that wine, while a gift, can also symbolize the consequences of sin, an agent revealing the moral state of the nation.

In Amos, the prophet's denunciation goes further, condemning excessive indulgence in wine as symptomatic of social injustice and spiritual blindness. The wealthy oppressors' revelry and drunkenness become inseparable from their neglect of the poor, portraying wine not just as a personal temptation but as a communal indictment. Here, wine's cautionary aspect sharpens, emphasizing that intoxicating pleasure, when divorced from ethical responsibility, leads to decay and divine disfavor. Hosea's lament also uses wine metaphorically to describe Israel's infidelity, illustrating a people intoxicated with idolatry and unfaithfulness to Yahweh. In this way, the prophets transform the discourse on wine from one of mere consumption to a profound commentary on covenant faithfulness and societal integrity.

Micah's poignant imagery of the "wailing of the winepress" combines agricultural reality with apocalyptic vision, suggesting the bitter consequences that arise when people trample on righteousness and justice. The winepress, a literal tool for crushing grapes into wine, becomes a metaphor for divine judgment pressing upon a rebellious people. This duality, wine as both joy and judgment, permeates the prophetic corpus, offering a complex portrayal that challenges simplistic assumptions. Wine is never merely alcohol; it is a symbol laden with theological and moral weight, demanding discernment from the faithful.

Beyond metaphor, the daily life and social customs of ancient Israel shaped biblical attitudes toward wine. Archeological and historical studies indicate that wine was a common and esteemed part of meals, religious offerings, and social gatherings, viewed as a cultivated fruit of the land that expressed gratitude toward God's provision. The climate and terrain of the Levant were conducive to viticulture, making wine accessible to many strata of society. However, the biblical narrative consistently parallels cultural acceptance with the ethical call to avoid overindulgence. Proverbs, often regarded as wisdom literature stratified alongside the Pentateuch in canonical order, elaborates this tension emphatically. The writer extols wine for its capacity to "gladden the heart," yet issues dire warnings against the "strange woman" of wine that ensnares and leads the naive astray, portraying intoxication as a pathway to destruction, a theme echoing the cautionary notes of the Torah and prophets.

Within these ancient texts, restraint emerges as a cardinal virtue. The ideal Israelite is depicted not as one who shuns wine altogether but as one who masters it, who drinks judiciously without surrendering to its illusions. This balanced approach seeks to honor the divine gift embedded in wine's creation while guarding against the spiritual and social harm that abuse inflicts. Ritual purity laws, priestly codes, and the prohibition of strong drink for Nazarites and certain officials articulate this concern at the highest levels of religious life, enforcing sobriety as a visible marker of holiness and devotion.

The Torah's influence extends beyond purely religious injunctions into the broader moral ethos of Israelite society, projecting values that reverberate throughout later biblical literature and into the Christian tradition. Its portrayal of wine as both a blessing and a potential snare reflects a theology deeply grounded in the human experience of temptation, discipline, and grace. Through its narratives and laws, the Torah invites believers to participate in sacred agriculture, the cultivation of not only the soil and vine but also of the inner life, where faith tempers desire and joy walks hand in hand with self-restraint.

In sum, the Old Testament's references to wine reveal an ancient people's complex relationship with a gift of nature that encompasses delight and danger, celebration and sobriety, covenant and judgment. Its writings resist simplistic reduction, offering instead a rich palette that portrays wine as a divine provision to be embraced with wisdom and an instrument of moral reflection when misused. The Torah and the prophets together shape a biblical vision inviting ongoing contemplation: to partake from the cup of blessing, not the cup of destruction; to celebrate God's bounty while holding fast to the disciplines of faith. This profound tension continues to challenge and inspire, inviting every generation of believers to navigate the delicate dance between faith and fermentation with reverence and resolve.

New Testament Views

In the tapestry of New Testament Scripture, wine emerges not merely as a beverage but as a profound symbol and a tangible element woven into the life and ministry of Jesus as well as the apostolic community that followed him. To comprehend the New Testament views on wine, one must immerse oneself in the dramatic encounters where wine serves both as divine provision and a mirror reflecting the complexities of human nature. The miracle at Cana, a scene brimming with symbolic resonance, stands as the inaugural public sign of Jesus' ministry, where the transformation of water into wine speaks volumes beyond the surface. This miraculous act, recorded with purposeful detail, reveals a God intimately involved with creation's good gifts, celebrating life's joys and blessings. Far from condemning wine outright, Jesus' initial miracle elevates the fermented grape's product into a sign of abundant grace, signaling that divine intervention is not devoid of joyful participation in earthly pleasures. The choice of wine, rich, robust, and often the drink of significance in cultural and religious festivities, was deliberate, affirming that the sacred and the celebratory are not mutually exclusive realms. This moment also subtly challenges later interpretations that would dismiss wine entirely, framing the fermented fruit as integral to the divine-human encounter.

Yet, the narrative does not shy away from wine's double-edged potential. Numerous teachings and parables throughout the Gospels cautiously acknowledge the dangers that accompany indulgence and excess. Jesus himself warns of the perils of drunkenness and moral laxity, intertwining ethical clarity with the broader theme of stewardship over one's body and spirit. The apostolic letters, flowing out of the early church's experiences and struggles, further refine this delicate balance. Paul, writing to various communities, does not outright forbid the consumption of wine but rather emphasizes moderation, self-control, and the avoidance of causing others to stumble in their faith. The apostle's admonitions recognize the cultural norms surrounding wine while urging believers to live distinctively, maintaining a witness that honors both personal sanctity and communal well-being. His counsel that "wine is a mocker," drawn from Old Testament wisdom, is echoed with measured concern, yet he also advises Timothy to use a little wine for medicinal purposes, underscoring a pragmatic approach rather than blanket prohibition.

In the Eucharistic traditions recorded by the Synoptic Gospels and Paul's letters, wine attains a sacred quality, becoming the blood of Christ, symbolizing covenantal renewal, sacrifice, and eternal life. This elevates wine from a mere drink to a sacramental element, steeped in theological depth and spiritual significance. The shared cup becomes a unifying emblem within the early Christian community, binding participants in a collective memory that transcends the material to touch the divine. Here, the fermented grape transforms into a conduit of divine grace, sacrificial love, and communal identity. The profound paradox encapsulated in this sacrament, a substance that, in excess, can destroy, yet, in measured use, mediate grace, invites believers into a nuanced appreciation of wine's biblical role.

However, the New Testament is not oblivious to the social realities surrounding wine consumption. The early church situated itself within a Greco-Roman milieu where drinking customs varied widely, from the restrained to the licentious. Against this backdrop, scriptural authors warn against behaviors that compromise witness or foster dependency. The pastoral epistles contain exhortations to temperance and vigilance, portraying drunkenness as antithetical to holy living and effective ministry. This ethical emphasis extends beyond individual conduct to communal responsibility, urging believers to cultivate environments where love, care, and mutual respect temper societal excesses. These teachings reflect a spiritual realism rooted in compassion, acknowledging human frailty while offering a higher calling to moral integrity and self-governance.

Moreover, the New Testament narratives reflect the complex interplay between Jewish heritage and emerging Christian identity concerning alcohol. Jewish festivals and rituals often incorporated wine as a symbol of joy and covenant fidelity, creating a theological framework that early Christians inherited but also reinterpreted. Jesus' participation in these celebratory occasions, and his reinterpretation of their meaning, points to a continuity and transformation, wine is not abolished but sanctified anew within the Kingdom paradigm. This dynamic invites a reexamination of wine's place not only as a cultural artifact but as a living signifier within the Christian story, one that accommodates both celebration and caution.

The nuanced witness of New Testament scripture, therefore, resists simplistic readings. It invites believers to engage wine with reverence and discernment, recognizing its capacity to enhance life and symbolize divine blessings while remaining vigilant against its potential to harm. In the hands of Jesus and the apostles, wine becomes a metaphor for the fullness of life in God's grace, a life marked by joy, sacrifice, and communal harmony. It is a mystery of both abundance and restraint, offering a spiritual lesson in balance and intentionality.

As we survey the apostolic teachings, the letters from Paul and others further reveal an awareness of alcohol's cultural weight and ethical implications in the nascent church. Believers were neither hermetically sealed from society nor blindly assimilated; instead, they navigated a path that upheld Christ's lordship over all areas of life, including matters as seemingly mundane as drinking. The apostolic voice consistently urges that all things, wine included, are to be engaged in a manner that reflects the new life in Christ, mindful of the Spirit's guidance and the community's witness. The epistle to the Ephesians, for example, forbids drunkenness, urging instead to be filled with the Spirit, indicating a transformative alternative to the empty excess often associated with alcohol. This contrast underscores the New Testament's ethical vision that places spiritual vitality over physical gratification.

Beyond the letters, the Book of Revelation introduces symbolic references to wine that further enrich the thematic tapestry. The vision of the wrath of God poured out like wine upon the sinful earth paints a stark picture of divine justice, suggesting that wine can also signify judgment and consequence. This dual imagery, wine as blessing and as wrath, evokes the full spectrum of human experience and divine response. It reminds readers that the symbol of wine in Scripture is neither univocal nor simplistic but complex and layered, capable of embodying grace and judgment, joy and sober reflection. This complexity invites believers to engage thoughtfully with their traditions, understanding wine not just as a physical substance but as a rich symbol that speaks to the depths of faith.

Within the New Testament, the social and communal dynamics surrounding wine are equally telling. The earliest Christian gatherings, often held in homes around meals, incorporated wine as part of shared fellowship and ritual. These communal meals were more than sustenance; they were acts of theology in practice, embodying unity, hospitality, and the anticipation of the Kingdom. The use of wine in these contexts is a tangible means of participation in the life of Christ and the community, reinforcing relational bonds and spiritual hope. Yet, these settings also demanded careful attention to inclusivity, prompting considerations about the impact of wine consumption on the vulnerable and those struggling with temptation. This sensitivity reveals a pastoral heart attuned to the well-being of all members, advocating love and mutual respect as guiding principles.

The New Testament, through its layered and multifaceted engagement with wine, ultimately presents a theology that balances celebration and sobriety, blessing and caution, symbol and substance. It does not cast wine as inherently sinful or pure but situates it within the broader context of human responsibility and divine grace. Jesus' miracles and teachings highlight the covenantal and communal significance of wine, while apostolic instructions mold these themes into practical wisdom for believers navigating a complex social world. The sacredness imparted to wine in the Lord's Supper further elevates its status, transforming it into a sign of profound spiritual realities that transcend mere consumption.

In this exploration, the New Testament encourages readers to view wine through a lens shaped by faith, moral awareness, and cultural context. It affirms the possibility of enjoying God's gifts with gratitude and joy while maintaining vigilance over the potential pitfalls of excess, addiction, and harm. This tension holds the promise of a mature, balanced faith, one that does not reject the good gifts of creation but engages them in the transformative light of the Gospel. Thus, New Testament views on wine invite us into a hospitality that is both celebratory and discerning, a faith that savors life's fullness with reverence and care.

Cultural and Historical Context

The presence of alcohol in ancient societies, especially as it pertains to the Bible, is a compelling and often misunderstood element that requires careful excavation through the layers of time, culture, and theology. To fully appreciate the biblical references to wine and fermentation, one must immerse oneself not only in the sacred texts but also in the multifaceted world from which these texts emerged. Ancient Near Eastern civilizations, including those of Israel's neighbors and predecessors, embraced fermented beverages as vital aspects of daily life, religious ceremony, and social order, shaping the texture of existence in ways that are sometimes lost to modern readers. Wine, in particular, carried an ambivalent character, simultaneously embodying blessing and danger, joy and caution; it was a symbol both of God's generous creation and human frailty. Understanding this duality requires a journey into the soil where vines were cultivated, into the festivals where wine was poured for gods and people alike, and into the homes where families navigated the pleasures and perils of fermentation alongside their neighbors.

In the ancient Near East, from Mesopotamia across to Egypt and the Levant, fermented beverages had long been appreciated not only for their intoxicating effects but also for their nutritional and ritual significance. Archaeological discoveries reveal wine jars in palace cellars, sacrificial contexts, and burial sites, testifying to the beverage's broad role in social and religious life. The production and consumption of wine were intertwined with agricultural rhythms and the religious calendar, often serving as a metaphor for divine blessing and human prosperity. In Israelite culture, the grapevine was among the most cherished cultivated plants, symbolizing the land's fertility and the covenantal relationship between God and his people. The vine's fruit was pressed into wine that would enliven feasts and offerings, bearing witness to God's provision. However, this very availability and blessing came paired with explicit wisdom literature and prophetic admonitions cautioning against excess and the degradation that could follow.

The biblical narrative reflects this cultural context with remarkable nuance. The Old Testament contains numerous passages where wine appears as a gift from God, emblematic of joy, celebration, and health. Psalm 104 extols God's provision of wine "that gladdens the heart of man," and Isaiah envisions an eschatological time when the mountains will drip with sweet wine, signaling renewal and peace. Proverbs includes admonitions warning that wine is "a mocker" and "a brawler," illustrating divine wisdom that recognizes wine's capacity both to delight and to destroy. The story of Noah's vineyards following the flood, or the celebratory drinking after harvest festivals, underscores an ancient worldview that embraces wine as a complex but integral aspect of life. Yet, nestled beside these affirmations are stern warnings. The Book of Proverbs and the prophetic writings continually remind the faithful of the dangers of drunkenness, portraying it as a source of folly, social upheaval, and even spiritual blindness. These texts present a delicate balance that honors the positive presence of wine while soberly confronting its potential for misuse.

Turning to the New Testament, the cultural role of wine continues to echo within a rapidly shifting religious and social landscape. Wine remains a customary element of meals and religious observance, carrying forward its Old Testament connotations of blessing and community. Jesus' first public miracle at Cana, transforming water into wine, is a powerful narrative moment, signaling celebration, transformation, and the inauguration of a new covenant. This episode invites readers to understand wine not simply as a commodity but as a symbol of divine abundance and joy. At the Last Supper, the shared cup of wine takes on a sacramental dimension, embodying Christ's blood and the establishment of a new covenant in his life and death. This ritual imbues wine with a sacred presence that transcends everyday consumption, placing it at the heart of Christian worship and theology.

Nevertheless, the New Testament is also candid in its portrayal of alcohol's potential for harm. Warnings by Paul, such as admonishing Timothy to "no longer drink only water but use a little wine for the sake of your stomach and your frequent ailments," suggest a practical medicinal application of wine while emphasizing moderation, not excess. The epistles contain several exhortations to avoid drunkenness, pointing to self-control, sobriety, and the maintenance of moral witness as essential virtues for the Christian community. The contrast between the celebration of wine as a gift from God and the warnings against abuse remains a thread woven through the early church's teaching, reflecting a continuity with the ancient wisdom underpinning Israelite tradition.

The surrounding Greco-Roman world also shapes the New Testament's cultural context of alcohol. Roman society's engagement with wine was deeply entrenched and socially significant, with symposiums, public banquets, and daily meals incorporating wine in ways that conveyed status, conviviality, and philosophy. While wine was widely consumed, excessive drinking could provoke social disapproval and regulation, balancing enjoyment with restraint. The early Christians inherited this milieu with its particular norms and controversies, negotiating a path that held to both continuity with cultural practices and the radical reorientation of values under Christ. This tension surfaces repeatedly in Scripture and early Christian writings, signaling the need for discernment in the face of familiar pleasures turned potentially dangerous when abused.

Beyond the texts themselves, ancient methods of winemaking and storage contribute to understanding the biblical imagery and attitudes. Fermentation was a natural, often imperfect process, less predictable than modern industrial methods, producing beverages varying from weak to potent. The terminology used in the Bible reflects diverse preparations, wine could be sweet, sour, or mixed with water or spices, each variant carrying different social and symbolic connotations. This reality complicates any simplistic modern equation of biblical references to alcohol with contemporary spirits or commercial products. Likewise, societal roles influenced drinking practices: elders, priests, and leaders often moderated their consumption as signs of wisdom or discipline, while celebrations could be raucous affairs where wine flowed freely, yet sometimes chaotically.

The socio-economic dimensions of alcohol further nuance its scriptural presence. Wine was both accessible and a marker of status, as vineyards represented wealth and productivity. Sharecroppers, laborers, and elites alike engaged with wine in distinct ways, embedding it into class dynamics and communal identity. Festivals and sacrifices routinely involved offerings of wine, linking agricultural bounty with divine favor and political loyalty. This nexus of economy, religion, and community life forms the backdrop against which biblical texts articulated their visions of wine as blessing and burden alike.

One cannot neglect the symbolic depth of wine across biblical genres. Prophetic literature frequently employs the imagery of winepresses and vats to depict divine judgment, with the crushing of grapes mirroring the crushing of nations under God's hand. Hymnic and poetic texts exalt wine as part of the good creation, a foretaste of heavenly joy, while wisdom literature cautions about wine's role in the moral life. Together, these layers create a tapestry of meaning wherein wine is not merely a beverage but a theological and ethical touchstone.

Throughout this exploration, it becomes clear that ancient societies understood alcohol through a prism both practical and spiritual, celebrating its gifts while guarding against its ruin. The biblical authors, shaped by this milieu, reflect a profound awareness that fermentation, like faith itself, is a process of transformation requiring stewardship, reverence, and clarity. As such, the scriptural portrayal of alcohol embraces complexity: wine is life-giving and cooling, festive and sacred, a symbol of blessing and a potential snare. This duality invites readers across millennia to wrestle with both the delights and dangers inherent in this ancient and enduring fruit of the vine.

As modern readers engage with these texts, appreciating their cultural and historical context allows for a richer understanding of the biblical witness on alcohol. Recognizing that ancient fermentation was embedded in relationships of community, worship, and daily sustenance helps to dismantle simplistic binaries of prohibition or permissiveness. Instead, it opens a space where faith and fermentation sit together as intricate, intertwined elements of human experience and divine revelation. This perspective is crucial for contemporary believers wrestling with their own convictions about alcohol, as it offers a foundation shaped by nuance, scholarship, and respect for the biblical narrative's depth.

In conclusion, the cultural and historical context of alcohol in ancient biblical societies reveals a world where wine functioned not only as a drink but as a symbol laden with spiritual significance and social meaning. The biblical texts reflect this ambivalence, celebrating wine as an expression of God's providence while simultaneously warning of its potential for harm. This balance invites us to approach the scriptural message with careful attention to both the blessing and caution inherent in the tradition. To understand wine in Scripture is to enter an orchard at twilight, where each ripe grape tells the story of joy, restraint, and reverence, a story whose sweetness and bitterness mingle to enrich the tapestry of faith.

Theological Interpretations: Blessings and Warnings

Wine as a Symbol of Blessing

Within the rich tapestry of biblical narrative and symbolism, wine emerges not merely as a common beverage of antiquity but as a profound emblem of blessing, joy, and divine favor. To understand wine's multifaceted role within Scripture, and by extension, its spiritual significance, one must journey beyond the mere physicality of fermented grape juice to embrace the layers of meaning that the biblical authors intended and that faith tradition has long cherished. From the vineyards of ancient Israel to the convivial feasts depicted in both Old and New Testaments, wine is woven into the fabric of worship, celebration, and covenantal relationship, signifying blessings that transcend the temporal and touch the eternal.

The positive connotations surrounding wine in biblical literature are evident across myriad passages that celebrate its presence at moments of communal rejoicing and personal gratitude. In the Psalms, for instance, wine is lifted up as a gift of God that gladdens the heart, a liquid joy that imbues feasts with warmth and camaraderie. The Psalmist writes of God preparing a table before His people, anointing their heads with oil, and filling their cups to overflow, images that speak of abundance and divine generosity, with wine acting as a tangible sign of God's providential care. It is no accident that wine so often accompanies the Psalms of thanksgiving and victory, serving as a metaphor for the fullness of life granted by God's kindness and mercy. The intoxicating gladness of wine parallels the joy that springs from experiencing divine presence and deliverance, reminding believers that earthly pleasures, when rightly appropriated, reflect heavenly realities.

More than a mere catalyst for revelry, wine's biblical symbolic weight also lies in its connection to covenant and sacred ritual. The Hebrew Scriptures describe occasions where wine is poured out as a libation, part of sacrificial offerings that ratify solemn promises between God and His people. The act of sharing wine in these contexts is deeply relational, embodying the bonds of trust, fidelity, and blessing that underpin the divine-human encounter. At the heart of these rituals is the recognition that blessing involves both giving and receiving; wine, as a gift of the earth, transformed by human hands, captures this dynamic interplay. It reminds worshipers that God's blessing flows freely, yet also invites responsible stewardship and gratitude.

This sense of wine as a sign of blessing finds its most iconic expression in the New Testament narratives surrounding Jesus and the Eucharist. The accounts of the Last Supper reveal wine as the blood of the new covenant, a symbol of salvation poured out for many. Here, wine transcends earthly hospitality and becomes sacramental, sealing a relationship of grace and atonement. Jesus' first recorded miracle at Cana likewise elevates the status of wine, transforming water into the finest vintage and thereby revealing the kingdom's abundance and joy. This miracle, laden with symbolic resonance, suggests that the messianic era will be marked not only by spiritual renewal but by deep human delight. Wine, therefore, signifies not only physical refreshment but the overflowing joy and fruitfulness of life in God's presence.

Delving deeper into scriptural insight, it is essential to recognize the moral dimensions tied to wine's symbolism. Biblical texts do not uncritically celebrate alcohol; rather, they acknowledge its capacity to bless and to betray, to bring joy and to invite excess. Yet the positive portrayals always present wine within a framework of balance and discernment, underscoring that true blessing arises only in temperance and proper context. For example, Proverbs advises the wise to enjoy wine in moderation, warning against the folly of overindulgence that leads to destruction. This ethical dimension is not a denial of wine's goodness; on the contrary, it insists that blessing and responsibility coexist. The moral texture of biblical wine imagery teaches that the joy wine imparts must be tempered by reverence and self-control, framing a wholehearted yet disciplined approach to God's gifts.

The celebratory role of wine is also intimately connected to the theme of covenantal joy that characterizes biblical worship. Festivals such as Passover and the Feast of Tabernacles are occasions when wine punctuates the liturgy and meal, reminding participants of God's deliverance and their ongoing communal identity. The wine cup, lifted and shared, is an outward sign of belonging and gratitude, a ritual act binding generations in memory and hope. This sacramental use of wine resonates deeply with the metaphor of the orchard at twilight, a place where ripened fruit is gathered in the golden light, symbolizing harvest, fulfillment, and the gentle balance of nature's gifts. In this light, wine epitomizes how temporal delights, harvested from the earth's bounty, can stir the soul toward the eternal, inviting believers into a rhythm of joy and restraint reflective of divine order.

Moreover, the spiritual significance of wine as an emblem of blessing is enriched when we consider its role in prophetic literature and wisdom traditions. Prophets frequently employ imagery of wine to illustrate both judgment and salvation, excess and restoration. While wine is at times a metaphor for impending doom when abused, it also serves as an optimistic symbol of future restoration and renewal, promising an age where joy will flow unabated from God's hand. The juxtaposition of wine's potential for blessing and destruction calls readers to a heightened awareness of God's holiness and the ethical demands of faithfulness. This tension, observable throughout Scripture, elevates wine from a mere drink to an icon of the covenant, both a gift to be treasured and a responsibility to be honored.

The positive spiritual connotations of wine extend into its contribution to fostering community and human connection. Within the biblical worldview, shared meals and cups of wine are relational acts that affirm identity, build fellowship, and celebrate communion with God and neighbor. The baptismal meal and early Christian agape feasts, as recorded in the New Testament, often included wine as a sign of unity and mutual care. Such moments reveal that wine's blessing is not limited to the individual's pleasure but is intimately connected to the well-being of the community. In this way, wine functions symbolically as a conduit of grace, both divine and interpersonal, reminding believers that spiritual health flourishes in the context of loving relationships and shared life.

Interpreted through the lens of faith, wine's positive connotations challenge contemporary readers to see beyond contemporary biases or fears surrounding alcohol. While modern Baptist traditions frequently emphasize abstinence as a mark of personal holiness, the biblical portrayal of wine as a blessing offers a complementary perspective: one that honors joy, celebration, and the sacredness of God's created gifts. This vision does not discount the risks but suggests that the moral and spiritual use of wine can be a means of reflecting the abundant life promised by Christ. The vineyard and its fruit become metaphors for God's providential care, calling believers to both delight and discipline in their engagement with creation.

Some contemporary voices within Baptist circles have begun to reclaim this biblical affirmation of wine's place within faith. They emphasize that understanding wine as a symbol of blessing invites a mature and grace-filled approach that integrates joy without guilt and restraint without repression. Such perspectives articulate a faith that embraces God's blessings holistically, recognizing that human flourishing includes celebrating the goodness of God's earth and participating in the communal rhythms of worship and fellowship marked by the vineyard's fruit. This approach fosters an ethic of grateful moderation, where wine's blessing is neither glorified nor demonized but appreciated as a spiritual gift to be carefully stewarded.

In the broader Christian tradition, wine's positive symbolism resonates deeply, uniting believers around shared narratives of covenant and grace. Its use in the Eucharist, its role in sacred story, and its presence in daily life remind the faithful that blessing often comes disguised in ordinary elements. It challenges believers to cultivate a spirituality that finds the divine in the commonplace and celebrates life's sweet moments with reverence. At the same time, wine functions as a mirror reflecting the condition of the heart, its potential to be a blessing depends on human intention and God's sustaining grace.

Thus, the spiritual significance of wine as a symbol of blessing within Scripture is complex and rich, encompassing joy, covenant, community, and moral responsibility. It is a testament to the biblical imagination's ability to embed sacred meaning in everyday experience, encouraging believers to approach life's gifts with both delight and discernment. Wine becomes a metaphor for the fullness of God's blessing, overflowing, life-giving, and deeply relational, inviting each generation to savor the divine presence in the fruit of the vine while honoring the call to wisdom and temperance. In this way, faith and fermentation entwine in a sacred dance, revealing the depths of blessing that accompany a life lived in gracious balance.

Warnings Against Excess

Amid the rich tapestry of biblical references to wine and fermented drink, one thread consistently warns against the perilous edge of excess, the descent into drunkenness, which Scripture portrays not merely as a physical failing, but as a profound moral and spiritual hazard. The biblical texts, imbued with poetic nuance and theological urgency, frame drunkenness as a multifaceted transgression that undermines individual dignity, disrupts communal harmony, and distances the soul from divine favor. This portrait of alcohol in the biblical worldview is complex: wine emerges as a gift, a symbol of joy and celebration, yet it simultaneously carries the potential for harm when embraced without restraint, embodying excess that leads to ruin. To apprehend this tension fully, we must delve into the vivid admonitions and narrative accounts that illuminate the consequences of drunkenness, tracing both the immediate social disorder it causes and the more insidious spiritual blindness it fosters.

Within the Old Testament, warnings against intemperance abound, underscoring the ancient community's awareness of alcohol's double-edged nature. Proverbs, a book rich in wisdom literature, repeatedly emphasizes the folly of excessive drinking. It speaks not only of the impairment of physical and mental faculties but also of the loss of honor and self-control. "Do not join those who drink too much wine or gorge themselves on meat, for drunkards and gluttons become poor, and drowsiness clothes them in rags" (Proverbs 23:20–21) vividly depicts the degradation that follows overindulgence, linking it directly to poverty and ruin. The imagery here is stark: the well-dressed figure, symbolizing social esteem and self-respect, stripped to rags by reckless appetite. This visual narrative warns readers that drunkenness is not a mere personal weakness but a pathway to social marginalization and moral decay.

The Book of Isaiah offers dramatic language when addressing this issue. In Isaiah 5:11–12, the prophet condemns those who "rise early in the morning to run after their drinks," who "stay up late at night till they are inflamed with wine," all the while neglecting their duties. These verses convey a powerful ethical indictment: the inebriated are depicted as neglectful citizens, whose impaired judgment leads to societal disorder. The imagery of rising early, ostensibly to seek sustenance, but instead pursuing intoxication, conveys the idea that drunkenness perverts the natural rhythms of life, twisting worship and work into empty or selfish pursuits. It suggests a fundamental inversion of priorities, where devotion to God and community is replaced by a self-centered indulgence in drink.

This message resonates across the biblical corpus, reinforcing the idea that excess drinking is not an isolated sin but one with wide ramifications.

Further entrenched in this moral matrix is the depiction of drunkenness as a veiled form of idolatry and spiritual blindness. Ephesians 5:18 instructs believers not to be "drunk with wine, which leads to debauchery. Instead, be filled with the Spirit." This New Testament exhortation elevates sobriety beyond mere self-control, linking it to spiritual vitality. Drunkenness, by contrast, is portrayed as a surrender to a power that dims clarity and fosters moral erosion. The apostle Paul's words articulate the spiritual consequences of excessive drinking: it dulls the conscious attunement to God and neighbor, opening a pathway to "debauchery," a term laden with implications of chaos and moral looseness. The contrast here is stark and purposeful: to be "filled with the Spirit" suggests a fullness of life, consciousness, and purpose rooted in divine presence, while drunkenness is a filling of emptiness, a surrender not to God but to fleeting, destructive impulses.

Extending beyond individual moral failure, biblical narratives often depict drunkenness as a cause and consequence of social distress, shame, and familial breakdown. The story of Noah in Genesis 9 provides a compelling example: after the flood, Noah becomes drunk, an event that leads to familial discord and disgrace. The text reveals layered symbolism, the first drinking episode recorded in Scripture, laden with ambiguity and a lesson. Noah's intoxication results in his exposure and subsequent humiliation by his son Ham, with repercussions rippling through the family line. This moment captures the vulnerability and confusion that excessive alcohol can elicit, tarnishing even those deemed righteous. It serves as a narrative caution, a proclamation that no one is immune to the dangers of drunkenness. The consequence is not only personal vulnerability but also relational fracture, illustrating the societal cost inflicted when self-control is abandoned.

In the prophetic literature, the role of drunkenness extends even to metaphors for national sin and judgment. The prophet Habakkuk, for instance, uses the metaphor of a man overwhelmed by wine to depict the inescapable consequences of excessive pride and injustice. The drunkenness here transcends the personal to become a vivid image of moral blindness inflicted upon a people or civilization straying from divine justice. The prophet's lament evokes a nation intoxicated, not on wine alone, but on its own self-destructive choices, blind to the peril ahead until calamity is inevitable. This metaphorical connection between drunkenness and societal downfall amplifies the biblical warning by situating individual excess within the broader sweep of communal decay. It invites readers to consider how unchecked indulgence and moral insensitivity can erode the very fabric of society.

Within the New Testament, the theme of self-control in the face of temptation is deepened, with Jesus' teachings frequently highlighting the dangers of loss of moderation. The parables and exhortations emphasize vigilance and preparedness, contrasting the wise steward who remains sober with the foolish one who is caught off guard by indulgence and distraction. Jesus' own transformation of water into wine at Cana celebrates wine's positive aspect, joy, hospitality, divine blessing, yet his ministry also warns implicitly against the misuse of such blessings. His call to "be wise as serpents and innocent as doves" (Matthew 10:16) aligns with the biblical tradition of moderation, urging followers to navigate the joys and risks of life with discernment and grace. The tension between joy and restraint in relation to alcohol underpins much of the biblical teaching on the subject.

Examining the epistles gives insight into the early church's grappling with alcohol's potential for harm. Paul's letters contain practical advice that underscores community well-being and individual responsibility. The admonition to avoid drunkenness in Romans 13:13, "Let us behave decently, as in the daytime, not in carousing and drunkenness", pairs sobriety with ethical living, linking personal choices to communal flourishing. In First Timothy, the counsel is more nuanced, advising Timothy to "stop drinking only water, and use a little wine because of your stomach and your frequent illnesses" (1 Timothy 5:23), revealing an acceptance of moderate consumption under certain conditions. Yet, this encouragement is carefully framed within a broader context that denounces drunkenness as sinful and socially disruptive, highlighting the importance of balance and wisdom. The early Christians were not in blanket prohibition but emphasized temperate use, always conscious of alcohol's capacity to both benefit and harm.

Drunkenness, then, is consistently equated with loss and danger in biblical texts, it brings on quarrels, reckless behavior, and a loss of honor. The book of Proverbs warns that "wine is a mocker and beer a brawler; whoever is led astray by them is not wise" (Proverbs 20:1), describing alcohol as a deceiving force that seduces the unwary and provokes conflict. The terminology here is compelling, the drink does not merely induce inebriation but mockery and brawling, personifying alcohol as a tempter with a will of its own, capable of leading people astray from wisdom. This personification serves to highlight the spiritual battle waged in the realm of human desires and the discipline required to live rightly.

Moreover, the metaphorical use of drunkenness extends beyond personal failing to symbolize those overwhelmed by sin and judgment. King Nebuchadnezzar's experience in Daniel 4, where he becomes like a beast for seven years after prideful excess, is narrated alongside his drunken debauchery, presenting intoxication as a symptom and expression of deeper spiritual fallenness and divine discipline. The story demonstrates how intoxication can be linked to hubris and punishment, illustrating the biblical theme that excess drinking can be both a cause and manifestation of estrangement from God's order. In such narratives, drunkenness is not a casual lapse but a symbol of catastrophic spiritual disorientation, a state to be avoided lest one lose not only worldly respect but spiritual footing.

The Psalms weave this theme into the fabric of personal lament and communal prayer. Psalm 107 recounts how some wander in deserts, hungry and thirsty, and "because of their dire straits he saved them from their distress." Verses that caution against drunkenness remind readers that those who "stagger like drunkards" fall into foolish ways and suffering. This mixing of metaphor and reality in the Psalms evokes a vivid emotional resonance; the staggering drunkard becomes emblematic of the vulnerable soul, susceptible to peril when restrained judgment fades. The Psalmist laments the frailty of humanity, yet also celebrates God's merciful intervention in delivering from the chaos wrought by folly and excess.

In the prophetic admonitions, the gravity of drunkenness is often interwoven with calls to repentance and restoration. The prophet Hosea juxtaposes Israel's spiritual adultery with drunken excess, implying that overindulgence in wine can be a reflection of alienation from God's covenant. Such abundantly used metaphors deepen the understanding that drunkenness is not merely a physical state but reflects a deeper spiritual condition, an unrooting from divine purpose and an embrace of worldly entanglement. This understanding enriches the moral texture of biblical warnings, provoking readers to see excess drinking as indicative of a wider spiritual crisis, one that requires restoration, not mere abstinence.

This biblical caution against excess extends into the symbolism of Sabbath and festival observances, where wine's role is sharply governed by measure and intention. In the joyful context of celebration, wine is embraced as a sacred element of communal delight, yet the intent and discipline around its use remain paramount. The narrative of the Passover, where wine is a ritual component, underscores that consumption must be within the bounds of remembrance and reverence. When these bounds are breached through drunkenness, the sacred is profaned, and the community's covenantal identity is threatened. This serves as a potent reminder that biblical temperance is not simply a personal virtue but sustains the communal and spiritual order.

Through this intricate web of admonitions, biblical writers reveal a consistent pattern: drinking wine or strong drink is often portrayed as natural and even good, yet always shadowed by the severe consequences of exceeding limits. Excessive drinking becomes a fissure through which sin, shame, and destruction enter both individual lives and the social fabric. This tension between celebration and caution underscores one of the Bible's deepest spiritual insights: genuine joy is inseparable from wisdom and self-control. The warnings against drunkenness demand that believers attend carefully to the stewardship of their desires and bodies, understanding that indulging without restraint imperils not only personal well-being but also the integrity of their relationship with God and community.

In sum, the biblical admonitions against drunkenness function as both practical guidance and profound spiritual teaching. They invite believers into a disciplined hospitality that honors God's gifts without succumbing to their dangers. They recognize the temptations inherent in human nature, the seductive yet destructive allure of excess, and they chart a course of temperance that fosters joy rooted in reverence, not abandon. Far from condemning the pleasures of drinking outright, Scripture's warnings reveal a deep care for human flourishing, a care that understands the fragile balance between delight and discipline, between celebration and self-denial. Through these warnings, the biblical worldview offers a timeless counsel: to embrace wine with gratitude and wisdom, never allowing it to become a snare that diminishes the soul or fractures the human community. This delicate balance invites ongoing reflection and humility, a guarding of the self, that resonates with believers as much today as it did in ages past.

Moral and Ethical Implications

Within the tapestry of biblical teaching, alcohol emerges not merely as a physical substance but as a profound symbol intertwined with the moral and ethical fabric of faith. The scriptures do not treat wine or fermented beverage consumption with a simplistic binary of right or wrong; rather, they engage with it in a nuanced manner that both celebrates its provision and warns against its dangers. This duality invites a deeper exploration of how scripture shapes enduring views on moderation and self-control, encouraging believers to navigate the landscape of joy and celebration without succumbing to excess and sin. The moral and ethical implications surrounding alcohol are thus wrapped in a complex interplay of divine blessing and human responsibility, a theme that resonates through both Old and New Testaments.

At the heart of Scripture's treatment of alcohol lies its association with joy and communal celebration. From the very first auspicious moments in biblical narrative, we see wine as a gift of divine benevolence. The vineyards of Israel, often portrayed as metaphors for blessing and prosperity, anchor this precious fruit in the spiritual imagination of God's people. Take, for instance, the Psalms, where wine is extolled for gladdening the heart, a symbol of God's generosity and the beauty of life that flourishes under His care. It is portrayed as a tangible manifestation of God's provision, a drink to be enjoyed in the fullness of life's blessings. This perspective locates alcohol not merely in the physical realm but as an emblem of divine favor, tied to the rhythms of fellowship, worship, and celebration. The wine at Cana, turned from water to the finest vintage, further cements alcohol's role as a sign of grace and joy in the ministry of Jesus, marking the inception of His public work in a moment brimming with festivity.

Yet, the moral compass of Scripture does not permit this celebration to drift unchecked into indulgence. The sanctified lens of faith discerns the shadow side of alcohol, its potential to enslave, destroy, and separate humankind from the very joy it promises. Proverbs, rich in wisdom literature, is unrelenting in its warnings against the overindulgence in wine. It calls the faithful to live cloaked in discretion, to eschew the folly of drunkenness, which clouds judgment and provokes strife. These admonitions are not cold legalisms but rather passionate entreaties from a

God deeply invested in the flourishing of human freedom and dignity. The biblical narrative reveals how excess leads not to happiness but to chaos: the weakening of self-control, the fracturing of relationships, and the perils of moral compromise. The imagery of intoxication is sometimes stark, staggering figures undone by folly, voices slurred, and honest judgment marred. The vividness of these depictions is a testament to the gravity of the consequences, prompting an ethical framework grounded in restraint.

This tension between divine blessing and human frailty is a cornerstone for understanding how scripture shapes the moral discourse on alcohol. The ethical demand placed upon believers is to embrace a posture of moderation, not merely for personal preservation, but as a witness to the transformative power of grace that fosters self-mastery. Paul's letters emphasize the fruit of the Spirit, where self-control stands among virtues that mark the life reconciled to God. Here, temperance becomes a sacred discipline rather than a restrictive rule. It is the visible manifestation of a heart attuned to God's will, a refusal to allow any earthly pleasure to become an idol or a stumbling block to spiritual integrity. In this light, moderation is less about legal limitation and more about an inner orientation that seeks the good of oneself and others, where joy is not diluted but refined by wisdom.

Moreover, the moral and ethical discourse surrounding alcohol in Scripture cannot be disentangled from its communal implications. Drinking, though enjoyed personally, belongs within the context of relationships and societal well-being. Scriptural exhortations repeatedly remind the faithful that their actions bear weight beyond private consequence; they ripple outward, influencing families, congregations, and the broader community. The Apostle Paul's counsel to the Corinthians concerning alcohol demonstrates this vividly. While acknowledging wine as a legitimate part of cultural and religious life, he warns against behavior that could cause others to stumble in their faith. Thus, the stewardship of alcohol consumption is anchored in love, responsibility, and accountability. The ethical Christian is called to a heightened sensitivity that surpasses self-regulation, tuning their heart to the needs and vulnerabilities of their brethren. By exercising moderation, they not only preserve their own spirit but also foster an environment of trust and mutual respect.

In the broader biblical worldview, alcohol occupies a symbolic space that reflects the moral trajectory of humanity itself, from blissful harmony to fractured existence. The vineyard serves as a metaphor not only for God's creative work but also for human stewardship and fallibility. Just as a well-tended vineyard flourishes and yields a harvest of delight, so too must humans tend their desires and impulses with conscientious care. The misuse of alcohol, likened at times to the unleashing of destructive forces, reflects the consequences of neglecting this divine stewardship. The prophet Isaiah's lamentations and warnings become parables of imbalance: excess that leads to immoral behavior, social injustice, and spiritual death. Yet, the hopeful resurrection of the vineyard theme points forward to restoration and redemption, urging faith communities to envision a future where joy and holiness are harmonized.

Interwoven with this symbolic discourse is the ethical challenge posed by the biblical witness to the dignity of the human person. Drunkenness is depicted not only as a personal failing but as an affront to the image of God within which every individual is created. To lose self-control under the influence is to forfeit a measure of the sacred freedom bestowed upon humanity. It diminishes one's capacity to love, to serve, and to reflect God's character in the world. Hence, the moral injunction against excess is deeply rooted in a theological anthropology that enshrines responsibility, both to oneself and to God, as intrinsic to faithful living. The ethical contours drawn by scripture reinforce the call to guard the sanctuary of the body and soul, to celebrate life's good gifts wisely, and to resist the lure of any addiction or bondage.

Furthermore, the biblical ethic surrounding alcohol invites reflection on the nature of sin and repentance. The Bible's candid portrayal of human weakness includes its encounters with temptation and failure. The occasional reference to wine-induced folly is balanced by the pervasive call to repentance and renewal. Within this ethical framework, grace remains the foundation, recognizing that while indulgence may lead to harm, restoration is possible through confession and transformation. The narrative is not one of unyielding condemnation but compassionate guidance toward healing and self-control that is empowered by the Holy Spirit. This balance between acknowledging human brokenness and offering hope underscores the relational dynamic between God and His people, a dynamic where moral discipline stems from love rather than fear.

It is this tension that informs the Baptist perspective, which has traditionally emphasized personal holiness and social responsibility in the sphere of alcohol use. Baptists, drawing from biblical admonitions and historical experience, have cultivated a theology that prioritizes ethical vigilance, advocating abstinence as a safeguard against the moral hazards embedded in intoxication. Yet, the moral foundation of this stance remains consistent with the biblical call to moderation and self-control, viewing temperance not as mere prohibition but as a spiritual discipline that honors God's intention for human flourishing. This perspective underscores the ethical mandate to protect oneself and the community from harm, to uphold the dignity of all persons, and to embody a faith that is responsible and socially engaged.

However, the ethical narrative is not monolithic. Scripture's rich and varied engagement with alcohol fosters an ongoing dialogue within faith communities about how best to live out these principles in contemporary contexts. The moral landscape surrounding alcohol use extends beyond mere personal choice into cultural, social, and pastoral realms, inviting believers into continuous reflection on how to reconcile scriptural wisdom with lived realities. The call to moderation and self-control thus becomes a dynamic journey rather than a fixed rule, encouraging a faith that is both discerning and compassionate, acknowledging diversity of experience and conviction while remaining anchored in the ethical vision of Scripture.

In sum, the moral and ethical implications of alcohol in biblical teaching invite believers into a profoundly thoughtful engagement with the gift and temptation of fermentation. It is a call to celebrate God's blessings with gratitude and joy while vigilantly guarding against the excesses that darken the soul and fracture communities. The scriptural mandate to embody moderation and self-control serves as a guiding light, illuminating the way toward a balanced spiritual life where faith and everyday practice coalesce in harmony. Wine, then, is more than a drink, it is a divine symbol, a moral test, and ultimately a sacred invitation to live in reverence, wisdom, and love. This balanced view, richly textured and deeply rooted in biblical truth, provides a foundation from which believers can navigate the complexities of alcohol with clarity, compassion, and conviction, fostering a faith that honors both joy and discipline in the pilgrimage toward holiness.

Gary E. Risenhoover

Baptist History and the Temperance Movement

Early Baptist Views on Alcohol

From the earliest days of the Baptist movement, the question of alcohol consumption emerged not only as a matter of personal conduct but as a significant marker of faithfulness and community integrity. The embryonic Baptist churches, forming in the turbulent religious landscape of seventeenth-century England, found themselves wrestling with moral, social, and theological challenges that inevitably included alcohol. To understand the foundation of early Baptist teachings on drinking, one must first grasp the complex interplay of doctrine, cultural context, and burgeoning social reform movements that shaped these formative convictions. Far from a mere reflection of individual preference, the Baptist emphasis on temperance sprang forth from a rich tapestry woven with fervent dedication to scriptural authority, a profound desire for holiness, and a drive to distinguish the community from a society often deemed morally compromised.

In the religious ferment that birthed the Baptist tradition, the roots of temperance were intertwined with the larger Puritan and Reformed milieu from which many Baptists emerged. The Puritan movement's intense concern with personal piety and social righteousness left an indelible mark. It is within this lineage of strict moral rigor that early Baptists inherited a cautious and often critical stance toward alcohol. Wine and spirits, though biblically acknowledged as blessings and symbols of joy, were considered susceptible to misuse and excess, threats not only to individual souls but to the spiritual health of the community. The earnest desire to live out a visible, exemplary holiness meant that believers were called to exercise self-control and avoid any behavior that might lead to temptation or scandal. From the outset, therefore, Baptists were orienting themselves toward a voluntary discipline where temperance was not merely advised but seen as an essential outworking of faith.

The transatlantic currents of the seventeenth and eighteenth centuries further animated this early Baptist posture. In England, the chaotic political and religious upheavals imbued the question of personal conduct with a heightened urgency. Baptists, who often faced persecution and social marginalization, were compelled to take a stance that reinforced internal cohesion and external witness. As congregations formed, their leaders began codifying expectations for members, and sobriety became a hallmark of the faithful. Notable early Baptist voices emerged, crafting sermons and treatises that intertwined biblical exegesis with practical exhortation. These figures drew heavily upon the New Testament emphasis on the fruits of the Spirit, particularly self-control, alongside Old Testament warnings against overindulgence and drunkenness. Temperance was presented not merely as a social virtue but as an indispensable element of the believer's sanctification.

Among the pioneering leaders who helped crystallize Baptist teachings on alcohol was John Smyth, often considered one of the earliest Baptist fathers. His vision of a regenerated church demanded holiness that extended to every facet of life, including the avoidance of intoxicants that could compromise one's testimony and spiritual focus. Smyth's commitment to believers' baptism by immersion also reflected a broader theological framework that insisted on the separation of the holy people from the profane world. Alcohol, then, was more than a personal choice; it was emblematic of a wider spiritual boundary defining the community. Such convictions, while rooted in scripture, were magnified by a sociocultural context that valorized sobriety as a countercultural statement, one that resisted the excesses of a hedonistic society.

As the Baptist movement migrated and blossomed in North America during the eighteenth century, its stance on alcohol was further shaped by the burgeoning evangelical awakening and the rise of social reform impulses. The Great Awakening instilled a sense of urgent personal conversion and holiness that reinforced temperance as an expression of true Christian renewal. Leading figures like Isaac Backus emerged, articulating a theology that harnessed revivalist zeal to promote moral reform, including caution or abstinence from alcohol. The realities of frontier life, where the availability of spirits often precipitated social disorder, gave practical impetus to these convictions. Baptist preachers wielded their pulpits as platforms not only for theological proclamation but for moral exhortation, inviting believers to envision temperance as a safeguard against the spiritual devastation wrought by excess drinking.

Indeed, in this era of awakening and reform, temperance among Baptists evolved into both a personal ethic and a communal standard. Baptist churches often established internal disciplines, such as church covenants and membership vows, which explicitly addressed drinking behavior. The notion that the church should be a sanctified people, visibly distinct and morally alert, galvanized efforts to curtail alcohol abuse within congregations and in the surrounding society. The rise of temperance societies, frequently intertwined with Baptist congregations, marked a shift from mere individual restraint to collective engagement. These societies were not secular clubs but spiritual disciplines incarnate, public testimonies that Baptists offered against the social ills believed to be propagated by alcohol. Thus, early Baptist temperance was both a confession of faith and an act of social witness.

The theological underpinnings that supported this were complex and compelling. Baptists, committed to the authority and sufficiency of scripture, wove together biblical admonitions with a lived ethic of holiness. On one hand, texts such as Ephesians 5:18, which warn against being drunk with wine but call believers to be filled with the Spirit, were foundational. On the other hand, the pervasive biblical motif of wine and joy was acknowledged, not ignored or condemned outright, but framed within the parameters of faithful moderation and avoidance of excess.

Early Baptists were, therefore, neither simplistic teetotalers by scriptural fiat nor indifferent to the cultural significance of fermented wine in biblical narrative. Their emphasis settled on responsible stewardship of the body and the potential spiritual hazards posed by alcohol's misuse. This balanced yet firm approach, enjoining both appreciation and restraint, became a defining feature of Baptist identity.

Simultaneously, the Baptists' radical commitment to religious liberty shaped their views. While firmly advocating temperance within their own communities, early Baptists were careful not to impose their convictions coercively upon the broader society. They championed voluntary Christian freedom, holding that each believer must answer to God regarding personal conduct. This nuanced position differentiated Baptists from other reform movements that tended toward legal prohibition or compulsory abstinence. It underscored the Baptist emphasis on conscience, individual responsibility, and the primacy of scripture as guidance rather than civil legislation as enforcement. Thus, early Baptist temperance was not born of authoritarianism but of heartfelt conviction and ecclesial care, guarding the purity and witness of the church while respecting the diverse freedoms of a pluralistic society.

Events and social realities throughout the eighteenth century only deepened this early Baptist approach. The deleterious effects of alcohol abuse on families and communities in America and England galvanized increasing advocacy for temperance, spurring Baptists to become early proponents of moral reform movements. Temperance was increasingly elevated as a distinct spiritual discipline, an act of fidelity to Christ that bore the fruit of self-command and charity. At the same time, the conflation of alcohol and moral decay became a cultural lens through which Baptists understood their mission in a world rife with temptation. The narrative of the believer as both witness and warrior against sin encompassed not only personal purity but social engagement, and alcohol was firmly positioned among the chief moral battlegrounds of the age.

Early Baptist teachings also engaged the communal dynamics of drinking, scrutinizing the social context in which alcohol was consumed. The convivial settings in taverns, where worldly distractions and sinful excess were common, were largely eschewed. Baptists urged their members to avoid environments where intoxication flourished and where the fragile bonds of Christian fellowship and witness might be compromised. This concern extended to the pastoral leadership of congregations, who were expected to model sobriety unequivocally. The intertwined relationship between moral example and communal discipline became a hallmark of Baptist ecclesiology, exemplifying how early Baptists viewed temperance as integral not merely to personal salvation but to the health and holiness of the body of Christ.

The trajectory of early Baptist thought on alcohol was not static. As the movement matured and spread, the diversity of experiences and contexts enriched the discourse. Some early Baptists, especially in rural or frontier regions, adopted a more cautious pragmatism, balancing cultural norms against spiritual priorities. Others, buoyed by revivalist fervor, embraced stricter prohibitions, advocating for total abstinence. The latter stance began to crystallize with the rise of nineteenth-century temperance movements, yet its roots were undeniably planted in the soil tilled by earlier Baptist theologians and congregations. This ebb and flow of interpretation and practice within early Baptist circles underscored a central tension, how to reconcile biblical teaching, denominational conviction, and complex social realities.

Integral to this evolving tapestry were the personal testimonies and pastoral writings recorded during the eighteenth century. Baptists frequently chronicled the struggles of believers grappling with alcohol-related temptations and consequences, embedding those accounts within sermons and church letters. These narratives highlighted the human cost of excess and the spiritual liberation found through temperance. They served as both cautionary tales and sources of encouragement, nurturing a culture where accountability and grace coexisted. The oral and written legacies of these testimonies formed a vital substratum that shaped congregational policies and individual behaviors alike.

Importantly, early Baptist teachings maintained a delicate balance between admonition and affirmation. While temperance was stringently upheld, moderate and responsible uses of alcohol, particularly wine symbolizing covenantal joy and sacred remembrance, were not categorically rejected. The Lord's Supper, central in Baptist worship, underscored this nuance. The fermented elements used in communion celebrated Christ's blood and the joy of salvation, affirming a theologically rich understanding of alcohol that transcended simple condemnation. This sacramental practice remained a steady counterpoint to the social and pastoral concerns informing Baptist caution, embodying a reverence that honored both tradition and temperance.

As the eighteenth century gave way to the nineteenth, the legacy of early Baptist views on alcohol continued to resonate, providing a solid foundation for subsequent temperance advocacy. It was within the crucible of these early teachings, imbued with scriptural fidelity, moral earnestness, and pastoral compassion, that the temperance ethos became indelibly imprinted upon Baptist identity. Far from a monolithic or simplistic stance, it was a complex and evolving conviction, shaped by biblical exegesis, cultural engagement, and heartfelt faithfulness. This dynamic heritage invites contemporary readers to appreciate not only the historical origins of Baptist temperance but also its enduring call to balance joy, restraint, and reverence in the lived experience of faith.

In essence, the early Baptist position on alcohol was a courageous and thoughtful response to the multifaceted realities of faith and society. It embraced the biblical narrative's full arc, from joyous blessing to prophetic warning, while navigating the perils and promises of a culture in flux. It was a stance born of deep scripture engagement and heartfelt concern for holiness, grounded in an ecclesiology that prized both freedom and responsibility. Early Baptists forged in the fires of religious upheaval and social change a vision of temperance as a vital expression of God's sanctifying work, one that continues to shape Baptist witness and dialogue today. This rich and textured legacy invites believers into a contemplative and compassionate engagement with faith and fermentation, one that honors tradition without rigidity and embraces grace without compromise.

Rise of the Temperance Movement

In the tapestry of nineteenth-century American society, where rapid industrialization, urban growth, and political change interwove with the fabric of daily life, the temperance movement emerged not merely as a crusade against alcohol but as a profound social reform rooted deeply in moral conviction and spiritual urgency. From its nascent beginnings, the movement found fertile ground within the Baptist tradition, whose adherents, galvanized by a call for holiness and social righteousness, became pivotal actors in driving the cause forward. The rise of the temperance movement cannot be separated from the broader cultural anxieties and shifting sensibilities of the era, a time when the effects of intemperance on families, communities, and the very soul of the nation were laid bare with stark clarity. In this social crucible, Baptists embraced temperance not only as a matter of personal piety but as an imperative for communal health, embodying a theology that fused the eternal and the earthly, sanctity and society, faith and public witness.

To comprehend the Baptists' embrace of temperance in the nineteenth century, one must first appreciate the theological soil from which this dedication sprouted. Baptist doctrine, historically emphasizing individual accountability, the authority of Scripture, and the transformative power of holiness, called believers to a life marked by moral clarity and discipline. Abstaining from alcohol was thus not merely a practical response to societal woes but a vivid proclamation of fidelity to divine commands and a testament to sanctified living. Yet, alongside this doctrinal framework lay a growing awareness of alcohol's corrosive effects beyond the spiritual realm. The social repercussions, domestic violence, poverty, broken homes, and public disorder became impossible to ignore, prompting Baptists to expand their concern from the private domain of the individual conscience to the broader public sphere. The temperance movement provided a platform where spiritual conviction coalesced with social activism, where sermons found echoes in petitions, and prayer mingled with reform legislation.

The rise of the temperance movement within Baptist circles thus occupied a liminal space between revivalism and reform, echoing the vibrant evangelical awakenings sweeping across the country but with a focused impetus toward moral legislation. Baptists were among the earliest and most fervent advocates of total abstinence, often surpassing other denominations in both fervor and organizational energy. This was not a mere reactionary stance but one incubated in decades of internal reflection and theological debate, which increasingly positioned alcohol as a barrier not only to personal holiness but to societal flourishing. The doctrines of sanctification and the visible church's purity demanded a decisive confrontation with what was understood as a demonic influence masquerading as benign pleasure. Baptists articulated their resistance through impassioned preaching, temperance societies, and the establishment of institutions aimed at rehabilitating those ensnared by intemperance. The growing network of temperance organizations often bore Baptist fingerprints, testifying to the denomination's deep investment in the movement's success.

Central to this movement were towering Baptist figures whose voices lent charismatic vigor and theological gravitas to the cause. Men like Lyman Beecher, though not denominationally Baptist, influenced many Baptists through his preaching and social activism, yet it was within Baptist homes and pulpits that the fire was kept alive and fanned. Leaders such as Francis Wayland and Richard Furman in earlier decades laid the groundwork by emphasizing social responsibility and the inseparability of faith and ethics, while later twentieth-century pioneers codified temperance as a denominational hallmark. The proliferation of Baptist publications, sermons, and educational materials disseminated a clear, uncompromising message that was rooted in Scripture and concerned with practical results. These leaders navigated the tension between pastoral care and prophetic challenge, often risking division within their congregations to uphold temperance as a moral imperative. Their stories reveal a complex interplay of conviction, cultural engagement, and personal sacrifice, underscoring that the temperance movement was no monolith but a vibrant conversation within the Baptist world, shaped by personalities as much as doctrine.

The societal context in which Baptists advanced temperance carried particular urgency, as nineteenth-century America wrestled with waves of immigration, urbanization, and shifting economic patterns that often inflamed anxieties about order and morality. Saloons and taverns became symbolic battlegrounds for competing visions of American identity and spirituality. For many Baptists, temperance was inseparable from the mission of Christianizing the nation and safeguarding the sanctity of home and family. The movement gained impetus from the burgeoning middle class, whose values aligned with evangelical Protestant ethics, and who viewed the moderation or elimination of alcohol as essential to progress and civility. The moral panic surrounding alcohol was undergirded by empirical observations of widespread social dysfunction, but it was likewise fueled by evangelical imaginations projecting a vision of a pure and prosperous America redeemed through faith and discipline. Baptist temperance advocates harnessed these currents, participating actively in conventions, public rallies, and legislative lobbying, animating a campaign that intertwined spiritual awakening with social reform.

Moreover, the organizational dimension of Baptist involvement was particularly remarkable, as temperance societies sprouted with Baptist leadership across the nation, interlacing with the denominational structure. Sunday schools, often dominated by Baptist influence, became arenas for inculcating temperance ideals among youth, inscribing these principles into the fabric of communal and familial life. The Women's Missionary Societies, growing in strength within Baptist circles, also became vital agents of temperance advocacy, embedding the movement within the rhythms of daily church life and women's expanding social roles. These organizational efforts reflected a broader trend of Baptist engagement with social reform movements, evidencing a theology that transcended isolated spiritual experiences to embrace social holiness, the idea that godliness manifests in just and compassionate societal relationships. Here, Baptists exhibited both innovation and tradition: leveraging new forms of activism while rooted in a theological conservatism that prized scriptural authority and personal conversion.

Yet, the rise of the temperance movement within Baptist ranks was not devoid of internal contestation and external critique. The movement was complicated by divergent regional experiences, theological interpretations, and social pressures. In the American South, for example, Baptists often balanced temperance advocacy with cultural traditions that included regulated social drinking, reflecting adaptations to local mores and economic realities. Debates raged within congregations and denominational bodies about the appropriateness of outright prohibition versus moderate use, with some factions warning against legalistic zealotry that might alienate believers or obscure the gospel's simplicity. Critics accused temperance advocates of fostering a spirit of control or moral superiority, challenging their assumption that legislation could successfully reorder hearts. These tensions illustrate that the temperance movement was a dynamic and, at times, contentious endeavor, a reflection of Baptists' attempts to navigate complex intersections of faith, culture, and power.

In tracing the Baptist temperance legacy, one encounters a complex mosaic of spiritual passion, social concern, and pragmatic reform. The movement's rise was marked by a blend of spiritual revivalism and emerging modern activism, an impulse to sanctify not only the individual soul but also the social order. The effort to curb alcohol's influence became a lens through which Baptists articulated broader commitments: to the sanctity of the home, the health of the nation, and the reality of divine rule in all spheres of life. Through sermons that framed temperance as a passport to moral and communal salvation, through organizational vigor that mobilized congregations and communities, and through personal witness that embraced sacrifice and resilience, Baptists indelibly shaped the contours of nineteenth-century American reformism.

This legacy, however, resists simplistic conclusions. The temperance movement, while inspired by a fervent desire for holiness, inevitably bore the marks of its cultural moment, its blind spots and breakthroughs, its divinely motivated zeal and its human imperfections. The entwinement of Baptist faith with temperance advocacy opened pathways for ethical engagement that continue to ripple into the present, inviting contemporary believers to ponder the intersections of faith, morality, and social responsibility anew. The nineteenth-century Baptist temperance crusade, with all its complexities and contradictions, stands as a testament to the power of religious conviction to animate public life and as an enduring chapter in the story of faith's encounter with fermentation.

Influential Baptist Leaders and Writings

Within the unfolding narrative of Baptist identity, the emphasis on temperance emerges not as a spontaneous mandate but as the fruit of a deeply rooted theological conviction intertwined with social consciousness. At the heart of this tradition stand towering figures whose insights, leadership, and writings sculpted the contours of Baptist temperance ideology, transforming it from a peripheral concern into a defining marker of faithfulness. These leaders, both pastoral and lay, engaged with the spiraling complexities of their times, cultural, moral, and spiritual, and their contributions resonate profoundly within contemporary Baptist reflections on alcohol.

One cannot begin this exploration without first acknowledging the indelible influence of figures like William Carey, often hailed as the "father of modern missions," whose embrace of sober living marked a significant moment in aligning evangelical outreach with personal holiness. Carey's conviction extended beyond missionary vigor to a lifestyle of disciplined temperance, which he viewed as essential in bearing witness to the transformative power of the gospel. His writings and correspondence reveal a man who understood that moral clarity was inseparable from spiritual authenticity, particularly within a colonial milieu rife with social upheaval and moral ambiguity. Carey's example set a precedent that saw temperance not simply as a private virtue but as a public testimony, a theme that would permeate Baptist consciousness in subsequent generations.

Following closely is the impact of Andrew Fuller, a contemporary of Carey, whose theological rigor and pastoral sensitivity crafted a vision of Christian living that seamlessly wove doctrinal orthodoxy with practical devotion. Fuller's extensive works emphasize the believer's sanctification, a concept inherently linked with moral restraint. While Fuller did not explicitly pen extensive treatises on alcohol, the tenor of his ministry and his writings on Christian discipline implicitly counseled sobriety and guarded behavior, laying a theological foundation that would implicitly support temperance movements arising later. His integration of evangelical zeal with a call for holy living fostered an environment within the Baptist community that was receptive to the developing temperance ethos.

Yet, it was in the 19th century that Baptist leaders truly galvanized a robust temperance movement, propelled by a confluence of revivalism, social reform, and emerging scientific understandings of alcohol's effects. The rise of evangelical revivals, marked by impassioned preaching and calls for personal renewal, found a natural ally in the virtuous call to abstain from intoxicants. Among the prominent voices was Lyman Beecher, though more broadly Presbyterian, whose moral crusades against alcohol profoundly shaped evangelical Protestants, Baptists among them. Within the Baptist tradition specifically, figures such as Francis Wayland emerged, whose writings on Christian morality engaged with the temperance cause not merely as a social undertaking but as a divine mandate. Wayland's intellectual contributions traced the destructive consequences of intemperance on families, communities, and spiritual health, weaving a compelling argument for abstinence or at least strict moderation rooted in Christian responsibility. His scholarly yet accessible prose galvanized Baptist academies and churches alike, stirring a deeper appreciation for temperance as a matter of both conscience and communal care.

Moving deeper into the Baptist heartland, the presidency of James M. Pendleton at prominent Baptist institutions exemplified the increasing institutionalization of temperance ideals. Pendleton's advocacy for temperance, backed by methodical theological reasoning, helped transition the movement from charismatic preaching circuits into the formal structures of Baptist life, embedding the cause within denominational conventions, seminaries, and publications. Such institutional backing lent momentum and durability, enabling temperance ideology to permeate Baptist consciousness not as an external imposition but as an internal conviction.

Pastoral leaders like J. H. Jowett further brought temperance into vivid pastoral focus, especially through sermons and devotional literature that intertwined warnings against the moral hazards of alcohol with invitations to deeper spiritual encounter. Jowett's ability to merge heartfelt compassion with rigorous moral appeal offered a template for subsequent Baptist preachers wrestling with the pastoral challenges alcohol posed, not least the tension between judgment and grace. His writings invoked the vineyard metaphor, a recurring biblical motif, to explore the ethical dimensions of wine and fermentation, holding up a vision of responsible joy unmarred by excess or addiction.

Parallel to these pastoral and academic contributions, Baptist women played a crucial yet often underappreciated role in advancing temperance ideology. Organizations like the Woman's Christian Temperance Union, heavily supported by Baptist women, provided grassroots vigor and moral clarity to the temperance cause. Leaders such as Frances Willard, though not a Baptist herself, influenced Baptist circles profoundly, inspiring women within the denomination to adopt temperance not only as a moral stance but as a vehicle for broader social reform. The writings and speeches emerging from Baptist women's temperance networks illuminated a faith that demanded active engagement with societal ills, reinforcing the conviction that moral stewardship extended beyond personal piety into communal advocacy.

Amid these historical currents, the theological elaborations of scholars such as Albert Henry Newman stand out for their precision and scope. Newman, an erudite Baptist historian and theologian, engaged the topic of alcohol not only as a social problem but from a biblical hermeneutic vantage point. His analyses dissected scriptural references to wine with an eye for nuance, distinguishing between the symbolic and the literal, between joyous celebration sanctioned by Scripture and the abuses abhorred by divine mandate. Newman's writings offered Baptist readers the intellectual tools to navigate the often polarized debates surrounding alcohol, encouraging a stance that was both rooted in tradition and open to critical engagement with emerging cultural realities.

Adding to this academic lineage, more recent Baptist scholars like Thomas C. Oden revitalized the temperance conversation by rooting it firmly in classical Christian virtue ethics. Oden's restorationist approach called Baptists back to the early church's emphasis on self-control and sobriety as spiritual disciplines essential for discipleship. His writings underscore that temperance transcends cultural regulation, it is a transcendent call to embody the fruit of the Spirit in a world rife with temptation. By framing temperance as a virtue in the lineage of wisdom and prudence, Oden helped revitalize Baptist engagement with the topic in the late 20th century, eschewing legalism in favor of grace-infused responsibility.

On the practical front, leaders like Dr. Augustus H. Strong, who combined theological scholarship with denominational leadership, leveraged temperance teachings as an integral part of pastoral formation. Strong's systematic theology, widely influential in Baptist seminaries, situated temperance within a broader moral and eschatological framework, emphasizing the believer's ongoing sanctification. His writings underscored that alcohol, while not inherently evil, becomes a decisive space where faith must express itself in disciplined choice, a juncture that carries profound implications for personal holiness and communal witness.

The educational sphere further advanced temperance ideology through the work of men like John A. Broadus, whose influence extended both as a seminary president and as a prolific writer and speaker. Broadus' pastoral ethos embodied temperance as part of a holistic Christian life, woven into the fabric of spiritual formation and church discipline. His essays and sermons, widely disseminated, offered practical guidance for congregations navigating alcohol's presence, consistently advocating for moderation but leaning toward caution and prudence. Broadus's legacy in Baptist life helped cement temperance as an intrinsic aspect of Baptist piety rather than a merely optional ethical stance.

Institutional dynamics also played a crucial role, with denominational resolutions and statements further espousing the temperance cause. The Southern Baptist Convention (SBC), for instance, increasingly formalized its position in the late 19th and early 20th centuries, propelled by the advocacy of leaders like Richard Fuller and James Thomas Draper, whose calls for abstinence were not only doctrinal pronouncements but pastoral appeals to safeguard families and churches. Draper's era witnessed the temperance ideal becoming practically synonymous with Baptist witness in many regions, a shift mirrored in the denomination's rising participation in the national temperance movement. These resolutions, while sometimes appearing rigid, reflect a discerning attempt to protect the spiritual and social well-being of congregations, rooted in centuries of theological reflection and pastoral experience.

It is impossible to overlook the complex contributions of Charles G. Finney, whose revivalist strategies and ascriptions to temperance influenced countless Baptists, even though his denominational ties lay elsewhere. Finney's passionate evangelism, which placed a strong emphasis on personal holiness and social reform, echoed deeply within Baptist circles. His insistence that conversion involved turning away from all sinfulness, including intemperance, permeated Baptist revivalism. His comprehensive vision merged spiritual renewal with moral reformation, inspiring Baptist leaders to adopt a more fervent stance on alcohol consumption within their communities.

The cumulative impact of these individual leaders and their writings cannot be overstated; together they weave a complex tapestry illustrating how Baptist temperance ideology progressively matured through theological reflection, institutional sanction, pastoral care, and cultural engagement. Their collective legacy embodies a spirited dialogue between biblical fidelity and lived experience, between conviction and compassion. Each leader, in their unique way, recognized that temperance was not merely a social issue but a spiritual discipline, essential for Christians navigating the challenges of a world where the line between blessing and curse often blurs within the chalice of fermented wine.

Thus, the history of Baptist temperance is revealed not as a monolithic position but as a rich, evolving conversation, a symphony of voices contributing harmony and dissonance alike, all striving toward a faith that honors both the sacredness of the body and the sanctity of community. Their writings invite modern readers into this ongoing dialogue, encouraging an understanding of temperance that balances joy and restraint, freedom and responsibility, tradition and innovation. The influence of these leaders endures, guiding contemporary Baptists as they continue to wrestle with the delicate intersection of faith, morality, and fermentation. They remind us that within the twilight orchard of belief, each fruit bears a story, a testimony to the enduring quest for a faith that embraces life's complexities with wisdom, grace, and unwavering devotion.

Impact on Baptist Communities

The impact of temperance views on Baptist communities stretches far beyond a mere matter of personal choice or isolated conviction; it is woven deeply into the very fabric of social interaction, communal identity, and spiritual discipline. From the earliest stirrings of Baptist emphasis on sobriety, these views have served as both a moral compass and a cultural boundary marker, shaping the contours of social life as much as religious observance. This impact emerges not simply as a static tradition but as a dynamic force, continuously influencing how Baptists envision their witness to the wider world, negotiate their internal diversity, and articulate their faith's practical implications.

At the heart of this influence is the conviction that sobriety is a sacred discipline, a reflection of the call to holiness that permeates Baptist theology. Early in Baptist history, temperance was not solely about avoiding the pitfalls of intoxication; it was intimately tied to the idea of moral clarity as evidence of a faithful soul. The Baptist tradition, with its emphasis on individual conscience and community accountability, embraced temperance as a means by which believers could embody purity, exemplify self-control, and avoid stumbling blocks that might endanger others. This moral posture gave rise to a distinct social ethic that moved beyond private restraint into collective responsibility. Within Baptist congregations, the avoidance or strict regulation of alcohol consumption became emblematic of a shared commitment to sanctification, a visible marker of communal identity distinguishing Baptists not only from the wider society but even from other Christian groups who might hold more permissive views.

The shaping of Baptist community life by temperance is evident in the rhythms of worship, fellowship, and governance. Churches often explicitly adopted policies restricting alcohol, embedding abstinence into church discipline and leadership qualifications. Ordained ministers and deacons were expected to model sobriety, reinforcing the theological teaching that temperance was inseparable from spiritual leadership. This standard created a culture in which the temptation or practice of drinking carried social consequences, sometimes resulting in exclusion or public admonishment, but also fostering a shared language of accountability marked by grace and restoration. Moreover, the temperance emphasis contributed to the way social events were structured. Weddings, celebrations, and church socials frequently centered around non-alcoholic beverages, creating environments where joyous fellowship was intertwined with the principles of restraint. This nurtured a communal ethos that celebrated joy and conviviality without excess, affirming the belief that faith and festivity need not depend on inebriation but find vitality in mutual respect and spiritual joy.

The broader societal reverberations of Baptist temperance views also become clear when one considers the way these convictions intersected with historical movements and cultural shifts. Baptists were often at the forefront of local and national temperance campaigns, galvanizing political advocacy rooted in religious and moral urgency. The nineteenth century, in particular, saw Baptists asserting their influence amid growing concerns about alcohol's destructive impact on families and communities. This engagement extended from small rural towns to burgeoning urban centers, where newfound social challenges posed fresh tests for Baptist temperance ideals. The struggle against saloons, public drunkenness, and licentiousness was not merely a question of morality but a fight for the preservation of social order, economic stability, and family welfare. Through this, Baptists forged an identity not only as spiritual caretakers but as active participants in the moral shaping of society. The temperance stance thus became a rallying point, uniting disparate Baptist communities under a shared banner of reform, social responsibility, and evangelical zeal.

Key figures within Baptist history played catalytic roles in elevating temperance from a personal conviction to a community-wide crusade. Revered leaders, pastors, and evangelists used their pulpits and publications to champion temperance as integral to Christian discipleship. Their voices rang with urgency, warning of alcohol's capacity to undermine faithfulness and calling believers to higher standards of living. These leaders often articulated temperance not as a burdensome restriction but as an expression of freedom, freedom from bondage to substances that enslave the body and dull the spirit. Their influence permeated Sunday school curricula, hymnody, and missionary endeavors, embedding temperance within the very language of Baptist spirituality. The formation of dedicated temperance societies and auxiliary organizations within Baptist circles provided structural support and communal reinforcement for these ideals. These societies fostered education, mutual encouragement, and public witness, further entrenching temperance as a normative expectation across age groups and social strata.

This emphasis on temperance also interacted in complex ways with Baptist views on freedom and conscience. Baptists have historically prized the autonomy of the believer and the sovereignty of conscience before God, yet this prized liberty found nuanced expression when it came to alcohol. While some Baptists have emphasized total abstinence as the ideal, others have allowed space for individual discretion undergirded by careful consideration of conscience and consequence. This tension between uniform standards and personal liberty animated ongoing debate within the community, driving a healthy engagement with the bounds of Christian freedom. Yet, even within this diversity, the social impact remained tangible: communities frequently negotiated boundaries through informal social pressure or formal disciplinary measures, seldom permitting ambiguity that might foster scandal or spiritual laxity. This balancing act reflected a communal sensitivity to the practical outcomes of drinking behavior, including the implications for witnesses, family health, and public perception.

Spiritually, the Baptist commitment to temperance has underscored a theology of the body and holiness that resonates across many aspects of church life. Abstaining from alcohol was often framed as a form of stewardship, caring faithfully for the temple God has given, guarding against anything that might harm or diminish it. This theology, deeply embedded within sermons and catechetical instruction, reinforced the connection between bodily discipline and spiritual vitality. It shaped prayer life, fasting practices, and approaches to temptation, embedding temperance within a holistic vision of life-giving faith. As a result, personal decisions about alcohol could not be easily separated from communal witness or doctrinal conviction. This created an environment where choices about drinking became part of a broad conversation about character, discipline, and witness, reinforcing a culture of intentional living that elevated temperance well beyond mere habit.

The social dimensions of these convictions often manifested in tangible ways within Baptist communities. Families found that temperance norms influenced courtship and marriage practices, with sobriety seen as foundational for stable households. Youth ministries and Sunday schools incorporated lessons on self-control and the dangers of drunkenness, fostering early inculcation of temperance principles that would shape lifelong habits. Baptists in leadership roles frequently reflected on the responsibilities inherent in representing the church, understanding that their conduct in matters of alcohol could enhance or diminish the reputation and effectiveness of their witness. In rural and urban congregations alike, temperance gatherings, revivals, and educational programs became occasions for binding the community tighter, where discipleship was expressed not only in word but in visible, embodied practice.

Nevertheless, the impact of temperance on Baptist social and religious life has not been without complexity and tension. As society evolved and questions about alcohol became more nuanced, Baptist communities grappled with evolving cultural contexts, legal frameworks, and shifting social attitudes. The rise of prohibition movements, legal battles over drinking laws, and the changing landscape of public morality introduced new challenges. Baptists found that maintaining a firm temperance position sometimes risked alienating others or creating divisions within their own ranks. Responses varied widely, from those who doubled down on strict abstinence to others who advocated for moderation or reconsideration of traditional stances. These debates, while at times contentious, reflected an ongoing effort to interpret faithfulness in light of changing times without compromising core convictions. In this way, temperance remained a living conversation, inviting continual reflection on how best to embody faith in service to both God and neighbor.

The legacy of temperance within Baptist communities is also marked by moments of profound grace and reconciliation. Stories abound of individuals and families whose lives were transformed by embracing sobriety, and whose testimony became a source of hope and encouragement for others. Within congregations, measures of pastoral care have often included compassionate outreach to those struggling with alcohol, integrating the temperance imperative with mercy and restoration. Such responses highlight that the Baptist approach to temperance, while deeply principled, is not merely rigid or punitive; it is infused with the gospel's call to healing, renewal, and community. This nuance has contributed to shaping Baptist social life in ways that balance firmness with kindness, discipline with empathy.

In sum, the impact of temperance views on Baptist communities has been profound and multifaceted, shaping not only religious doctrine but also the rhythms of daily life, social cohesion, and communal identity. It has provided a framework within which Baptists navigate theological convictions, personal morality, and public witness. Far from a mere relic of the past, the Baptist emphasis on temperance continues to influence how communities live out their faith amid changing cultural landscapes. As a living tradition, it invites believers to engage with enduring questions of moderation, holiness, and social responsibility, nurturing a faith that is both grounded in scripture and responsive to the complexities of human experience. Thus, temperance in Baptist life stands not only as a testament to historical teaching but as a vibrant, ongoing expression of devotion, a testimony of faith's power to shape character, community, and conscience across generations.

Gary E. Risenhoover

Scripture and Baptist Doctrine: Points of Convergence and Divergence

Baptist Confessions and Statements

Within the Baptist tradition, the conversation about alcohol consumption has often been shaped and defined not merely by personal conviction but significantly through formal confessions and statements of faith that reflect communal theological discernment. These documents have served as both mirrors and molders, reflecting prevailing convictions about alcohol while simultaneously helping to shape Baptist identity and practice. When one probes deeply into these confessions and doctrinal declarations, a complex and dynamic picture emerges: one marked by a profound reverence for Scripture, a commitment to moral clarity, and yet an underlying tension as Baptists wrestle with how best to interpret biblical references to wine and strong drink within a modern cultural framework.

Historically, Baptist confessions of faith have consistently emphasized sobriety and temperance, issues entwined with broader concerns about holiness and sanctification. From the earliest expressions of Baptist thought, there is a notable effort to uphold both the goodness of God's creation, including the fruit of the vine, and the grave moral dangers associated with its abuse. The London Baptist Confession of 1689, for example, stands as a seminal document that reflects the doctrinal heart of Baptist theology. In this confession, wine and strong drink are not condemned outright; rather, they are acknowledged as lawful and even beneficial when used appropriately under God's providence. Yet the confession simultaneously condemns drunkenness as a sin, warning believers to exercise self-control and restraint. This dual stance, affirming the goodness of creation while denouncing excess, captures a recurring theme throughout Baptist confessional literature: the call to balance joy and discipline, celebration and sobriety.

Such founding confessions reveal the deep textual roots upon which Baptist theology of alcohol rests, yet they do not fully eliminate differences of interpretation and emphasis. The 19th and 20th centuries witnessed the rise of the temperance movement, which dramatically influenced Baptist thought and practice, especially in the United States. With an increasing awareness of alcohol's social consequences, Baptists, along with other evangelical Protestants, frequently adopted a more stringent stance. Many Baptist state conventions and associations began issuing formal statements advocating for total abstinence, seeing it as not only a personal virtue but a necessary public witness to holiness and social reform. These statements, while not confessional in the strictest technical sense, carry immense weight within Baptist circles, as they embody communal values and pastoral concerns. The fundamental idea that alcohol, although not inherently evil, has become a spiritual stumbling block for many and thus should be avoided became prominent. This position is often justified through a theological lens that prioritizes the avoidance of scandal and the promotion of purity over nuanced engagement with biblical texts that appear more ambivalent toward wine and strong drink.

Yet, in the midst of such clarity, tensions surface as Baptist formal statements sometimes struggle to reconcile cultural pressures with biblical nuance. While some confessions and statements explicitly urge total abstinence, others adopt a more moderate approach, emphasizing personal conscience and Christian liberty. This divergence reflects the Baptist commitment to the autonomy of the local church and the priesthood of all believers, which allows varying interpretations and applications to coexist within the broader denominational family. The Southern Baptist Convention's historical documents, for example, reiterate the sinfulness of drunkenness and commend moderation but have at different times in history expressed both strict prohibitionist and more permissive attitudes toward alcohol. This oscillation reveals an underlying tension: how to uphold a witness of holiness without alienating those who might use alcohol responsibly and under conscience.

The Baptist Faith and Message, the confessional statement of the Southern Baptist Convention, articulates a position that combines biblical fidelity with pastoral caution; it rejects drunkenness as sinful while not explicitly condemning the use of alcohol. The language here is careful and measured, reflective of a tradition aware of its diverse membership yet striving to maintain consistent ethical guidance. This document's phrasing encourages believers to approach alcohol with sobriety and self-control rather than blanket prohibition, signifying a theological priority on wisdom and community impact over dogmatic enforcement. Such language is crucial because it implicitly acknowledges the complex biblical witness, including scriptures that affirm wine's place in celebration and blessing, as well as warnings about its dangers. It thus positions the Baptist tradition not as rigidly legalistic but as thoughtfully engaged with Scripture, tradition, and contemporary realities.

One cannot overlook the critical role that Baptist leaders and theologians have played in developing and disseminating these confessional viewpoints on alcohol. Their sermons, articles, and pastoral guides often accompany or influence formal statements, bringing a lived and practical dimension to doctrinal positions. Throughout Baptist history, influential figures have argued for temperance both on biblical grounds, citing prohibitions against drunkenness and exhortations to holiness, and on the basis of social and pastoral concerns. These voices frequently emphasize that while wine in biblical contexts often symbolizes blessing and joy, modern alcoholic beverages and the cultures surrounding them bring real dangers of addiction, family disruption, and moral decline. Consequently, many Baptists see formal temperance confessions not as mere doctrinal assertions but as pastoral necessities amid the evils and temptations of contemporary society's drinking culture. In this way, confessional language does much more than state theological truths, it seeks to nurture community health and personal discipleship.

Yet, as such formal statements and confessions continue to shape Baptist identity, they also invite critical scrutiny and dialogue about their scriptural interpretation and pastoral application. Some contemporary Baptist voices argue that traditional confessions too readily adopt a monochrome moral position that underestimates the complexity of biblical texts and cultural changes. They challenge the tendency toward prohibitionist extremes by highlighting biblical passages where wine is portrayed as a gift from God, to be enjoyed with gratitude and moderation, such as the wedding at Cana or the psalmist's acknowledgment of wine gladdening the heart. These critics advocate for confessions and statements that better capture this balance, fostering a faith that does not fear alcohol per se but calls for sober wisdom and responsible stewardship. Such perspectives often urge Baptists to replace rigid prohibitions with nuanced frameworks that respect individual conscience and communal accountability, reflecting a holistic understanding of biblical teaching that embraces joy without slackening moral rigor.

Ecumenical dialogues have brought further perspective to Baptist confessions regarding alcohol. When positioned alongside confessions from other Protestant groups, Catholic traditions, or Orthodox churches, the Baptist approach appears both distinct and part of a broader Christian conversation about alcohol, morality, and spirituality. For instance, while some Catholic documents commend the moderate use of wine within the Mass and daily life, they equally caution against excess, thus sharing with Baptists the dual themes of blessing and temperance. However, Baptists' historic emphasis on personal conversion and sanctification lends a particular ethical urgency to their statements on alcohol, often infusing them with a reformist zeal. These ecumenical conversations encourage Baptists to reconsider their confessional language in light of a wider

Christian witness, recognizing that unity in core faith doctrines can coexist with diversity in practical approaches to alcohol.

Moreover, the evolving cultural landscape challenges Baptist confessions and statements to remain relevant and compassionate in addressing alcohol-related issues. Increasing awareness of addiction, mental health, and social injustice invites Baptist communities to expand their doctrinal reflections beyond prohibitions and personal restraint toward more comprehensive pastoral responses. Formal statements are thus beginning to include acknowledgments of the complexities surrounding alcohol use, including recognizing those struggling with dependency and the significance of grace and redemption. This pastoral sensitivity enriches traditional confessions, moving them from static declarations into living documents that engage the realities faced by believers and their families. The challenge remains to balance scriptural authority with compassionate application, so that confessions can inspire not only moral discipline but also healing and hope.

The way Baptist confessions address alcohol also reverberates in local congregations' life and witness. Churches often adopt or adapt confessional statements to guide their policies, worship practices, and community outreach, making these documents influential beyond mere theological texts. For many congregations, the confessional stance on alcohol shapes social events, pastoral counseling, and communal expectations around personal behavior. This practical outworking means that formal doctrinal positions underpin how faith communities embody their moral commitments, contributing to a collective ethos about sobriety, celebration, and self-control. Here the tension between tradition and contemporary context can be most acutely felt, as congregations navigate diverse member convictions and the societal norms surrounding alcohol. The success of confessions in these settings depends largely on their capacity to articulate principles that inspire faithful living without imposing unnecessary division or alienation.

Ultimately, the formal doctrinal positions encapsulated in Baptist confessions and statements reflect a rich tapestry of biblical interpretation, theological conviction, pastoral concern, and cultural engagement. They affirm a God-centered worldview wherein alcohol is neither demonized nor trivialized but placed within a framework of covenantal obedience and ethical responsibility. These documents call for believers to honor God's creation by exercising restraint and wisdom, acknowledging the gift of life's pleasures while guarding against their potential for harm. Yet they also reveal ongoing tensions within the Baptist tradition: between sobriety and joy, discipline and liberty, communal witness and personal conscience. Engaging seriously with these confessional texts invites Baptists, indeed all readers, to appreciate the depth and nuance of their inherited wisdom while remaining open to growth and dialogue. In doing so, the tradition strengthens not only its theological coherence but also its capacity to nurture communities faithful to Christ's call in a complex and evolving world.

Scriptural Interpretations in Baptist Thought

Within the Baptist tradition, scriptural interpretations concerning alcohol have long been a topic of profound theological engagement, moral reflection, and ecclesial prudence. The way Baptists read and apply biblical teachings on drinking is a tapestry woven with threads of reverence for the sacred text, historical context, pastoral concern, and denominational identity. This tapestry reveals both a deep commitment to Scripture's authority and a complex relationship with the text's ambiguities regarding wine, strong drink, and their appropriate use. At the center of Baptist hermeneutics is the conviction that the Bible, as the infallible Word of God, must guide Christian life entirely, yet this guidance demands careful exegesis, spiritual discernment, and practical wisdom. Baptists approach scripture with a desire to honor both God's revealed will and the gospel's transformative power, engendering a dynamic interpretative process that balances doctrinal fidelity with pastoral sensitivity.

Traditional Baptist readings often affirm the biblical acknowledgment of alcohol's existence and its role in ancient cultures, notably in celebratory, medicinal, and ritual contexts, yet simultaneously emphasize the sober warnings the Bible issues about drunkenness and moral decay. This duality shapes the Baptist theological stance: alcohol itself is not inherently sinful, but its misuse undoubtedly is. Many foundational texts, such as Ephesians 5:18, where Paul exhorts believers not to be drunk with wine but filled with the Spirit, Luke 1:15 referring to John the Baptist abstaining from wine, and Proverbs 20:1's caution that wine is a mocker and strong drink a brawler, are wielded within Baptist communities as scriptural pillars underscoring the perils of intemperance. These passages carve out a moral framework that demands personal restraint, community accountability, and an avoidance of anything that might cause spiritual harm, whether to oneself or to another. Thus, Baptist thought often elevates the virtue of temperance as an essential expression of Christian discipleship, rooted deeply in scriptural witness.

However, Baptists have not always read these Scriptures monolithically. Historical Baptist theologians and denominational leaders have conversed vigorously over the permissibility and prudence of personal alcohol consumption. Some strands within the tradition have espoused strict abstinence, interpreting biblical warnings as imperative commands for believers to shun alcohol entirely to safeguard personal holiness and public witness. This position correlates with the temperance movements that gained momentum in the 19th and early 20th centuries, where Baptists played a significant role advocating for sobriety, both as a spiritual discipline and social reform. For these adherents, biblical texts that celebrate wine, such as Jesus turning water into wine at Cana (John 2) and Paul's advice to Timothy to use a little wine for his stomach's sake (1 Timothy 5:23), are often understood symbolically or strictly limited to their cultural context, considered exceptions rather than normative endorsements of drinking. This interpretive lens prioritizes the moral risk inherent in alcohol use and elevates abstention as the spiritually safest and most responsible course.

Yet this latter-day abstinence-centric hermeneutic is not without tensions and counterpoints within Baptist circles. A more moderate and nuanced approach has gained traction over recent decades, one that advocates for responsible drinking within the parameters of biblical caution and conscience. Proponents of this view argue that a wholesale rejection of all alcoholic beverages risks imposing cultural biases onto the text and overlooks the rich biblical texture wherein wine functions as a sign of God's blessing, joy, and covenantal life. They highlight passages such as Psalm 104:14-15, where wine is described as gladdening the heart of man, and Ecclesiastes 9:7, which urges enjoyment of life's pleasures in the fear of the Lord, as legitimate expressions of God-ordained joy that He permits and even ordains as part of human experience. This cohort within Baptist theology insists that Scripture's condemnation is reserved primarily for excess and addiction, not the moderate use that can coexist with a Spirit-filled life. This view functions not only as a corrective to legalism but also as an invitation to trust the believer's conscience and God's grace, allowing for a diversity of practice without fracturing fellowship.

Navigating these interpretive disputes, Baptist theologians often turn to the Bible's broader narrative of redemption and holiness to inform their stance on alcohol. The call to holiness in Leviticus, the wisdom literature's counsel on discernment and self-control, and the New Testament's portrayal of the Spirit's transformation all coalesce to set a high bar for moral conduct. Within this framework, alcohol consumption becomes a meter not simply of behavior but of the believer's heart alignment. Does drinking foster love, edification, and community, or does it give rise to judgment, harm, and spiritual stumbling? The Apostle Paul's instruction in Romans 14 about not causing others to stumble often receives special emphasis among Baptists, ensuring that liberal or moderate drinkers prioritize the spiritual well-being and conscience of more cautious members. This principle of mutual love and communal care tempers personal liberty with responsibility, sustaining unity amid diversity. Thus, scriptural interpretation is not merely an intellectual exercise but a practical, relational endeavor grounded in pastoral concern.

Despite these careful conversations, areas of tension persist within Baptist communities due to variances in scriptural emphasis, cultural backgrounds, and personal experience. For some who have witnessed personal or familial devastation through alcohol abuse, biblical warnings resonate with concrete, immediate urgency, leading to calls for absolute prohibition within church life. Others, shaped by different cultural milieus or theological traditions, perceive a more permissive or celebratory scriptural tone concerning wine and derive comfort in moderate consumption, viewing it as a gift rather than a trap. These divergent readings invite robust dialogue but also risk misunderstandings or judgments that fracture fellowship. The challenge for Baptist communities is to hold firmly to scriptural truth while extending grace and patience to those wrestling with the implications of these sacred texts in their lives. Many churches have found that fostering open, respectful conversations that acknowledge the pain and faith of all participants leads to healthier relationships and deeper spiritual maturity.

In addition to theological interpretation, Baptists also bring a distinctive ecclesiological lens to the topic of alcohol. Emphasizing congregational autonomy, Baptists empower individual churches and believers to discern their own path regarding alcohol, often guided by local context and collective conscience rather than a centralized doctrinal imposition. This decentralized approach allows for pluralism within the broader Baptist movement yet sometimes exacerbates discrepancies in practice and belief. While some congregations maintain strict prohibitions of alcoholic beverages in all church-sponsored events, preaching abstinence as a moral imperative, others adopt a more accommodating stance, permitting responsible use while emphasizing personal holiness and witness. This structural characteristic reflects Baptists' commitment to the priesthood of all believers, affirming that scriptural interpretation is a communal labor requiring humility, dialogue, and the Spirit's illumination. The result is a spectrum of responses, all claiming fidelity to Scripture yet articulating its implications differently.

Moreover, Baptist interpretations often manifest a profound concern for the witness of the church in the world. Baptists traditionally value personal morality highly as a testimony to the transforming power of the gospel. Therefore, reading Scripture about alcohol is never abstract but intimately tied to questions of evangelism, community reputation, and ethical engagement with society. When Baptists teach abstinence, they often do so not only on grounds of personal conviction but also out of a desire to display holiness visibly as a countercultural witness against societal excess and immorality. Conversely, where more permissive views prevail, the argument is made that rejecting all alcohol alienates potential seekers and disregards biblical assurances that thanksgiving wine can be part of God's good creation. These practical pastoral reflections shape how biblical texts are applied and underscore that scriptural interpretation serves the gospel mission.

Importantly, Baptist interpreters have also engaged critically with the original languages, historical usage, and cultural milieu of the biblical references to alcohol, revealing subtleties often lost in simplistic readings. The Hebrew word "yayin," typically translated as wine, denoted a range of fermented beverages whose alcoholic potency varied greatly. The Greek terms "oinos" and "sikera" similarly referred to wine and strong drink but also carried connotations of both celebration and excess. Understanding these socio-linguistic nuances allows Baptists to appreciate the biblical text's multifaceted attitudes toward fermentation products, not merely as prohibitions or endorsements but as part of the fabric of life in ancient Israel and the early church. This scholarly depth encourages believers to resist reductionist interpretations and to embrace the richness of biblical theology about the created order, human pleasure, and divine discipline.

Complementing theological and lexical considerations is the pastoral narrative that colors Baptist interpretations of alcohol. Personal testimonies within Baptist communities often illustrate how scriptural convictions shape lives profoundly. Stories of addiction overcome through faith, families healed by sobriety, and individuals wrestling with conscience on the drinking question reveal the lived dimension of scripture's authority. These narratives bring to life the dialectic tension in the text between blessing and burden, joy and judgment, liberty and responsibility. They also serve as powerful hermeneutical guides, reinforcing scriptural calls to love and compassion while warning against self-destruction. Through such stories, the Bible transcends a book of ancient rules, becoming a living Word speaking into contemporary struggles and hopes.

Despite the earnest attempts at clarity, the question of alcohol in Baptist scripture interpretation remains a continuing conversation, inviting each generation to listen anew. Emerging voices within Baptist scholarship seek to reclaim a balance between biblical faithfulness and cultural engagement, challenging older abstinence paradigms by re-examining scriptural texts in their historical breadth and narrative integrity. These contemporary theologians argue that an overemphasis on prohibition risks obscuring the Gospel's fullness, which incorporates joy, celebration, and God's provision alongside moral discipline. Simultaneously, they caution against laxity that could undermine spiritual vitality and community witness. This renewed conversation reframes Baptist engagement with Scripture as a living dialogue, ever seeking to reconcile divine truth with human frailty, tradition with cultural change, and holiness with hospitality.

In sum, Baptists read and apply biblical teachings on drinking through a kaleidoscope of interpretive methods, theological convictions, cultural sensitivities, and pastoral realities. Their scriptural engagement is marked by an earnest effort to honor the Bible's authority while wrestling with its intricacies and implications. The Baptist tradition's hallmark has been a spirited commitment to temperance as a virtue deeply rooted in Scripture's cautionary tone, yet this commitment is far from monolithic. Whether emphasizing abstinence or moderation, the underlying thread is a desire to live faithfully under God's Word, embody Christ-like love, and maintain an honest, joyful, and holy life amid the complexities that alcohol presents. As such, these scriptural interpretations continue to shape Baptist identity, provoke thoughtful dialogue, and encourage communal growth on a topic that is as ancient as the vineyards and as current as today's congregations. In this ongoing quest, faith meets fermentation in a dance of restraint and celebration, inviting believers to hold both the cup of blessing and the call to holiness with equal reverence and courage.

Points of Agreement and Disagreement

Within the complex matrix of faith and fermentation, the interplay between scriptural text and Baptist doctrine unspools as a rich tapestry threaded with both harmony and tension. The dynamic relationship between these two pillars, ancient biblical teachings and centuries-old denominational convictions, calls for a nuanced examination, one that reveals not only points of agreement but also the inevitable areas where discord emerges, reflecting the living, breathing nature of theological interpretation. The Baptist tradition, shaped decisively by its historical commitment to moral clarity and temperance, finds itself wrestling with scripture that speaks with varied voices on the subject of alcohol, at times blessing wine, at times warning against its abuse, and at other moments offering ambiguous allusions that require careful theological navigation.

The sacred texts of the Bible present a multifaceted picture of alcohol, one that resists simplistic categorization. From the celebratory cups of wine poured at wedding feasts and sacramental rites to the sober admonitions against drunkenness and dissipation, the scriptures offer a spectrum that Baptist theology must negotiate with both respect and discernment. Baptists, rooted deeply in the principle of *sola scriptura*, the authority of scripture alone, find themselves compelled to wrestle with every relevant verse through the lens of faithful interpretation and contemporary moral application. At the heart of this discourse lies a fundamental point of convergence: the acknowledgment that alcohol in its essence is neither inherently evil nor condemned outright by God. This shared understanding with the biblical text forms the cornerstone of Baptist reflections on alcohol; the substance itself, a natural product of fermentation, is regarded as a creation within God's good order, deserving neither complete vilification nor unrestrained consumption.

This harmony finds strong support in several passages that affirm wine as both a gift and a blessing. Psalm 104 exalts the vine and wine as joy for the heart of man, highlighting the natural world's provision for human delight. Likewise, the apostle Paul's commendation of wine for medicinal purposes in the pastoral epistles presents a tacit acceptance of alcohol's rightful place when used judiciously. Baptists echo these scriptural affirmations through their categorical rejection of total prohibition as an absolute biblical mandate, an important doctrinal concession that recognizes the biblical wine culture of ancient Israel and the early church's tacit tolerance toward moderate use. Here, agreement is clear and robust: alcohol, in measured and respectful quantities, is compatible with a devout Christian life. It is this rooted acknowledgment that allows Baptists to navigate the complex waters of alcohol with a degree of grace and reason, rather than rigid legalism.

However, it is the very place where this grace operates that tension intensifies, for Baptist doctrine stands equally firm on the principles of personal holiness and social responsibility. Drunkenness is unequivocally condemned throughout scripture, and Baptists elevate these prohibitions to a paramount place in their ethical framework. The pastoral epistles' repeated warnings to avoid excess resonate loudly, underscoring the dangers alcohol poses when abused, physical ruin, spiritual dullness, broken relationships, and public scandal. Baptist theology's emphasis on personal and communal holiness compels its adherents to adopt a posture of caution and abstinence, not merely as a private virtue but as a public witness. This sacred imperative often results in the tradition's characteristic promotion of total abstinence or at a minimum, a strong temperance ethic, particularly in communities deeply scarred by alcohol-related harm. The tension here is real and palpable, as doctrine pulls against the scriptural acknowledgment of alcohol's permitted use, erecting walls of prudence that sometimes border on prohibitionist tendencies.

Complicating this further is the ongoing interpretive effort within Baptist circles to distinguish between "wine" in biblical times and modern alcoholic beverages. Many Baptist scholars and theologians argue that the intoxicating strength of current drinks far exceeds that of ancient drinks, thereby justifying a stricter approach as a response to changed circumstances rather than scriptural prohibition. This point of difference underscores a broader dynamic: the ever-present tension between the timeless truths of scripture and the mutable realities of cultural context. While scripture never lists a blood alcohol content or distinguishes between fermented grape juice and distilled spirits, Baptist doctrines and conventions often make this pragmatic distinction, reflecting a commitment to moral stewardship in light of empirical knowledge about alcohol's effects in the present age. This practical divergence from textual literalism to contextual morality reveals an interpretive elasticity that, while not undermining scripture's authority, calls into question whether Baptist doctrinal stances are absolute or adaptive, an ambivalence that continues to inspire debate within the denomination.

Further areas of discord emerge in the contrasting theological emphases on individual liberty and communal welfare. Baptist tradition profoundly affirms the believer's conscience and the right to personal decision-making in matters not expressly forbidden by scripture. Yet, this respect for individual freedom exists in tension with a communal ethic that prioritizes protecting the vulnerable and fostering spiritual edification. The apostle Paul's letters, particularly in Romans and 1 Corinthians, grapple with this delicate balance, advocating for liberty tempered by love, warning believers to refrain from actions that might cause a weaker brother to stumble. Baptist doctrinal teaching grapples with this paradox: how to honor personal liberty regarding alcohol while simultaneously upholding the broader mission of church discipline and witness. This dynamic fuels vigorous ongoing dialogue within Baptist communities, sometimes leading to divergent practices ranging from full abstinence to moderate participation in social drinking, each sincerely grounded in a scriptural reading that emphasizes either liberty or responsibility. The discord here is less about the foundational truths than about their prioritized application within specific cultural and pastoral contexts.

Moreover, interpretations of biblical metaphor and symbolism around wine introduce additional complexities. The wine of the Eucharist, as celebrated in many Christian traditions, symbolizes Christ's blood, a sacred, transformative element of worship that brings spiritual life and renewal. Baptists, while sharing reverence for such symbolism, diverge in their understanding of the ordinance of the Lord's Supper, often resisting sacramental analogies that conflate the physical substance of wine with spiritual efficacy. Some Baptists utilize grape juice instead of wine in communion to avoid association with alcohol altogether, reflecting a doctrinal predisposition toward avoidance rooted in concerns over scandal and unity. This practice, though not scripturally mandated, reveals a theological hesitation that contrasts with biblical images celebrating wine's joyous and life-giving qualities. The tension between symbolic practice and textual imagery exposes a subtle but significant divergence in how doctrine crystallizes worship experience, further complicating the conversation.

In the realm of pastoral care and social ethics, further points of disagreement become evident. The Baptist insistence on temperance has traditionally extended into vigorous opposition to alcohol-related social problems, family disruption, poverty, and moral decay, manifesting in historical support for the temperance movement and even prohibition. These social convictions have sometimes translated into doctrinal rigidity, marginalizing those struggling with addiction or those choosing a more moderate path, revealing an undercurrent of judgment that contrasts with the gospel's call to grace and restoration. Scripturally, the call to compassion and mercy toward the weak is clear, inviting believers into ministry and healing rather than condemnation. Yet, the Baptist approach has often wrestled with balancing these dual demands of holiness and mercy, producing ecclesial responses that invite both embrace and estrangement. The fault line between doctrine's protective instincts and the inclusive love of scripture continues to shape Baptist conversations about alcohol.

Contemporary voices within the Baptist tradition increasingly champion a more nuanced dialogue, emphasizing grace-filled engagement over legalistic division. These perspectives highlight scriptural passages that speak to the abundant life and the celebration of God's good gifts, suggesting that fear and prohibition need not define the entire conversation. They call for a restoration of joy and reverence coexisting within the sphere of fermentation, advocating for informed, responsible, and communal discernment that acknowledges human fragility without succumbing to harsh judgment. This emerging tendency seeks to reconcile longstanding doctrinal disagreements with scriptural honesty, fostering a posture of humility that honors diverse convictions as part of the Baptist family tapestry. In doing so, it exemplifies an evolving hermeneutic that underscores unity through diversity, inviting believers to embrace a faith that is both practiced with restraint and lived with joy.

Yet, even as these more inclusive approaches gain traction, they are met with concern and resistance by segments of the Baptist community committed to preserving the tradition's hallmark of temperance as a sacred boundary marker. For them, any softening of stance risks compromising moral witness and inviting theological ambiguity. The debate turns, again and again, on the question of where to draw lines, between acceptable use and misuse, freedom and bondage, testimony and temptation. Scripture provides the foundational parameters, but doctrine and pastoral practice struggle to translate these into a consistent, lived reality. This tension exemplifies the vibrant struggle within a faith community seeking to remain faithful to ancient texts while responding to contemporary challenges with wisdom and love.

Ultimately, the intricate dance of points of agreement and disagreement between scripture and Baptist doctrine concerning alcohol reveals not a simple binary of right and wrong but a dynamic interplay shaped by historical memory, theological conviction, cultural context, and pastoral care. It is a landscape marked by shared commitment to scripture's moral vision and an earnest desire to live holy lives, yet simultaneously characterized by honest recognition of the complexities inherent in interpretation and application. Recognizing this, the conversation must be held in a spirit of charitable engagement, not to erect barriers but to build pathways toward understanding and mutual respect. As readers journey together through this dialogue, they are invited to see the orchard at twilight, a place where the fruit is both sweet and tart, where joy and restraint coexist beneath the spreading branches, and where reverence for God's word and compassionate pastoral care meet in a dance as timeless as faith itself. In this light, the points of harmony become anchors, the points of tension become openings for growth, and the entire discourse emerges as a testament to the living, breathing nature of faith seeking understanding within the sacred sphere of fermentation.

Cultural Influences on Baptist Perspectives

Cultural Norms and Drinking Habits

Through the centuries, the tapestry of Baptist identity has been intimately woven with threads of cultural customs, regional traditions, and social mores that have shaped, and continue to shape, collective and individual understandings of alcohol and its place within the life of faith. To truly comprehend how Baptists have approached the subject of drinking, often with a marked sobriety and restraint that some might mistake for rigid abstinence, it is essential to first peer beyond doctrinal formulations and theological treatises into the vibrant, multifaceted world of cultural norms that have long influenced behavior and belief. In this intricate dance between belief and environment, it is not merely scripture alone that has dictated practice but an ongoing dialogue with the customs, fears, revelries, and concerns of surrounding society. The manner in which Baptists relate to alcohol is, therefore, a reflection as much of their faith commitments as it is a mirror of the cultural landscapes they inhabit.

Historically, Baptists emerged from Protestant dissenters, often rooted in English, Scottish, and later American frontiers, where social context was both a crucible and a canvas for religious expression. In many of these environments, patterns of alcohol consumption were already deeply embedded in daily life and community practice. Wine, beer, cider, and later spirits were common accompaniments to meals, celebrations, and communal gatherings. However, Baptists, particularly from the 18th and 19th centuries onward, cultivated a distinctive ethos that elevated moral clarity and personal piety as bulwarks against the social ills they perceived to be linked to alcohol, excess, licentiousness, and disruption. This ethos found fertile ground in regions where alcohol use acquired symbolic and practical associations with disorder, poverty, and family breakdown, phenomena that Baptists sought to counteract with a rigorous moral framework.

As waves of revival and reform swept through Baptist communities, particularly in the American context, temperance became more than a personal choice; it transformed into a cultural ideology. This ideology was shaped, reinforced, and disseminated through churches, schools, and social organizations, embedding a shared value system in which abstinence, or at least moderation, was not just encouraged but often expected. Yet, these positions were not adopted in a vacuum. They interacted dynamically with broader societal narratives about alcohol. For example, in many rural Southern Baptist strongholds, the temperance movement coincided with agrarian values of hard work, self-discipline, and family stability. Here, refraining from alcohol reinforced social identity, a signifier of respectability and spiritual seriousness, especially as communities sought to distinguish themselves from urban centers associated, rightly or wrongly, with vice and decadence.

Regional distinctions have further nuanced Baptist perspectives. Whereas Southern Baptists historically *dipped heavily into* calls for abstinence, Baptists in New England or parts of the Midwest sometimes exhibited more nuanced attitudes, reflecting a cultural milieu where wine and beer were less stigmatized and occasionally integrated into customary hospitality and fellowship. In such contexts, alcoholic beverages could carry social meanings that were less about moral struggle and more about communal bonding and celebration. This diversity within Baptist culture underscores how deeply cultural surroundings act as an interpretive lens through which scripture and doctrine come alive, often magnifying some themes while muting others. At the same time, the infiltration of popular culture, mass media, and increased urbanization has complicated these once-clear-cut regional paradigms, presenting new challenges and opportunities for Baptist communities navigating the waters between tradition and modernity.

Moreover, the social identity of Baptists has frequently been rooted in countercultural narratives, resisting mainstream societal indulgences to preserve a distinct ethical witness. Alcohol, therefore, became symbolic of this boundary, a line demarcating the sacred from the profane, discipline from indulgence. This boundary was not only individual but communal. Churches served as social hubs where collective norms surrounding drinking were reinforced, and where deviations were often met with disapproval or correction. This function as moral gatekeepers contributed to a strong internal culture of accountability, but it also risked fostering social stigma and alienation for those who struggled with or simply chose to engage differently with alcohol. The tension between maintaining community identity and accommodating diverse experiences has been a persistent undertow within Baptist cultural fabric.

The phenomenon of cultural transmission also sheds light on this complex relationship. As Baptist congregations expanded globally, crossing continents into vastly different cultural contexts such as Latin America, Africa, and Asia, they encountered varied traditions regarding alcohol consumption. In some of these settings, wine and beer are integral to social rituals and celebrations, and outright abstinence could risk alienating converts or seeming culturally blind. In response, many Baptist missionaries and local church leaders have had to reinterpret and adapt temperance teachings, balancing scriptural fidelity with cultural sensitivity. This intercultural encounter has enriched Baptist perspectives, fostering an awareness that views on alcohol are not monolithic but deeply contextual. Such interactions invite a humility that recognizes the interplay between eternal principles and temporal realities.

Within contemporary Baptist communities, cultural factors continue to exert strong influence, even as globalization, migration, and technological connectivity bring new voices and experiences into the fold.

Digital media platforms expose Baptists around the world to a myriad of attitudes toward alcohol, from evangelical leaders advocating strict abstinence to progressive voices encouraging thoughtful moderation. This exposure precipitates dialogue and sometimes confusion, as younger generations wrestle with inherited cultural norms that may seem at odds with lived realities among peers and neighbors. The resultant diversity fosters both tension and opportunity, tension in the form of intra-community debate and opportunity in the potential for richer, more nuanced expressions of faith that respect individual conscience alongside communal well-being.

Societal attitudes toward alcohol beyond the church walls also bear heavily on Baptist perspectives. The legal framework, public health messaging, and media portrayals all contribute to shaping communal perceptions. In societies grappling with alcoholism, addiction crises, and the social fallout of substance misuse, Baptists often feel a prophetic impulse to call for sobriety and promote restorative support. Conversely, in cultures where wine is celebrated as part of culinary heritage or religious ceremony, complete prohibition may appear unnecessarily austere or discordant with cultural beauty and joy. Such cultural ambivalence pushes Baptists toward a dialogue that weighs the biblical calls for wisdom, restraint, and love against the realities of social practices and human experience.

The role of family and upbringing cannot be overstated in shaping Baptist attitudes toward alcohol. In many Baptist households, stories of personal struggle or family hardship related to alcohol have forged strong commitments to temperance, often motivated by a desire to shield future generations from harm. Rituals of faith, including baptism and Sunday worship, frequently serve as platforms reinforcing these values. Yet alongside such cautionary narratives, there often exists an undercurrent of celebration for the goodness of creation, including the fruits of the vine, when such blessings are honored responsibly. This duality, affirming joy and hospitality while warning against excess, reflects a cultural dance shaped by both personal memory and collective wisdom.

Finally, the social role of alcohol in fostering relationships and community life challenges Baptists to reconsider strict positions. Fellowship meals, weddings, and celebrations frequently feature wine and beer as gestures of hospitality and markers of joy. The question emerges: can faith engage with alcohol not only as a potential source of harm but as an emblem of celebration that glorifies God through gratitude and communal bonding? Emerging voices within the Baptist tradition advocate for such a balanced view, urging communities to embrace both tradition and contextual learning, to see alcohol neither as inherently sinful nor as harmlessly neutral but as a gift demanding discernment, grace, and communal care.

In sum, Baptist beliefs and practices concerning alcohol cannot be fully grasped without understanding the powerful currents of culture, regional, social, familial, and historical that shape how scripture is read and how faith is lived. The landscape of Baptist drinking habits is as variegated and vibrant as the twilight orchard where joyful fruit coexists with thorn and restraint. Grappling openly with these cultural forces invites a richer, more compassionate faith that honors both divine wisdom and human complexity, fostering communities where sobriety and celebration, discipline and delight, can find a harmonious dance. This nuanced exploration opens doors for deeper dialogue, inviting Baptists and all readers to savor not only the fruits of fermentation but the fruits of understanding nurtured in the fertile soil of culture and faith.

Regional Variations within Baptist Communities

In unraveling the intricate tapestry of Baptist perspectives on alcohol, one cannot overlook the profound influence of geography and regional culture. The Baptist tradition, far from homogenous, is diffused across a broad spectrum of societal contexts, each imparting its distinctive flavor to how alcohol is perceived, practiced, and preached against or in favor of. From the rolling hills of the American South to the urban enclaves of the Midwest, from the sun-drenched plantations of the Caribbean to the more austere landscapes of parts of Africa and Asia, the constellation of Baptist communities reflects a mosaic of interpretations and lived realities. The role that geography plays is thus not peripheral but central, functioning almost like a prism through which biblical teachings on alcohol are refracted, yielding variations of hue and intensity in belief and behavior.

In the southeastern United States, often referred to as the "Bible Belt," where Baptist churches predominate in numbers and influence, a legacy of antebellum social structures and pietistic fervor has historically cemented a conservative stance on alcohol. This regional context has long associated temperance with moral vigilance and communal stability, intertwining alcohol abstinence with ideals of righteousness and social cohesion. Here, the Baptist prohibitionist ethos manifests not only as a theological conviction but as a cultural identity marker. Drinking is frequently framed as antithetical to faithful living and social order, linked to temperamental outbreaks, family disruption, and spiritual decay in community narratives. The regional culture, shaped by a collective memory of revivalist camps and fire-and-brimstone preaching, reinforces a sobriety that is as much outwardly observable behavior as it is inward moral resolve.

Yet, even within this regional stronghold of temperance, important diversities emerge. Urban centers in the South, such as Atlanta or Charlotte, have witnessed a gradual shift amid modernization, population diversification, and economic change. Younger Baptist congregants, influenced by global cultural interactions and more liberal social milieus, often adopt more moderate and less *absolute-driven* approaches to alcohol. While official doctrine may remain conservative, personal and communal practices reflect an accommodation with the realities of social drinking, hospitality, and celebration. This nuanced blend of restraint and engagement illustrates how geographical space is not static but dynamic, reacting to demographic changes and cultural influxes. The interplay of rural conservatism with urban cosmopolitanism within a single region reveals the complexity of regional variations even beneath the broader banner of Southern Baptist identity.

Moving northward toward the Midwest, Baptist communities encounter a different cultural and historical landscape that colors their views on alcohol. The region's immigrant heritage, comprising German, Scandinavian, and Eastern European influences, brought with it traditions of beer brewing, wine making, and communal drinking as social customs rather than moral dilemmas. Such backgrounds tend to dilute the strict dualism familiar in the Bible Belt by emphasizing moderation and communal celebration over outright abstinence. These cultural inheritances have contributed to a somewhat more permissive stance within many Baptist circles, where alcohol is often present at gatherings and worship-related fellowship events in modest amounts. The Midwestern Baptist ethos frequently balances temperance with an acknowledgment of alcohol as a culturally embedded social norm, thus encouraging individual responsibility without blanket prohibitions. It is a posture that tempers doctrinal strictness with pragmatic acceptance, reflecting geography's shaping hand in directing the lived expression of faith.

Urban-industrial centers in this region, such as Chicago, Minneapolis, and Detroit, further complicate the picture, introducing factors such as ethnic diversity and socioeconomic stratification that significantly inform Baptist attitudes toward alcohol. In immigrant-heavy communities or economically challenged urban neighborhoods, alcohol can be laden with symbolic weight: it may represent social bonding and ethnic identity, yet also struggles with addiction and marginalization within the community. Here, Baptist congregations often become bastions of both advocacy and pastoral care, preaching restraint and moral uprightness alongside social services aimed at recovery and rehabilitation. The geography of these community realities, where towering factories meet tight-knit ethnic enclaves, frames a Baptist discourse on alcohol that is deeply contextualized, tenderly walking the line between condemnation and compassion.

Crossing over to the western regions of the United States, the picture shifts considerably again. Western Baptist communities, influenced by pioneering individualism and frontier ethos, often embody a spirit of personal decision-making tinged with libertarian nuances. The relative novelty of settlement in many western states and the freer social structures characteristic of their development have often resulted in diverse and less stringent attitudes toward alcohol. Whereas church doctrine may echo traditional Baptist warnings about misuse and excess, there is often a greater emphasis on personal responsibility and less on institutional enforcement of temperance. Hospitality, celebration, and cultural pluralism underpin community life in these areas, subtly reconfiguring how Baptists relate to alcohol, not as a categorical evil, but as potentially enjoyable when engaged in wisely. Sometimes, this latitude brings about tension within Baptist circles, as elder leadership wrestles with balancing tradition with evolving community norms, but it also paves the way for dialogue that appreciates complexity over binary moralism.

The West Coast, with its motley of ethnicities and progressive social movements, adds yet another layer of regional variation. Baptists here navigate a cultural milieu infused with lifestyle experimentation and spiritual eclecticism. This environment fosters a more relaxed, often ambivalent attitude toward alcohol, aligning with wider regional trends that view alcohol more secularly than spiritually. Church communities may emphasize grace and freedom in Christ, interpreting biblical cautions about alcohol as warnings against excess rather than divinely mandated prohibition. Such perspectives sometimes contrast sharply with the more ascetic tendencies of traditional Baptists elsewhere, provoking internal denominational debates about the stewardship of bodies and spirits. Nevertheless, these Western Baptists often champion an approach that centers on informed choice and mutual respect, reflecting their region's broader ethos of diversity and inclusion.

Delving into the Caribbean and parts of Latin America, Baptist communities encounter yet another set of cultural scripts. In these tropical regions, fermented beverages such as rum and local fruit wines have historically played a significant role in rituals, festivities, and daily life. Here, alcohol is entwined not only with economy and culture but also with colonial legacies and missionary histories. Baptist churches in these areas often wrestle with the tension between inherited cultural customs surrounding alcohol and the strict moral codes implanted by evangelical mission efforts. How Baptists here negotiate indigenous respect with imported temperance ideals vividly underscores how regional heritage shapes religious outlooks. Many congregations seek a middle path, recognizing the cultural significance of alcohol yet advocating prudent use and awareness of its potential for harm. This balancing act reflects the Baptists' broader struggle to contextualize faith within vibrant, multifaceted cultures rather than impose rigid dogmas alien to local life.

Exploring Africa, where Baptist missions have profoundly planted roots, regional variation reveals itself in how economic, cultural, and social realities converge to influence perspectives on alcohol. In rural areas where traditional fermented drinks are common, Baptists often confront the challenge of integrating biblical morality with longstanding indigenous practices. Alcohol here possesses dual functions: as a medium of social bonding and as a spiritual risk. Baptist churches, influenced both by global evangelical norms and by local cultural wisdom, strive to articulate theology that respects tradition yet calls for responsible stewardship. In urban African Baptist communities, issues linked to rapid modernization, poverty, and urban stress introduce new concerns about alcohol abuse, prompting churches to emphasize health, family welfare, and rehabilitation alongside spiritual exhortation. The regional conditions, markedly different from Western contexts, reveal how geography not only frames attitudes toward alcohol but compels adaptive theology that responds to real-world challenges.

Asia's Baptist communities, though comparatively smaller and more diverse, add a further dimension to regional variation. Countries such as the Philippines, South Korea, and parts of India with Baptist presence reflect cultural attitudes where alcohol carries varying degrees of social acceptability. In some areas, drinking is an integral part of social rites; in others, sobriety aligns closely with local moral codes and religious syncretism. Baptist churches in these settings often navigate a path that incorporates both scriptural fidelity and cultural sensitivity, recognizing that a doctrinally blind importation of temperance ideals may alienate rather than edify. Here, geography intersects with religion to produce forms of Baptist witness that value relational harmony and practical wisdom. This global perspective reminds readers that the Baptist relationship to alcohol cannot be divorced from the textures of place and culture but must be read as a dialogue between faith and environment.

Within these variegated global and national geographies, one discerns that the Baptist communion is less a monolith and more a constellation of communities, each orbiting local cultural, economic, and societal forces. These forces sculpt attitudes toward alcohol through a complex sedimentation of history, ethnicity, social class, and regional identity. For example, a Baptist in rural Alabama may inherit a tradition in which abstinence is a carefully guarded virtue tied to family honor and communal reputation. Meanwhile, a Baptist in metropolitan Seattle might view alcohol through lenses shaped more by individual conscience and contemporary health awareness than by inherited cultural strictures. Both experience the same overarching scriptures, yet their interpretive communities animate those scriptures differently through the crucible of distinct geographical realities.

Furthermore, regional variations also illustrate how Baptists address the tensions between personal liberty and communal accountability regarding alcohol. In regions marked by more rigid social controls and homogeneous populations, the watchful communal eye often reinforces strict temperance. Conversely, in more pluralistic and mobile urban areas, the emphasis tends toward personal freedom balanced by exhortations to wisdom and moderation. This dichotomy often reflects the broader cultural politics of the locale, either prioritizing collective conformity or individual autonomy. In this way, geography informs not only practical behavior but theological emphases, with regional Baptists differently parsing concepts like holiness, self-control, and love for neighbor as they relate to alcohol use.

Yet it is important to recognize that these regional repertoires are not fixed. Migration, digital communication, and denominational interchanges continuously reshape Baptist views, creating hybrid forms and eclectic practices. The regional vineyard, then, is not enclosed by fences but connected by pathways that allow ideas, and wines, literally and metaphorically, to flow and ferment anew. Southern Baptists moving to the Pacific Northwest bring their conservative temperance perspectives into dialogue with more permissive contexts; Midwestern Baptists relocating abroad negotiate former cultural norms with fresh community realities. These exchanges provoke re-examination, sometimes resistance, sometimes renewal, evidencing geography's ongoing dynamic relationship with Baptist convictions on alcohol.

The metaphor of the "twilight orchard" resonates deeply here. Just as fruits hanging in a dimming orchard cannot be categorized into singular varieties by light alone, so too Baptist communities, under the setting sun of tradition and dawn of contemporary culture, display a spectrum of colors and flavors concerning alcohol. Each region's unique climatic conditions, historical, social, and economic, nurture different fruit, while all remain connected by the root systems of shared biblical heritage and Baptist identity. This orchard is neither perfectly ordered nor randomly scattered; it is an intentional cultivation where restraint, joy, and reverence intermingle according to soil and season. Geography, therefore, is more than a backdrop; it is an active cultivator in the spiritual and practical attitudes that Baptists bring to the subject of alcohol.

Moreover, the regional nuances often manifest in denominational governance and local church autonomy, hallmark strengths of Baptist polity. Regional conventions and associations exert considerable influence on the framing of alcohol policies, ranging from outright prohibitions in some locales to more permissive guideline structures elsewhere. Local churches, exercising freedom within these parameters, reflect their community's cultural dispositions and pastoral priorities. In some regions, this has resulted in robust support networks for sobriety and abstinence advocacy, while in others, it encourages educational programs centered on responsible use and harm reduction. Again, the geography of these communities steers the dialectic between doctrinal fidelity and pastoral care, shaping the lived experience of faith amid the realities of alcohol.

At the intersection of regional variation and individual experience stand the personal testimonies that animate Baptist perspectives with human complexity. Stories of believers in Tennessee recount how regional expectations of abstinence shaped not only their choices but identity formation within family and church. Testimonies from Baptist young adults in California often reveal a journey of wrestling between inherited convictions and contemporary social practices involving alcohol, leading to nuanced reconciliations. Such narratives underscore the inseparability of local culture and personal faith journeys, invigorating the theological discourse with practical realities. Geography emerges not just as a macro-level influence but as an intimate storyteller weaving with the threads of individual conscience.

Additionally, the role of Christian education and theological training within each region cannot be overstated. Seminaries and Bible colleges, reflecting their regional contexts, impart doctrinal teachings and cultural attitudes about alcohol that permeate local churches and communities.

For example, institutions situated in strongly prohibitionist areas emphasize holiness codes that stress avoidance, while those in more moderate contexts may offer courses exploring biblical moderation and cultural engagement. These educational factors feed back into regional variations, fostering churches whose approaches to alcohol correspond closely with their theological formation environments.

Conversely, the advent of technology and media has introduced a convergent force, narrowing some geographic gaps as Baptist communities worldwide can access similar sermons, Bible studies, and theological debates. Yet even here, regional cultures selectively consume and adapt these inputs, reaffirming local distinctiveness amid global connectivity. Thus, the tension between geography's centrifugal pull and digital connectivity's centripetal force continually reshapes Baptist interactions with alcohol, creating a dynamic ecology of faith and ferment.

Regional variations within Baptist communities also reveal the multiplicity of responses to societal challenges linked to alcohol. In places grappling with addiction crises, economic hardship, or public health concerns, Baptist churches often become active agents of social intervention, advocating for sobriety and providing care for those affected. Conversely, in regions where alcohol is a cornerstone of cultural celebration and socializing, Baptists may focus on fostering responsible enjoyment, hospitality, and awareness. These differing emphases illuminate how geography shapes both the problematics addressed by the church and the pastoral strategies employed, blending theology with social realities in regionally specific ways.

It is essential, finally, to acknowledge that the regional diversity in Baptist alcohol perspectives invites greater humility and openness within the denomination's wider conversations. Recognizing that faithful interpretation and practice cannot be disentangled from the soil in which it takes root encourages an ethos of listening and learning across regions.

Such an attitude resists monolithic pronouncements and fosters the dialogical community the Baptist tradition esteems, whereby unity in essentials coexists with liberty in nonessentials. Geography thus becomes a gift, an opportunity to witness how faith in Christ navigates diverse cultural streams, enriching rather than dividing the fellowship.

In conclusion, the profound impact of geography on Baptist perspectives and practices concerning alcohol forms an indispensable lens through which to understand the rich variation within the tradition. The contours of belief and behavior are shaped by historical legacies, cultural customs, socioeconomic conditions, theological education, and personal narratives, all flowing through the filter of place and community. This kaleidoscopic view challenges simplistic binaries and invites a deeper appreciation for the nuanced interplay between faith and environment. Where one Baptist orchard may yield the fruit of absolute abstinence, another produces the ripened flavor of careful moderation; both reflect, in their own way, a sincere pursuit of divine guidance illuminated by the lights of geography and grace.

Modern Cultural Challenges

In contemplating the modern cultural challenges that shape Baptist perspectives on alcohol, it is essential to appreciate that these views are far from static; rather, they are vibrant, living reflections of broader societal currents, historical pressures, and deeply rooted theological convictions that have evolved over generations. The contemporary American landscape, in particular, serves as a complex tapestry of varied influences, ranging from legal frameworks and public health initiatives to popular media portrayals and shifting social attitudes, that collectively contribute to an intricate dialogue on alcohol within Baptist communities. This dialogue, often marked by tension between tradition and progress, underscores how cultural shifts threaten to destabilize established norms while simultaneously opening pathways to new understandings and empathetic engagement.

One of the foremost cultural forces molding Baptist attitudes toward alcohol today is the pervasive presence of alcohol in mainstream society. Unlike earlier eras when drinking was often confined to specific social contexts or rituals, alcohol now saturates everyday life in nearly every corner of American culture. From ubiquitous advertisements showcasing glamorous lifestyles associated with wine, beer, and spirits, to the celebratory ubiquity of alcohol at social gatherings, corporate functions, and media portrayals, the cultural message tends to normalize drinking as an integral facet of sociability and success. For many Baptists steeped in a tradition emphasizing temperance and moral clarity, this normalization poses an existential challenge. It demands that adherents calibrate their responses carefully: how might one maintain fidelity to a legacy that cautions against the spiritual dangers of alcohol when society seems to embrace its consumption with such enthusiastic ubiquity? This question resonates profoundly not only within individuals but across congregations grappling to uphold doctrinal teachings while engaging effectively with the world around them.

Moreover, the proliferation of craft brewing and artisanal fermentation movements in recent decades has complicated the cultural landscape significantly for Baptists. This burgeoning trend, while celebrating heritage, creativity, and local community life, entwines alcohol with identity, craftsmanship, and hospitality in novel ways that are difficult to neglect or outright reject. Many younger Baptists, especially those whose lives intersect with these evolving cultural values, find themselves drawn into conversations that challenge the binary notion of alcohol as inherently sinful versus harmless. Instead, they encounter narratives valuing moderation, intentionality, and respect for tradition coupled with cultural innovation. This evolving discourse is accompanied by a generational gap, wherein older members of the faith might view any engagement with alcohol as perilous, while younger believers seek a more moderate and nuanced approach embodying grace and wisdom without fear or shame. Navigating this intergenerational tension requires careful listening and humility, as it raises profound questions about how culture informs theology and vice versa.

Regional differences within Baptist communities also play a significant role in shaping how alcohol is perceived and integrated into faith practice. In the American South, where Baptist life has historically dominated the religious and cultural fabric, a legacy of prohibitionist values remains prominent, interwoven with socio-political identities and local traditions. Here, alcohol often carries a heavier symbolic burden, tied not only to moral concern but to cultural memory and communal identity that resists accommodation. Conversely, in more urban or diverse regions of the United States, as well as among Baptists with more ecumenical or global identities, attitudes toward alcohol tend to be more permissive, reflecting local norms that view moderate consumption as acceptable or even customary. These regional variations produce a patchwork of beliefs and practices that can complicate denominational unity, sparking debates over control, witness, and pastoral care. One can observe a tangible struggle within regional expressions of Baptist faith as they negotiate fidelity to denominational standards while responding pastorally to their unique social milieus.

Another critical cultural dimension influencing Baptist perspectives concerns the public health discourse surrounding alcohol use. In recent decades, new findings emerging from medical and psychological research have intensified public awareness of alcohol-related health risks, addiction potential, and social harms such as impaired driving, domestic violence, and community disintegration. These sobering realities resonate deeply within Baptist circles, where concern for holistic well-being, spiritual, physical, and relational, is a defining hallmark of faith practice. As awareness grows, many Baptist leaders and congregations have become more proactive in promoting abstinence or responsible drinking as acts of stewardship and witness. The church increasingly finds itself in the challenging position of advocating for compassion and support for individuals grappling with addiction, while maintaining clear moral boundaries to protect vulnerable members from harm. This tension sharply reveals the intersection between faith, scientific knowledge, and social responsibility, demanding that Baptists engage thoughtfully with public health initiatives without compromising core convictions.

Simultaneously, the shifting cultural attitudes toward sexuality, gender, and individual autonomy intersect with discussions about alcohol in significant ways. In a society increasingly attentive to identity politics and personal freedoms, the act of drinking or abstaining from alcohol is no longer merely a moral or religious choice; it becomes a potential statement about individuality, community belonging, and social identity. Baptists face cultural pressure both to honor the individual conscience shaped by personal background and experiences and to nurture a sense of collective accountability grounded in biblical instruction. This dynamic is especially salient among younger generations who may resist what they perceive as authoritarian or restrictive religious norms, advocating instead for a faith that embraces complexity and respects plurality. The challenge for Baptist churches and theologians is to articulate a vision of temperance that embraces freedom and responsibility without falling into relativism or legalism, thus fostering a vibrant, lived faith that engages lovingly with cultural diversity.

Technology and social media form another modern front in the cultural battleground over Baptist views of alcohol. The digital age accelerates the exposure of individuals to diverse perspectives, temptations, and testimonies relating to drinking. Online platforms offer spaces where Baptists can share personal stories of struggle, recovery, and reflection, but they also expose believers to secular messages glamorizing alcohol or promoting risky behavior. The virtual realm, therefore, acts as a double-edged sword, providing unprecedented opportunity for community building and pastoral care, while also necessitating vigilant discernment and proactive education to counter misinformation or harmful cultural narratives. Furthermore, social media magnifies the visibility of personal choices to broader audiences, where decisions about drinking can become points of critique or division within faith communities. This dynamic challenges Baptists to cultivate resilient and compassionate approaches that honor individual struggles and triumphs while maintaining communal bonds.

Economic factors add nuanced layers to the cultural context as well. In some Baptist communities, socioeconomic status profoundly influences how alcohol is regarded. In regions afflicted by economic hardship, alcohol abuse may be linked visibly to family breakdown, poverty, and despair, reinforcing stricter communal attitudes against its use. Conversely, affluence can coincide with sophisticated drinking cultures where moderation and connoisseurship are the norm, complicating straightforward prohibitive stances. The church's response in such varied economic contexts must be both prophetic and pastoral, addressing systemic causes of alcohol problems and offering healing and restoration. This economic dimension amplifies the need for a contextualized, empathetic approach that considers the lived realities of congregants and their communities.

Legal and political developments also exert considerable influence over contemporary Baptist positions on alcohol. Changes in legislation around alcohol sales, distribution, and consumption reflect shifting societal norms that intersect with religious ethics. In some states and municipalities, laws permitting or restricting alcohol mirror regional religious demographics and cultural values, creating environments either hospitable or hostile to open dialogue about drinking. Baptists, often deeply invested in civic life, find their theological commitments tested as they navigate advocacy for temperance alongside respect for individual freedoms enshrined in law. Furthermore, contemporary debates on issues such as addiction recovery programs, mental health resources, and responsible advertising regulations challenge Baptists to participate thoughtfully in public policy, striving to witness ethically within pluralistic societies.

An additional dimension of cultural challenge arises from interfaith and ecumenical interactions. As Baptist communities increasingly encounter Christians from traditions with differing views on alcohol, ranging from conservative abstinence to sacramental use, the resulting conversations stimulate reexamination of entrenched perspectives. Encounters with Catholic, Orthodox, and mainline Protestant practices of incorporating wine into worship and communal life invite Baptists to reflect more deeply on the biblical foundations and theological meanings of alcohol consumption. Sometimes these dialogues provoke internal tension, while at other times they yield opportunities for enriched understanding and unity across denominational lines. This intersection of faith traditions presses Baptists to hold their convictions with humility and openness, appreciating the diverse ways Christians live out their beliefs about alcohol.

Furthermore, the challenge of pastoral care around alcohol use continues to present modern Baptists with profound opportunities and dilemmas. Pastors and church leaders must walk the delicate line between pastoral sensitivity and doctrinal integrity when addressing congregants struggling with alcohol. Stories of redemption and fall, of painful consequences and miraculous recovery, are emblematic of the human condition within faith communities. The diversity of experiences within Baptist churches means that a one-size-fits-all approach is impractical and often harmful. Instead, nuanced, empathetic ministries that include counseling, support groups, and community education programs are emerging as vital components of contemporary church life. These programs seek to create safe spaces where questions about alcohol can be honestly discussed without judgment, fostering healing and growth. Such pastoral initiatives embody the tension between justice and mercy, discipline and grace, which remain central to the Baptist spiritual journey.

Cultural dynamics related to racial and ethnic diversity within Baptist congregations further complicate the discussion of alcohol. African American Baptists, Hispanic Baptists, and others often bring unique cultural traditions and historical experiences that influence their views on drinking. For some, alcohol consumption is intertwined with cultural identity and social cohesion; for others, historical trauma related to substance abuse in marginalized communities shapes a more cautious approach. Recognizing and respecting these nuances encourages Baptists to transcend simplistic generalizations, promoting intercultural dialogue and inclusive pastoral strategies that acknowledge diverse lived realities. This inclusivity bolsters the church's witness as a place of unity amid diversity, a sanctuary where complex cultural narratives about alcohol are met with understanding and hope.

The relationship between alcohol and spirituality emerges **as another** critical site of modern cultural challenge. Some Baptists wrestle with the idea of whether drinking wine or beer under certain circumstances might be not only permissible but spiritually enriching, invoking biblical imagery of joy, celebration, and blessing. Others hold firmly to sobriety as a pathway to holiness, emphasizing self-control and avoidance of temptation. These divergent views reflect an underlying spiritual tension about how the use of created good things interacts with sanctification and holiness. Contemporary cultural conversations pushing for a more holistic, integrated spirituality inspire some Baptists to revisit their assumptions, seeking to balance reverence, freedom, and joy in faithful living. Navigating these spiritual nuances demands a charitable listening ear and a theological imagination willing to hold apparent contradictions in creative tension.

Finally, the generational transformation of faith expression profoundly shapes how Baptists today engage alcohol and related cultural questions. Millennials and Generation Z bring fresh perspectives shaped by digital connectivity, global awareness, and evolving social values. Many reject the rigid dichotomies of past eras, preferring a faith that embraces complexity, personal integrity, and inclusivity. At the same time, they face unique pressures, mental health crises, substance misuse epidemics, and cultural fragmentation that complicate their relationship with alcohol.

The Baptist church's mission includes discerning how to support these generations in forming healthy habits and spiritual practices around alcohol, without alienating them through outdated or overly rigid teachings. This frontier calls for creative pastoral vision, innovative educational frameworks, and dynamic community engagement that honor both tradition and change.

In sum, the modern cultural challenges confronting Baptist views on alcohol are neither simple nor monolithic. They reflect a rich interplay of societal trends, regional identities, public health concerns, theological convictions, economic realities, legal frameworks, and diverse cultural narratives. This complexity pushes Baptist believers toward a more nuanced, empathetic, and dialogical stance, one that resists reductionism and embraces the mystery and tension inherent in faithful discipleship. Grappling with alcohol in contemporary culture invites Baptists to embody a faith that is both rooted and adaptive, disciplined and joyful, clear in moral conviction yet gracious in communal engagement. It is within such a spiritual posture that Baptist communities can move forward with hope, unity, and integrity amid the ferment of modern life.

Personal Stories: Faith and Alcohol in the Baptist Experience

Stories of Temperance and Commitment

In the quiet corners of countless Baptist homes, in the gentle pulse of Sunday morning gatherings, within the whispered prayers of small groups and the determined resolve of youth leaders, there unfold stories, intimate and profound, of men and women who have taken up the mantle of temperance not simply as a social custom or a traditional expectation, but as a deliberate, deeply ordained act of faith. These narratives, woven into the very fabric of their spiritual journeys, speak volumes about the complex relationship between personal conviction, communal witness, and the ever-present challenge of navigating a world in which alcohol often looms as both a cultural constant and a spiritual battleground. The tapestry of these lives reveals the kaleidoscope of motivations, struggles, reconciliations, and unwavering commitments that define the lived experience of choosing abstinence as an expression of devotion.

One cannot begin to trace these stories without first meeting Sarah, a middle-aged woman whose serene presence belies the fierce determination born from years of wrestling with family inheritance and faith. Raised in a household where alcohol cast long shadows of conflict and sorrow, Sarah's path was marked early by a personal vow: to safeguard her soul and family from the destructive cycles her parents could not escape. Her choice of abstinence was less about judgment of others and **was deeply rooted** in a longing to honor God through stewardship of her own body and mind. In her local congregation, Sarah has become both a silent sentinel and an active voice, quietly exemplifying how the call to temperance can be a beacon of hope rather than condemnation. Her story is not one of denial but of liberation, demonstrating the serenity that can bloom when one embraces restraint as a form of worship. She speaks candidly about moments of tension, when social pressures swirl thick, when invitations to celebrate seem laden with compromise, but also about the grace that sustains her, knitting strength into solitude and resilience into fellowship.

Then there is Thomas, a young Baptist pastor navigating the delicate balance between tradition and pastoral care, whose journey into temperance is marked by theological inquiry and pastoral sensitivity. For Thomas, the decision to abstain from alcohol was born not merely from inherited denominational norms but from a close reading of scripture that led him to a nuanced understanding of holiness, stewardship, and community health. His seminary years were punctuated by spirited debates on Romans and Ephesians, yet his resolve solidified when confronted with the reality of addiction in his ministry context. He shares with humility how his commitment to temperance deepened as he witnessed firsthand the havoc wrought by alcohol abuse among his congregants and beyond. Yet Thomas also recognizes the diversity within his church, the ones who responsibly partake, the ones who abstain, and the ones struggling within. His story invites reflection on the pastoral tensions that arise when doctrinal convictions meet the variegated realities of human experience. In his preaching and counseling, Thomas errs on the side of grace, encouraging open dialogue while modeling the peace he finds in his own abstinence, illustrating how faith can guide moral clarity without fracturing community bonds.

Margaret's story unfolds along a different trajectory, one marked by cultural history and personal heritage. Coming from a lineage of Southern Baptists steeped in a tradition of temperance, Margaret's abstinence is a heritage inherited with fierce pride and personal empathy. Yet her narrative is not static; it is alive with the complexities of modern life and cultural shifts. She recounts the celebrations and tensions of family reunions, where the clinking of glasses often signals joy but also stirs old wounds. Her commitment to abstinence is intertwined with a sense of responsibility to bear witness to the covenant her community holds with God, upholding a standard that has defined Baptist identity for generations. Yet Margaret's reflections also reveal a compassionate awareness of the need for humility in judgment, a humility grounded in the recognition that faith journeys are deeply personal and often fraught. Through her, we glimpse the delicate dance of honoring tradition while extending grace, of standing firm on principles without erecting walls that isolate. Her life story is a testament to the endurance and adaptability of faith lived honestly within the messy contours of human relationships.

Cameron's experience adds yet another layer, he is a young man whose decision to embrace temperance emerged from a crucible of temptation, failures, and redemption. Raised in a Baptist community that valued sobriety, Cameron nonetheless found himself drawn into the allure of alcohol during his college years, a period as much marked by spiritual searching as by the hazards of newfound freedom. His honesty about the confusion, the mistakes, and ultimately his recommitment to abstinence draws the reader into a personal battleground where faith both falters and fortifies. His testimony resounds with the rawness of vulnerability, revealing how the decision to abstain is not a one-time event but an ongoing, sometimes grueling process of daily surrender and renewal. Cameron's story challenges simplistic stereotypes of temperance as mere abstinence, showing instead how it can be a vibrant, courageous stance of faith, with struggles that many face silently and victories that emerge slowly. He advocates a theology of grace and restoration, emphasizing that abstinence, far from a mark of perfection, can be the sign of a heart that yearns for wholeness and is willing to fight for it.

Evelyn, a grandmother whose years span the changing landscapes of Baptist thought and culture, offers a wisdom steeped in longevity and humility. Her choice to abstain from alcohol was never a burden but a joy, an offering that connected her to a host of biblical women who found strength in obedience and clarity. Evelyn's story is rich with memories of a church that once barked firmly against liquor stores and now navigates a world more fragmented and less certain. She recalls how the value of temperance was taught not only through sermons but through community example, church dinners without wine, social events where sparkling cider signaled celebration without excess. Evelyn reframes temperance as a gift, one that is as much about self-control and discernment as it is about self-denial. Her reflections inspire contemplation on the ways older generations can nurture younger believers, passing down traditions that balance reverence with relevance. Through Evelyn's voice, we hear the heartbeat of enduring faithfulness that spans eras, offering continuity amid change.

Among the voices converging are those of contemporary women leaders like Jasmine, a vibrant youth minister whose ministry is defined by openness and dialogue. Jasmine's approach to temperance is informed by a conviction that faith must engage honestly with culture, not retreat from it. She shares how her own abstinence is an intentional act of ministry, a way to stand as a distinctive witness amid peer pressure and shifting social mores. Yet Jasmine is quick to emphasize the importance of empathy, recognizing the varied experiences of her congregation, many of whom come from families where alcohol is woven tightly into **the social fabric** and stories of pain. Her story is a call to conversation, a plea to keep the doors of dialogue open, to listen more than judge. Jasmine embodies a vision of temperance that is as much about connection and care as it is about conviction, encouraging young believers to anchor their choices in faith while honoring the journeys of others.

Intertwined with these personal testimonies are accounts of couples who have found unity and strength in mutual commitment to temperance. Their shared stories often echo with the power of partnership, two souls journeying together in a vision of faith that renounces excess to embrace health, joy, and witness. These couples speak of the strength born in shared discipline, the grace that softens moments of temptation, and the joy uncovered in celebrations unmarred by dependency. Through their lives, temperance becomes a communal experience, a sacred covenant that deepens marital bonds and models a life of balance for children and community alike.

Across these diverse narratives, a common thread emerges: temperance for these individuals is never a restrictive imposition but a liberating choice fueled by faith's call to holistically love God and neighbor. It is an act of spiritual intentionality, a daily embodied prayer that resonates far beyond the physical abstention from alcohol. These lived experiences illuminate how personal narratives intersect with theology, culture, and church practice, revealing that the path of temperance is as richly textured and uniquely navigated as any spiritual discipline.

Moreover, these stories challenge reductive portrayals of abstinence as merely legalistic or outdated, displaying instead a mosaic of faith journeys marked by honesty, grace, and courage. They confront the complexity of human weakness and strength, of societal pressures and divine calling, offering a hopeful vision where commitment and freedom coexist. In their accounts, we witness the transformative power of faith that guides moral resolve while embracing compassion, a harmony that breathes life into what could otherwise be a source of division.

In contemplating these stories, readers are invited into a twilight orchard of the soul, where each fruit is a story of joy, restraint, and reverence, a sacred space where faith and fermentation meet not as adversaries but as companions on the journey toward spiritual maturity and communal harmony. These personal portraits, vibrant and varied, beckon us to listen with open hearts, to understand complexities without haste, and to honor the commitment that so many embrace with quiet dignity as an offering of love to God and neighbor alike.

Navigating Social Drinking and Faith

In the intricate dance between social engagement and spiritual conviction, many believers find themselves walking a delicate tightrope when it comes to alcohol. The social world often pulses with occasions that seem inextricably tied to the ritual of sharing drinks, whether at weddings, community gatherings, or moments of celebration and commiseration alike. Within these settings, the tension between cultural participation and personal faith becomes palpable, raising poignant questions about identity, belonging, and moral integrity. For some, abstinence is a clear line drawn, a protective boundary cultivating spiritual discipline and testimony. Yet for others, the question is murkier, marked by a nuanced grappling that resists simplistic categorization, inviting a thoughtful reconciliation between outward practice and inward grace instead.

One such narrative emerges from a woman who grew up within a Baptist household where sobriety was preached as both a moral imperative and a communal standard. Her adolescence was shaped by sermons underscoring the dangers of alcohol and the virtues of temperance, making her keenly aware of the cultural divide she would later navigate. In her young adult years, entering a university setting where social drinking was prevalent, she faced the challenge of reconciling her upbringing with her desire to forge authentic friendships and community ties. At first, she chose a path of strict avoidance, mindful of not compromising her beliefs. However, over time, through thoughtful reflection and conversations with classmates from diverse backgrounds, she began to discover a more textured understanding. She realized that for her, the crucial issue lay not in the presence of alcohol itself but in the manner and motives governing its use. Attending a party, she might decline a drink yet remain present, engaging honestly and fully in fellowship without participating in excess or pretending to be something she was not. This balance, she found, nurtured both her spiritual integrity and relational openness, allowing her faith to witness amid cultural context rather than retreat in isolation. Her journey illustrates a dynamic tension, one not resolved by rigid abstinence alone but by a conscientious navigation responsive to both conviction and community.

Contrasting this experience is the testimony of a Baptist youth minister who, having witnessed the ravages of alcohol abuse in his family and congregation, embraces a firm stance on abstention. For him, social drinking is inseparable from the risks of addiction and moral failure, and he advocates for clear boundaries as a safeguard of personal holiness and pastoral responsibility. He recounts stories of congregants struggling to maintain sobriety, whose faith was deeply tested by the very social spheres where drinking was the norm. To mitigate these challenges, he organizes gatherings focused on wholesome fellowship devoid of alcohol, offering alternative spaces where the community can gather in joyous celebration and mutual support without the entanglements of fermentation. His narrative underscores that within Baptist circles, the choice to abstain often stems from both theological conviction and pastoral care, informed by painful realities rather than mere cultural conformity. Yet even in his firmness, he acknowledges the complexity of the modern social landscape and the importance of compassionate dialogue with those whose experiences diverge from his own.

Amidst these testimonies is a voice from a suburban Baptist who approaches the matter with a hermeneutic of moderation, emphasizing the biblical affirmations of wine as a gift and symbol of joy. Drawing on scriptural passages where wine plays a positive role, from the celebrations at Cana to the exhortations to enjoy life's blessings, he interprets the call to sobriety as a call to self-control rather than outright prohibition. His social circles often include those who drink responsibly, and he believes excluding oneself entirely risks forfeiting the relational bridges that can lead to meaningful spiritual conversations. Nevertheless, he exercises caution and prayerful discernment, recognizing the individual accountability embedded in scriptural warnings against drunkenness. His life exemplifies a faithful integration of cultural participation and spiritual vigilance, walking a path that honors both the richness of tradition and the demands of holiness.

These divergent accounts illuminate the profound complexities entwined in the lived experience of navigating social drinking and faith. They testify that this balance is rarely a static resolution but an ongoing negotiation shaped by personal history, theology, community influences, and the ever-shifting terrain of cultural norms. For many, it is entwined with questions of witness, how does one embody a faith that calls for temperance without alienating those who choose otherwise? How can believers foster fellowship that is inclusive yet faithful, celebratory yet sober-minded? The metaphor of the twilight orchard, shimmering with ripe fruit and whispered boundaries of shadow and light, finds its echo in these real-world stories where joy, restraint, and reverence coalesce in varying degrees.

In exploring these lived realities, some find that early rigid stances soften with maturity, as faith deepens and expands to embrace complexity. Others find resolve fortified through struggle, perceiving the challenges of social drinking not as mere trials but as crucibles shaping character and testimony. There is an undeniable interplay between individual conscience and communal ethos, a tension that calls for humility, patience, and a willingness to listen as much as to speak. Within Baptist communities, where strong convictions about temperance have shaped identity for generations, this dialogue is both vital and delicate, carrying the weight of inherited wisdom alongside the winds of contemporary cultural shifts.

Moreover, the role of grace emerges as a luminous thread weaving through these testimonies. For those wrestling with the temptation or legacy of alcohol-related harm, it becomes a beacon of hope and restoration rather than condemnation. One family's story recounts how a grandfather's decades of sobriety, grounded in faith, inspired younger members to approach social drinking with serious intentionality. Yet it also tells of moments when failure and forgiveness intertwined, when a youthful misstep was met not with ostracism but with redemptive love, opening pathways for healing and renewed commitment. These narratives resonate with the biblical themes of mercy and redemption, highlighting the church's role not only as a moral tribunal but also as a compassionate community embodying Christ's reconciling love.

Interestingly, the crossroads of social drinking and faith also invite creative expressions of fellowship that transcend the binary of drinking versus abstention. Some Baptist churches have embraced social spaces where non-alcoholic beverages, such as grape juice, artisanal sodas, or fermented teas, become symbols of shared celebration without the attendant risks of inebriation. These spaces cultivate conviviality grounded not in the buzz of alcohol but in the warmth of kinship and common purpose. In doing so, they embody a visible testimony of how faith can shape cultural participation thoughtfully, inviting all to the table with dignity and joy. These pioneering efforts suggest that the tension between culture and conviction need not produce division but can inspire innovation, fostering communities where every member's path is honored and the fruits of the Spirit, love, joy, peace, and patience, collectively flourish.

The stories of individuals who attend social events, like weddings or holiday gatherings, reveal the nuanced choreography involved in managing expectations and internal convictions. One young man recalls attending a cousin's wedding where the toasts flowed as freely as the wine, yet he chose simply to raise his glass of water, feeling both the sting of social awkwardness and the peace of staying true to his conscience. Over time, he developed a gracious confidence that disarmed curiosity and respected his boundaries without alienating others. His experience highlights the importance of presence over participation, a powerful witness that authentic engagement need not require compromise but rather the courage to embody one's convictions with kindness and humility.

Conversely, experiences also abound where faith communities have struggled with judgment or misunderstanding toward members whose attitudes toward alcohol differ. A middle-aged woman's story speaks to the pain of alienation when her choice to enjoy an occasional glass of wine was met with suspicion and distancing by her church family. Her journey toward reconciling her personal convictions with her place in the faith community involved confronting assumptions, fostering open conversations, and ultimately finding spaces where diverse perspectives could coexist. Her story underscores that the navigation of faith and fermentation is not only a personal matter but also a communal challenge, requiring the church to evolve in wisdom and grace, learning to embrace complexity without fracturing unity.

Underlying these individual and communal stories is a broader cultural backdrop that shapes perceptions and choices. In societies where alcohol holds a prominent social and economic place, abstinence can sometimes feel countercultural or isolating. Particularly among younger generations, there is an increasing awareness of health considerations, mental wellness, and responsible consumption that shapes new paradigms of engagement. These cultural currents ripple through faith communities, prompting reassessment and dialogue. Within Baptist circles, this has fueled conversations about how to best articulate a biblically grounded yet culturally sensitive approach, one that acknowledges the dangers of alcohol misuse while appreciating its place in cultural expressions of hospitality, celebration, and fellowship.

The theological reflections accompanying these narratives further enrich the conversation. The Baptist theologian's insights remind us that scriptural admonitions against drunkenness coexist harmoniously with affirmations of wine as a symbol of God's blessing, thereby framing the issue not as a simplistic prohibition but as an invitation to live in balanced holiness. Understanding this balance helps believers negotiate the space between legalism and permissiveness, cultivating a moral discernment anchored in love and self-control. In this moral economy, social drinking is not inherently sinful but carries responsibility and vigilance, avoiding excess and fostering a heart attuned to God's guidance.

Thus, the lived experience of navigating social drinking and faith is richly textured, marked by stories of steadfastness and flexibility, caution and openness, exclusion and inclusion. It challenges believers to embody a spirituality that is neither rigid nor lax but marked by wisdom, grace, and courage. The plurality of convictions within the Baptist tradition reflects a tapestry rather than a monolith, each individual weaving their own thread into a collective narrative that honors both faithfulness to Scripture and sensitivity to culture.

In the end, this navigation is much like the twilight orchard itself, a space where the sweetness of the fruit coexists with shadows, where moments of light invite reflection on restraint, and where the horizon beckons toward unity amid diversity. It is a journey less about definitive answers and more about ongoing dialogue, where faith illumines the path, and fermentation becomes not a source of division but of enriched fellowship. As believers engage with these realities, walking the balance between social participation and spiritual conviction, they treasure the grace that sustains them, cultivating communities where temperance and joy, discipline and delight, reverence and celebration find harmonious expression.

Challenges and Transformations

The journey of faith is often marked by moments of profound challenge and transformation, and when alcohol enters the picture, these moments can become particularly complex and deeply personal. For many within the Baptist community, the struggle to reconcile personal experiences with alcohol and the spiritual convictions rooted in tradition poses a dynamic tension that resists simple resolution. The narratives captured here are not merely anecdotal; they are living testimonies that weave together the threads of joy, temptation, restraint, failure, and ultimately, renewal, reminding us that the path of faith is rarely linear or predictable. Each story reveals a distinct facet of the multifaceted relationship between belief and drinking, offering rich insight into the human spirit's capacity for growth amidst tension and contradiction.

Consider first the account of James, a man who grew up steeped in Baptist culture, where the message about alcohol had been clear and unwavering: abstain. For James, this clarity provided a firm moral compass during his turbulent youth, yet as he ventured into adulthood, the rigid boundaries of prohibition began to feel constraining. His first encounter with wine did not come in a moment of rebellion but rather in a quiet setting, sharing a modest glass of red wine with his wife at a meal, celebrating a milestone that felt sacred in its own right. The experience marked a subtle but significant shift. James wrestled with the inherited scriptural warnings and the lived experience of savoring the elements of creation with a spirit of gratitude rather than excess. Over time, this tension evolved into a nuanced position, one that honored the cautionary wisdom in scripture while also allowing space for mindful enjoyment that neither compromises faith nor personal integrity. James's narrative illustrates a transformation of understanding from a black-and-white worldview toward one delicately shaded in grace and discretion, embodying the struggle many face as they seek to integrate cultural tradition with personal revelation.

In stark contrast stands the testimony of Maria, whose story centers on a profound struggle with the destructive side of alcohol. Raised in a Baptist household that vehemently opposed any consumption of spirits, Maria's earliest memories of church were imbued with stern sermons about the perils of drunkenness. Despite, or perhaps because of, this environment, she found herself entangled in the very behaviors her faith warned against, using alcohol as a refuge from pain and isolation. Her journey through addiction was fraught with despair and alienation, compounded by the stigma present within her faith community. Yet, it was precisely this atmosphere that eventually became the crucible for her transformation. Drawing upon her faith's message of redemption and forgiveness, Maria engaged in a difficult process of self-examination, healing, and reconciliation with both God and the church community. Her story is not one of condemnation but of mercy, the hard-earned restoration that flows from a faith willing to confront brokenness and offer hope. Maria's experience challenges simplistic judgments and calls believers to a posture of compassion, recognizing the complexities that underlie every person's encounter with alcohol.

Then there is Elijah, whose narrative navigates the space between cultural identity and personal conviction. As a young pastor in a Baptist church within a community where alcohol was interwoven with social and familial occasions, Elijah found himself at a crossroads. The church's official stance was aligned with abstinence, reflecting generations of temperance advocacy, yet in his pastoral care, Elijah witnessed the nuanced realities of his congregants' lives. Some valued the tradition wholeheartedly while others wrestled with feelings of exclusion or judgment. Elijah's transformation was less about changing personal habits; he remained abstinent but more about reshaping his approach toward pastoral empathy and dialogue. His reflections led him to foster conversations that acknowledged the grace-filled possibilities within the biblical texts, the diversity of the Baptist experience, and the call to love without conditionality. Elijah's story reveals a leadership shaped by humility, bridge-building, and the courage to embrace complexity rather than demand conformity, an evolution vital for communal health and spiritual depth.

Among these varied journeys, Renee's story shines a spotlight on the role of women in navigating faith and alcohol, a dynamic frequently laden with unique social and theological pressures. Raised in a conservative Baptist environment that prescribed strict roles and expectations, Renee initially viewed alcohol through a lens of moral suspicion and potential threat to familial harmony. Her transformation was sparked by her inquisitive nature and academic pursuit of biblical hermeneutics, which exposed her to the richness and ambiguity of scripture regarding alcohol's role in worship, medicine, and celebration. Moving beyond inherited taboos, Renee embraced a vision of faith that welcomed critical inquiry and personal freedom balanced by responsibility. Yet her journey was not without tension, as a mother and a believer, she grappled with the implications of her evolving views within her family and church, facing skepticism and opposition. Renee's narrative underscores the profound challenge of embodying transformation in contexts where tradition weighs heavily and invites readers to consider the courage needed to live authentically amidst contested convictions.

Equally compelling is the testimony of Thomas, whose experience speaks to the broader societal shifts impacting Baptist perspectives on alcohol. As a youth minister in a rapidly changing urban setting, Thomas noticed that younger generations often lacked the deep cultural memory of temperance that shaped their elders. Many young Baptists viewed moderate drinking as a normative part of social life, even as their older mentors upheld abstinence as a non-negotiable virtue. Thomas's transformation involved bridging this generational divide by fostering open conversations that honored both convictions. Hesitant at first to challenge longstanding prohibitions, he gradually recognized the opportunity for richer, more honest dialogue that tackled not only alcohol use but the underlying values of respect, self-control, and grace. His story reflects a broader transformation within Baptist communities striving to stay faithful to core principles while engaging meaningfully with contemporary culture, insisting that such balance is not a dilution but a deepening of faith's relevance.

Additionally, Marissa offers a powerful reflection on the spiritual dimension of transformation as it relates to alcohol. Having grown up in a Baptist family where wine appeared solely as an emblem of temptation or sin, she recounts her awakening during a spiritual retreat where she encountered a more textured understanding of biblical wine as a symbol of joy, covenant, and healing. This experience prompted Marissa to unlearn long-held biases and embrace a spiritual maturity willing to hold paradox, recognizing wine as both a blessed creation and a potential snare. Her transformation involved not merely reinterpreting scripture but cultivating a personal spirituality marked by discernment and gratitude rather than fear or prohibition. Marissa's narrative invites believers to contemplate how faith matures not through rigid rules but through humility, wrestling with mystery, and the grace to accept complexity.

The collective resonance of these narratives reveals a kaleidoscopic view of transformation, one that engages heart, mind, and community in evolving attitudes toward alcohol within the Baptist tradition. Far from a single trajectory, these stories highlight the interaction between inherited doctrine, personal experience, cultural context, and spiritual reflection. They chart the difficult process of questioning and reshaping convictions in light of lived realities, often accompanied by resistance, doubt, and vulnerable honesty. Yet, they also radiate hope, illustrating faith's power to nurture growth, forgiveness, and wisdom even amid uncertainty. They challenge readers to resist simplistic dichotomies of right and wrong, temperance and indulgence, instead encouraging a posture that embraces nuance and complexity with grace.

Individual transformations also highlight the communal dimension vital to understanding faith and fermentation. The stories show that changes in belief about alcohol rarely occur in isolation; they ripple through families, congregations, and wider Baptist circles, challenging traditions and fostering dialogue. This relational aspect calls for patience and empathy as communities navigate new understandings, balancing respect for heritage with openness to evolution. The painful tensions these transformations can generate become invitations for deeper connection, as believers learn to listen deeply, honor diverse journeys, and pursue unity without uniformity.

Moreover, these narratives voice a critique of rigid structures that too often eschew pastoral care in favor of legalism. They underscore the need for churches to offer safe spaces for honest conversations about alcohol, temptation, and freedom in Christ. Transformation emerges not from judgment but from relationships grounded in love and grace, enabling individuals to confront struggles without shame and to celebrate milestones without fear. Such environments embody the very heart of the gospel, where transformation is ongoing, God's mercy is abundant, and faith embraces the fullness of human experience.

The journey through challenges and transformations in relation to alcohol within the Baptist tradition ultimately points toward a richer, more mature faith, one marked by humility, compassion, and thoughtful engagement rather than simplistic mandates. It calls believers to a deep listening that honors both scripture's wisdom and the lived realities of the faithful. This process may be slow and uneven, often fraught with tension, but it is also deeply life-giving, inviting the church to embody more fully the reconciling power of Christ in a world marked by both joy and struggle. The evolving stories of James, Maria, Elijah, Renee, Thomas, and Marissa remind us that faith and fermentation together invite a sacred dialogue, one that nourishes the soul and strengthens community, even as it challenges us to wrestle honestly with our fears, hopes, and convictions.

Gary E. Risenhoover

Balancing Joy and Restraint: The Spiritual Discipline of Temperance

Temperance in Historical and Theological Context

Temperance, often viewed in the public imagination as a stern and austere commandment to abstain, harbors a far richer and more nuanced heritage within the spiritual roots of Christianity, particularly within the Baptist tradition. When the word is unpacked, it reveals not merely a legalistic restriction on indulgence but a profound discipline that encompasses self-control, wisdom, and reverence. Temperance, therefore, is less about denial and more about the deliberate cultivation of character, a measured harmony between joy and restraint that opens the soul to deeper spiritual growth.

Tracing this discipline back to its historical origins requires us to peer into the ancient world, where the human need for balance amidst physical appetites was first explored. The biblical narrative, beginning in the Old Testament, already showcases a complex relationship with wine and fermented beverages, highlighting their capacity to bring blessing, social joy, and sacred symbolism while cautioning against their potential to breed excess and moral decay. The Psalmist's celebration of wine as "gladdening the heart of man" (Psalm 104:15) sits alongside Proverbs' warning that "wine is a mocker, strong drink is raging" (Proverbs 20:1). This dual tension sets the stage for an overarching spiritual posture: the body's appetites are gifts to be stewarded with discipline, not denied out of fear or indulged without reverence.

In the intertestamental period and the nascent Christian church, this posture matured into a more defined theological framework. Apostolic teachings scattered throughout the New Testament reinforce the centrality of self-control, a fruit of the Spirit described by Paul as an essential feature of the believer's character (Galatians 5:22–23). The early church fathers, grappling with a pagan culture rife with debauchery, adopted a stance that saw temperance as a key virtue. It was not simply about moral avoidance but about cultivating a life that reflected the order and holiness of God. The pursuit of temperance was a pursuit of alignment with divine intention, an expression of freedom rather than bondage, where the believer lived not to serve impulses but to honor God with mind and body alike.

Within the Baptist tradition, this concept of temperance was further shaped by theological convictions emerging from the Reformation and beyond. Baptists, emphasizing the authority of Scripture and the necessity of personal faith commitment, regarded temperance as a discipline rooted deeply in the individual's response to God's holiness. Unlike some Christian traditions that sanctioned moderate drinking under regulated conditions as acceptable, many Baptists in subsequent centuries intertwined their understanding of temperance with strong convictions about holiness, social responsibility, and the dangers of addiction. This was not an arbitrary imposition but a theologically grounded response to the biblical call towards sanctification, a process by which believers are progressively conformed to the character of Christ.

Historical circumstances amplified this theological emphasis. The temperance movement of the nineteenth and early twentieth centuries, in which Baptists were prominently involved, propelled these convictions into the public square. The temperance crusade, often led by motivated believers longing to redeem society from the scourge of alcoholism, sought to contextualize spiritual restraint within practical reforms. Yet, even in this heightened social activism, the roots of temperance remained profoundly spiritual. It was not mere prohibition but a vision of human flourishing that was pursued, a flourishing grounded in self-mastery, in the freedom from the enslaving grip of excess, and ultimately in the cultivation of deeper communion with God and neighbor.

The theology underlying temperance is intricately woven with the doctrine of creation and the imago Dei, the belief that humanity is made in the image of God. This belief asserts that every human impulse, including the enjoyment of food and drink, is a gift intended to be ordered rightly. When a person practices temperance, they echo the divine nature of harmony and orderliness, exercising the dominion over creation that God intended, but in a way that respects limits and honors sacred gifts. It is, in essence, a form of worship, as much an act of reverence as prayer, acknowledging that the human body is a temple of the Holy Spirit and must be treated with care and respect.

Moreover, temperance intertwines closely with the concept of stewardship. The steward, biblical in origin, is one who manages resources entrusted by God with wisdom and accountability. In this sense, the ability to moderate alcohol consumption, or to abstain entirely, is a vital dimension of managing one's own life as a gift from God. This stewardship transcends self-interest and radiates outward to community and society, fostering relationships built not on excess and recklessness but on mutual respect, care, and holiness.

In the spiritual discipline of temperance, self-control operates not as a cold, mechanical restraint but as a dynamic engagement of the will empowered by grace. Faith, in this context, acts as both the soil and the water for the growing of this fruit. Without faith, temperance becomes mere human willpower prone to failure and frustration; with faith, it becomes a transformative journey where weakness is met with divine strength. The believer learns that temperance is not to be understood as mere asceticism but as a joy-infused practice of freedom, where boundaries become the framework for life's beauty rather than its limitation.

From a theological perspective, this discipline also bears eschatological significance. The call to live soberly is not only a present moral ideal but points toward the coming fullness of God's kingdom, a time when all appetites and desires will be perfectly ordered in harmony with divine will. Temperance is thus a foretaste of that future condition, a mini-kingdom living out the hope of redemption and restoration amid present struggles. It beckons believers into a lifestyle where faith is embodied, where spiritual maturity is measured by one's ability to inhabit freedom without succumbing to enslavement, whether to wine, wealth, or any other worldly pleasure.

Historic voices within the Baptist tradition echo these insights. The writings of theologians such as John Gill, William Carey, and later leaders in the temperance movement capture a consistent pattern: temperance serves as both a protective hedge against sin and a pathway toward spiritual health. This is echoed in sermons, treatises, and personal correspondence where the discipline is portrayed not just as an ethical duty but as a means of grace. Such writings reveal a vision of temperance that honors both individual holiness and communal wellbeing, highlighting the interwoven nature of personal choices and their wider relational impact.

In juxtaposition to other Christian traditions, Baptists have often held a more rigorous position, emphasizing personal purity and social witness. Yet, this position has not been devoid of nuance. Within the community, diverse voices have emerged, pointing out that temperance does not demand prohibition in all circumstances but calls for wisdom married to compassion. This internal dialogue reflects an understanding that temperance, while grounded in firm biblical and theological soil, must be attentive to the complexities of human experience and cultural context.

Such a perspective invites believers to consider temperance not only as a commandment to abstain but as a lifelong spiritual discipline, akin to prayer and fasting, that shapes character and molds the soul into the likeness of Christ. It becomes an avenue toward greater inner peace, clearer conscience, and more vibrant service. The spiritual roots of temperance, then, stretch deep into the history of God's people, inviting all who follow to partake in this rich heritage of self-mastery, joy harnessed by reverence, and freedom fashioned through grace.

Ultimately, temperance in the historical and theological sense is a call to live in harmony with God's created order, embodying love through restraint, and walking faithfully in the tension between freedom and obedience. It is a vibrant, living tradition that transcends mere abstinence and opens a pathway to spiritual flourishing, a journey marked by grace, wisdom, and an ever-deepening reverence for the gifts God has entrusted to human stewardship. In embracing this discipline, believers echo the Psalmist's declaration of wine as a blessing, while heedfully living out the Proverbs' caution, discovering in this balance an invitation to a life both joyful and reverent, both spirited and sober.

Practical Applications of Temperance

Temperance, far from being a mere prohibition or a set of external restrictions, is a profound discipline that permeates the very essence of spiritual growth and self-mastery. It is often facile to reduce temperance to a simple refrain of "don't drink" or "avoid excess," but to do so is to miss the vibrant spiritual life that blossoms when self-restraint is embraced not as a burden, but as a pathway to freedom. To practice temperance is to embark on a journey where one cultivates balance, nurtures reverence for the body and soul, and learns to navigate the complexities of human desire with wisdom and grace. Within the Baptist tradition, and indeed across many Christian circles, this discipline takes on nuanced shapes, serving both as a safeguard against the potential harm of alcohol and as a testament to living out a faith that honors God in every choice, no matter how seemingly mundane.

Individuals who embrace temperance often find themselves walking a delicate tightrope between joy and restraint. This balance is a daily exercise, frequently invisible to the casual observer but profoundly transformative to the practitioner. It demands a high degree of self-awareness, knowing one's limits, recognizing triggers, and fostering a spirit attuned to God's guiding presence. The practice of moderation is less about vigilant prohibition and more about cultivating the fruit of the Spirit, self-control, so well articulated in Galatians 5. This spiritual fruit is not simply an internal prowess; it is a manifestation of grace working through human weakness, enabling believers to choose what edifies rather than what destroys. One poignant way this insight takes form is in the mindful consumption of alcohol: choosing to partake, to abstain, or to moderate not out of fear or social pressure, but out of reverence for God's gift of health, clarity, and the well-being of one's community.

To live temperately does not mean dwelling in a joyless asceticism. Quite the opposite, it is an embrace of liberty underpinned by discipline, a joyful freedom that flows from knowing one's boundaries and respecting them. For many individuals, especially within Baptist communities, this involves deliberate choices around social situations. The contemporary Christian who practices temperance learns to face worldly pressures with firm but gracious boundaries. At church gatherings, family celebrations, or moments of leisure, the art of saying "no" or "enough" is a sacred exercise. Far from alienation, it transforms these moments into opportunities for testimony, showing that joy and moderation can coexist harmoniously. Through such examples, others are encouraged, compassion is cultivated, and a culture of responsible enjoyment takes root.

Moreover, temperance extends beyond the question of alcohol to shape an entire lifestyle of thoughtful consumption and ethical decision-making. The individual committed to self-restraint often finds that the principles of moderation radiate outward, affecting attitudes toward food, entertainment, work, and speech. A person practicing temperance becomes adept at discerning excess in all forms, realizing that overindulgence in any domain can dull spiritual senses and erode community well-being. Temperance nurtures an overarching posture of mindfulness, where impulses are observed and filtered through the lens of faith. It is this holistic disposition that enables believers to integrate the discipline naturally, avoiding the alienation that rigid or legalistic approaches often cause.

The cultivation of temperance is deeply rooted in prayer and reflective practices. The believer who seeks to grow in self-restraint turns often to Scripture and spiritual disciplines not merely for rules but for strength and inspiration. The Psalms, Proverbs, and New Testament narratives offer vivid portraits of wisdom's counsel: to seek balance, to guard the heart, and to live with integrity before God and neighbor. Many find that daily moments of meditation, quiet reflection, journaling, or even spiritual fasting, reinforce the commitment to moderation by sharpening awareness and inviting God's presence into the struggles of temptation. Such practices transform temperance from a cold rule into a warm embrace of divine empowerment. They also create space to rehearse gratitude for blessings, which paradoxically lessens the desire for excess by cultivating contentment with enough.

In practical terms, this might look like deliberate preparation before occasions involving alcohol. For example, some believers choose to fast from alcohol not simply as a test of willpower but as a spiritual discipline of humility and dependence on God's provision for satisfaction and joy. Others take proactive steps by setting personal limits, deciding beforehand how much to drink or in what contexts to abstain, thereby exercising forethought and accountability. This approach acknowledges human fallibility and creates safeguards against succumbing to peer pressure or emotional impulses. Accountability partners or spiritual mentors often play a crucial role here, providing encouragement and gentle correction, reflecting the communal nature of temperance practiced within the Body of Christ.

Another important but often overlooked dimension of practicing temperance is the cultivation of empathy and social responsibility. Alcohol is not experienced in isolation; it touches families, friendships, and communities, sometimes bringing joy and other times causing harm. Those who embrace temperance deeply understand that their choices ripple outward. By practicing restraint, the individual honors not only personal health and spiritual clarity but also models care for others, especially for those who struggle with addiction or who have been hurt by excess. This posture of compassion reflects the heart of Christ's call to love one's neighbor. It transcends judgment and invites a shared journey of healing, respect, and restoration. Through such acts, temperance becomes more than self-discipline, it becomes a channel of grace flowing into the wider world.

The metaphor of an orchard at twilight from earlier chapters carries particular resonance here: just as fruit must be carefully tended, harvested at the right time, and preserved thoughtfully, so too must the virtues of moderation and celebration intertwine gracefully. Cultivating temperance requires nurturing the inner spiritual life, honoring the 'soil' of one's conscience and faith, and responding to the rhythms of life with patience and wisdom. It is in this orchard, where temptation and grace dance, that self-restraint is not a form of scarcity but a fertile ground of abundance. In the harmonious interplay of faith and fermentation, believers find a dynamic equilibrium where joy is not sacrificed but deepened by reverence and responsibility.

Furthermore, engaging with temperance invites believers to question societal narratives that often glorify excess or equate freedom with uninhibited pleasure. Through spiritual reflection, Christians learn to distinguish cultural pressures from kingdom values, reclaiming a posture of freedom defined not by indulgence but by allegiance to Christ. This countercultural stance is not withdrawal but an intentional participation in a community that values health, holiness, and mutual care. It challenges the pervasive dichotomy that frames pleasure and piety as opposites, revealing instead that disciplined joy is a higher form of happiness, one that enriches both the individual and the community while honoring divine intention.

Amidst this practice, many believers discover unexpected joy in everyday moments. The simple ritual of sharing a modest cup of wine or cider with family and friends can become, through temperance, a sacred act, a celebration of creation, relationship, and gratitude. These occasions carry a profound symbolism, echoing biblical imagery where wine often signifies blessing, abundance, and covenant joy. The temperate Christian, therefore, navigates a middle path that neither demonizes alcohol nor capitulates to its dangers but honors it as part of God's good gifts when handled wisely. This wisdom imbues social interactions with a richer texture, transforming them into occasions of intentional blessing rather than careless excess.

Importantly, temperance practiced individually gains deeper vitality when it is embraced communally. Within Baptist churches and fellowship gatherings, creating environments that support moderation rather than encourage overindulgence becomes a practical outworking of faith. Leaders and laypersons modeling temperance inspire confidence and create safe spaces where all can participate without fear of judgment or pressure. Such communities nurture the gifts of hospitality, respect for diverse convictions, and celebration of restorative joy. By weaving temperance into the fabric of community life, believers embody the kingdom's call to love and care for one another holistically, fostering a culture where physical, emotional, and spiritual well-being flourish side by side.

Self-restraint, therefore, is neither a superficial exercise nor an isolated ideal but a transformative lifestyle deeply embedded in faith. The individual who walks this path becomes a beacon of God's sustaining power, showing how human freedom is amplified, not diminished, by discipline. This journey requires humility, recognizing when to seek help or to say no, as well as courage to stand firm amid contrary voices. Embedded in this practice is the recognition that true liberty lies not in unchecked desires but in the harmonious ordering of life's pleasures under divine guidance.

As the narrative of faith and fermentation unfolds, it becomes clear that temperance is more than a reaction to excess; it is a proactive embrace of wholeness. For believers, this means learning to savor what is good, holy, and life-giving with intention and depth. It means practicing gratitude in every sip and every choice, allowing the discipline of moderation to cultivate a sacred space where faith and flesh meet harmoniously. Thus, temperance unfolds as an art, a spiritual craftsmanship that, far from constraining life's joy, refines and ennobles it, enabling each person to drink deeply of God's blessings without losing themselves in the flood.

Ultimately, practicing temperance is a daily, sometimes hourly, decision, shaped by prayerful discernment, community wisdom, and personal resolve. It is a path walked with grace, marked by moments of triumph and times of struggle, and sustained by the unshakable hope that self-restraint opens the door to fuller communion with God and neighbor. The believer who embraces this path discovers that through temperance, not only is the excess tamed, but the soul's deepest hunger for meaning, purpose, and love is tenderly nourished. It is in this sacred balance that faith and fermentation find their fullest expression, inviting all who journey to partake in the abundant life that self-control and joyful celebration together create.

Spiritual Benefits and Challenges

Temperance, often perceived narrowly as a strict moral boundary or a set of prohibitions, reveals itself upon closer spiritual examination as a profoundly positive discipline that nurtures the soul, cultivates deeper faith, and invites believers into the sacred rhythms of reverence and self-mastery. Rather than a mere external restraint imposed on behavior, temperance unfolds as an internalizing grace, a transformative practice that shapes character, emotional awareness, and one's relationship with God. This subtle yet powerful dimension of temperance manifests as a crucible wherein spiritual growth is forged through the tensions and triumphs of everyday living, especially when facing the allure, challenge, and complexities that alcohol presents within the Christian journey.

The spiritual benefits of temperance emerge most vividly when its practice aligns with the biblical portrayal of the fruit of the Spirit, particularly self-control. Self-control is not a harsh prohibition but a freeing gift, enabling believers to navigate the vicissitudes and temptations of life without succumbing to excess or dependency. In this sense, temperance bridges the visible and invisible realms: it is manifested by tangible choices, opting for sobriety or moderation, but its roots run deep into the heart's cultivation of discipline, discernment, and trust in God's sovereignty. By choosing temperance in the face of cultural norms that often glorify indulgence, the faithful open a pathway toward greater awareness of the Spirit's leading, an expanded capacity for resisting temptations that ultimately enslave, and an enhanced sense of dignity that honors the body as a temple of the Holy Spirit.

Within the Baptist tradition, which reveres moral clarity and personal accountability, temperance carries an added spiritual weight. The decision to abstain or consume alcohol responsibly resonates beyond personal health; it becomes an act of worship, a declaration that life's fullness is not found in fleeting pleasures but in steadfast communion with God and community. This perspective reframes temperance from mere restriction into a joyful discipline that reveals and exercises faith itself. Each moment of resistance becomes a spiritual triumph, echoing the Psalmist's refrain of delighting in the law of the Lord, which is sweeter than honey to the soul. By embracing temperance, believers cultivate the spiritual muscle to say "no" to what diminishes life and "yes" to the abundant life promised by Christ.

The challenge inherent in temperance lies precisely where its benefits are most profound: it demands vulnerability, intentionality, and ongoing conversion of the will. This challenge is visible in the spiritual journey of many who wrestle with alcohol's place in their lives, whether struggling with past excesses, navigating cultural pressures, or discerning how personal convictions align with denominational teachings. The paradox is rich: temperance invites a fidelity that confronts weakness without shame, transforms struggle into grace-filled perseverance, and nurtures a faith that is both realistic and hopeful. This wrestling becomes a sacred dialogue between God and soul, where each choice is a step toward maturity, reflecting Paul's exhortation to "live by the Spirit" and not gratify the desires of the flesh.

Moreover, temperance as a spiritual discipline fosters a deeper appreciation for the ordinary moments of life, those seemingly mundane opportunities where faith is lived out in practice. The restraint practiced over a glass of wine or a fleeting craving becomes a meditation on discipleship itself, how to honor God through stewardship of the body and mind, how to model integrity for others, especially the vulnerable, and how to embody love that sometimes means saying no to self for the good of neighbor. In this way, temperance reveals itself as a vehicle for sanctification, the ongoing process of becoming Christlike in thought, word, and deed. It aligns the body's habits with the soul's longings, harmonizing desire with divine purpose.

One cannot overlook the communal dimension in the spiritual benefits of temperance. In Baptist fellowship, where mutual accountability and shared testimony carry sacred weight, the practice of temperance contributes to the health and unity of the faith community. Choosing temperance can be an act of solidarity with those who suffer from addiction or who have been wounded by misuse of alcohol. It embodies the biblical call to "bear one another's burdens," offering a living witness to the grace that empowers transformation. The collective cultivation of temperance creates a sacred space where joy and restraint coexist, where celebration does not drown in excess but sings with gratitude and moderation, inviting all into a fuller participation in divine life.

Tempering desire through temperance also sharpens spiritual senses, enabling believers to attune more keenly to God's voice and presence. In a culture saturated with sensory overload and instant gratification, the practice of self-restraint paradoxically opens the door to spiritual attunement. It fosters a holy quietness, allowing room for prayerful listening and deeper meditation on Scripture. This is not a withdrawal from joy but an invitation to savor joy more profoundly and discern its divine source. Wine, in biblical images, symbolizes blessing, celebration, and even the new covenant in Christ's blood; temperance creates space where such sacred symbols are not trivialized but honored in their fullest spiritual meaning, untouched by misuse.

The challenges of temperance also intersect with the reality of freedom in Christ. The New Testament portrays Christian freedom not simply as liberty to indulge but as freedom to serve one another in love, which sometimes calls for voluntarily putting aside certain liberties for the sake of others. This spiritual paradox, freedom exercised through self-limitation, is central to understanding the role of temperance. It exposes the heart's motives and calls believers to examine what truly enslaves or liberates. The struggle to maintain temperance provokes honest reflection about deeper spiritual attachments and dependencies. It invites embracing a freedom that is measured not by license but by love, not by satisfying personal desire but by seeking God's will and the flourishing of community.

At times, embracing temperance can be isolating, especially when cultural narratives pressure conformity to indulgence. This isolation highlights the need for spiritual resilience grounded in firm conviction and grace-filled community support. The practice of temperance thus becomes a spiritual discipline that tests faith's endurance and persistence. It calls upon believers to renew their minds continually, draw strength from Scripture, recall God's faithfulness, and rejoice in the power of the Holy Spirit to sustain them. Within this endurance emerges a refined faith, one that stands undeterred amid cultural currents and personal trials.

The spiritual benefits of temperance also weave tightly into the broader narrative of Christian witness and mission. Believers are called not only to personal holiness but to be lights in the world, exemplifying ways of living that point beyond themselves to God's kingdom. Temperance shapes this witness by highlighting a lifestyle marked by intentionality, responsibility, and reverence rather than by heedlessness or excess. It contributes to a testimony that godliness is practical and lived in the ordinary choices as much as in grand declarations. Through this lens, temperance assumes a prophetic dimension, challenging societal norms that idolize consumption and immediacy, inviting the world to glimpse a different order based on sacrificial love and wisdom.

As the spiritual journey deepens, temperance can become a form of spiritual artistry, a dance between desire and discipline, joy and restraint, celebration and sobriety. It teaches the soul to delight in God's presence beyond external stimulants, to discover the feast set before it that no earthly wine can replicate. This artistry is often cultivated through prayer, fasting, contemplation, and communal worship, all practices that accompany temperance and enrich its spiritual significance. The story of faith and fermentation thus unfolds not as a harsh tale of denial but as a rich narrative of transformation and wholeness.

The dialectic of benefit and challenge in temperance invites believers into a posture of humility and grace. Recognizing that temperance is not always an achieved state but a lifelong pursuit, believers are encouraged to rely on God's mercy and the strength of the Spirit. They are reminded that moments of failure do not signify defeat but opportunities for renewed commitment and growth. This grace-centered approach fosters a spiritual environment where confession, encouragement, and healing coalesce, sustaining the journey toward greater maturity and freedom.

In daily life, the impact of temperance on personal faith often surfaces in subtle yet profound ways. It may shape how one participates in social rituals, approaches hospitality, or navigates moments of temptation. It influences how individuals pray about their desires and boundaries, how they seek accountability and support, and how they cultivate gratitude for the body and soul God entrusted to them. Over time, this consistent practice reveals itself as a cornerstone of spiritual integrity, a foundation upon which trust in God is built, and a beacon for others seeking to live faithfully amid complexities.

The narrative of temperance also invites reflection on the meaning of joy in a Christian life. It challenges the assumption that joy must be equated with uninhibited pleasure and suggests instead that true joy often arises from disciplined freedom. This perspective aligns with biblical themes where joy is a deep spiritual fruit that flourishes in the soil of obedience, faithfulness, and trust. Hence, temperance, far from quenching the spirit, ignites joy by enabling believers to savor life's blessings with clear minds and grateful hearts, undistracted by the fog of excess.

Furthermore, temperance intersects with the call to holiness, being set apart for God's purposes. The disciplined life models the radical commitment to embody God's kingdom in the here and now, resisting cultural pressures that dilute faithfulness. It becomes a sacred testimony that holiness is both an inward transformation and outward expression, lived in everyday choices including how one approaches alcohol. This dynamic reinforces the Baptist emphasis on personal and communal holiness sustained through the Spirit's power.

Ultimately, the spiritual benefits and challenges of temperance illuminate the profound intertwining of faith and freedom, strength and vulnerability, joy and restraint. They reveal a journey that is not about rigid rules but about relationships, relationships with God, self, and others, shaped by trust, humility, and love. Temperance stands as a spiritual pathway, inviting believers to walk thoughtfully, prayerfully, and joyfully into lives that honor God's design for flourishing in all dimensions. It calls forth a faith that is at once disciplined and deeply compassionate, capable of confronting the complexities of alcohol's presence in faith communities with wisdom, grace, and hope.

This understanding forms a bridge between ancient scriptural wisdom and contemporary experience, offering a way forward in conversations often marked by division and misunderstanding. It reframes temperance as a profound blessing, a source of spiritual vitality that enriches personal faith and strengthens communal bonds. In embracing this fuller picture, believers find themselves not constrained but liberated; not burdened but buoyed; not isolated but embraced by a faith that celebrates life's fullness through both restraint and celebration. Through the lens of temperance, faith and fermentation harmonize, offering a rich symphony of worship, witness, and well-being in the tapestry of Christian life.

Temperance as a Path to Holiness

Within the enduring tapestry of Christian spirituality, temperance emerges not simply as an exercise in moral restriction but as a vibrant pathway toward sanctification, a dynamic dance of devotion that intertwines self-mastery with divine alignment. For many believers, this virtue transcends mere abstention or avoidance; it blossoms into a discipline that refines the soul, cultivates spiritual maturity, and nurtures an intimacy with God that radiates through all aspects of life. Temperance, in this deeper and richer sense, becomes both the soil and the fruit of holiness, a sacred rhythm where restraint is not a burden but a deliberate embracing of freedom in Christ.

At its core, temperance is often misunderstood as a negative formula, a set of prohibitions meant to constrain human desire and deny pleasure. Yet, this view misses the expansive and liberating truth that Scripture reveals. The biblical witness presents temperance as a fruit of the Spirit, a hallmark of a life being transformed by grace. This transformation unfolds not through external imposition but through internal surrender, an ongoing conforming to the image of Christ. In this light, restraint does not cloak deprivation; it unveils a richer relationship with God, where freedom is found in submission, and joy is deepened by discipline.

The Apostle Paul, in his epistles, consistently weaves temperance into his exhortations on holy living. It sits among virtues like love, patience, and faithfulness, signaling that self-control is not incidental but essential in the believer's journey of sanctification. To practice temperance is to recognize one's body and spirit as temples of the Holy Spirit, entrusted not for reckless indulgence but for sacred stewardship. It is a conscious acknowledgment that the choices concerning earthly desires and pleasures bear eternal significance. In choosing restraint, believers echo Christ's own self-emptying, embracing a modesty and respect for their created nature that mirrors obedience and devotion.

This pathway toward holiness through temperance becomes particularly poignant when considering the cultural context in which the issue of alcohol often arises. Within Baptist tradition, temperance has historically signified a robust and sometimes rigorous standard of conduct, especially regarding abstaining from alcoholic beverages. Such discipline is not merely a social stance but a spiritual posture rooted in the desire to embody Christlike character. Yet temperance here is not understood narrowly as legalism or prohibition but as a deliberate cultivation of self-control that protects the soul from bondage to sin and promotes the flourishing of the Christian witness. From this perspective, temperance embodies a sanctifying grace, empowering believers to navigate temptation with clarity and integrity while honoring God with their bodies and choices.

The link between temperance and sanctification is also profoundly psychological and relational. Self-control fosters a mind renewed and a heart attuned to God's will, enabling believers to transcend the immediate gratifications that often distract from spiritual goals. Practicing temperance becomes an exercise in heightened awareness, a spiritual discipline that sharpens discernment and softens the grip of cravings that can fracture fellowship and wound testimony. Through this restraint, individuals often find an unexpected peace and joy, a freedom from the anxieties that accompany uncontrolled indulgence, a freedom that opens space for greater dependence on God's providence and power.

Furthermore, temperance as a spiritual discipline draws believers into a more profound rhythm of prayer, meditation, and sacramental life. It invites a daily dying to self-will, aligning desires with divine desires. In moments of resisting temptation, the soul is forged in ways that mere intellectual assent cannot accomplish. This experiential involvement in holiness nurtures humility, acknowledging human weakness while celebrating God's sustaining strength. In restraining one's appetites, the believer simultaneously embraces vulnerability and trust, finding that true strength flows not from self-sufficiency but from reliance on God's grace.

Critically, temperance also preserves the communal and relational dimensions of holiness. Within the church, individual discipline affects the health of the whole body. Choosing temperance, therefore, is not isolated but relationally responsible, a testament to love for others, preventing scandal, encouraging spiritual integrity, and fostering an environment where the gospel can be faithfully proclaimed. It strengthens the bonds of community, demonstrating that spiritual maturity is not just personal accomplishment but shared flourishing. In this way, temperance weaves together the threads of personal devotion and corporate witness, embodying the kingdom's values in tangible ways.

In embracing temperance as a positive virtue, the believer reclaims the garden of Eden's original vision, not a life shackled by prohibition but a life marked by flourishing in God's created order. Just as the fruit of the vine can symbolize blessing and joy, so too does the thoughtful exercise of self-control signal reverence and respect for the divine gifts of sustenance and celebration. Temperance is, paradoxically, an act of honoring pleasure rightly ordered by wisdom and love. This gift of disciplined enjoyment reflects the very nature of God's intention for human delight and fulfillment, free from the corruption of excess.

Moreover, as the spiritual journey deepens, temperance becomes entwined with a broader theology of embodiment and incarnation. Recognizing that God became flesh and dwelt among us, sanctification involves honoring the material as a vessel of divine presence. Thus, temperance is not asceticism that denies the body but rather a reverence for the body as an integral part of incarnational faith. It calls believers to steward their bodies with care, knowing they are instruments of worship and service. This perspective fosters a holistic spirituality where mind, body, and spirit coexist in harmonious devotion, enriching the believer's capacity for love, ministry, and witness.

The practice of temperance also cultivates patience and perseverance, qualities indispensable to the Christian life. In a world marked by instant gratification and relentless consumption, temperance stands as a countercultural witness, reminding believers that holiness often requires waiting, enduring, and thoughtful restraint. It impresses upon the heart the value of delayed reward and persistent faithfulness, transforming not only appetites but character. This long arc of spiritual growth demonstrates that sanctification is less about isolated moments of virtue and more about the steady march toward Christlikeness, propelled by disciplines that sustain and shape the soul across time.

Importantly, temperance holds a liberating dimension that challenges simplistic notions of sin and freedom. It confronts the tyranny of desire by offering a way into authentic freedom, a freedom that is not the license to indulge but the power to choose what aligns with God's will. In this, temperance becomes a co-creative act with God's Spirit, where human agency is preserved and empowered within the framework of divine purpose. Believers find in this discipline a joyful obedience that frees them from the chains of compulsive behavior, enabling a richer, fuller experience of life in Christ.

This spiritual discipline also invites believers into reflective self-examination, a necessary step in sanctification that temperance encourages. Through the lens of temperance, individuals become more attuned to the subtle motions of the heart and the triggers that prompt excess or imbalance. It fosters a gentle but honest self-awareness that does not judge harshly but seeks understanding and healing. This introspective aspect of temperance deepens the journey toward holiness by uncovering hidden idols, false dependencies, and areas where grace can heal and transform. It nurtures spiritual maturity by opening pathways for confession, repentance, and renewal.

Moreover, temperance intersects powerfully with the practice of gratitude. Restrained indulgence naturally cultivates a disposition of thankfulness, an appreciation for God's blessings that is not taken for granted but savored with mindfulness. This attentiveness to God's providence enriches worship and daily life, transforming ordinary moments into sacred encounters. Temperance, therefore, functions as a gateway to a heart of gratitude, deepening relationship with God and enhancing spiritual joy. This thankful orientation reinforces the sanctifying process, binding believers ever closer to the source of all goodness.

The biblical narrative beautifully encapsulates this holistic vision of temperance as a sanctifying grace. From the wisdom literature that extols moderation as understanding, to the prophetic condemnations of drunkenness and excess, Scripture offers a balanced portrayal of alcohol and desire, not as inherently evil but as forces to be skillfully and reverently managed. The vineyard imagery itself evokes a spiritual metaphor where vineyards must be carefully tended to produce good fruit, just as the soul must be nurtured through discipline. This delicate balance challenges believers to partner with God in cultivating a holy life marked by both joy and restraint.

Within the Baptist tradition, this nuanced understanding of temperance enriches the historical emphasis on moral clarity and communal responsibility. Here, temperance is championed not solely as a preventive measure against vice but as a proactive spiritual cultivation that fosters vibrant faithfulness. It is the soil in which the seeds of sanctification take root and flourish, enabling believers to embody the gospel with integrity and love. While the denomination has often highlighted abstinence, the deeper theological current points toward the transformative power of temperance as a positive discipline, one that shapes character, preserves witness, and glorifies God.

The tension between abstinence and moderation within Baptist circles further illuminates how temperance operates as a dynamic spiritual practice. It invites ongoing dialogue and discernment, pushing believers to engage Scripture, tradition, and experience with humility and openness. In navigating this complex terrain, temperance challenges rigid stereotypes and encourages compassionate understanding, revealing a rich spectrum of faithful responses united by a commitment to holiness. This vibrant conversation itself becomes a sign of spiritual vitality, where the church wrestles with cultural realities while seeking to honor God in all things.

Personal testimonies within Baptist and wider Christian communities illustrate the lived reality of temperance as a pathway to holiness. Stories of individuals wrestling with temptation, learning to say no, and finding new depths of reliance on God bring warmth and texture to theological principles. These narratives reveal that temperance is neither easy nor merely a theoretical ideal but a courageous, daily endeavor that transforms lives. They underscore the paradox that in choosing limitation, believers often discover an unexpected abundance of peace, clarity, and spiritual strength.

Ultimately, temperance as a discipline invites believers into a relationship marked by reverence, not only for God but for their own humanity and for the sacredness of life's gifts. It cultivates a posture of worship where every act of self-control echoes a deeper submission to divine authority and love. Through this lens, holiness is not a distant abstract but a present reality, lived moment by moment in choices large and small, including those surrounding alcohol and other desires. Temperance, then, is a sacred rhythm of the soul, a gentle yet powerful heartbeat that sustains faithfulness and draws the believer into an ever-deepening union with God.

In reflecting on temperance as a path to holiness, one discovers that the journey itself is both challenging and profoundly rewarding. It requires vigilance against complacency, courage to confront temptation, and grace to endure failures. Yet, it also offers richness, freedom, and profound joy. Through temperance, believers participate in the ongoing work of sanctification, partnering with the Spirit to cultivate a life that honors God, edifies the church, and blesses the world. It stands as a testament to the transformative power of faith, where self-restraint is no longer a mere rule but a radiant expression of love, devotion, and holiness in the fabric of everyday living.

Contemporary Debates within the Baptist Community

Advocates for Strict Abstinence

Within the vibrant tapestry of Baptist communities, firmly woven strands of conviction advocate for strict abstinence from alcohol, a position deeply rooted not only in theological tradition but also in pastoral care, social ethics, and historical precedent. Advocates for total avoidance do not merely espouse a personal preference or cultural habit; rather, they articulate a pastoral theology that intertwines scriptural interpretation with concern for individual and communal well-being. This perspective often springs from a profound sense of duty to protect the vulnerable, those whose lives can be ravaged by alcohol's insidious grip, and to uphold a moral clarity that witnesses to the holiness expected in Christian discipleship. From these devout voices arises a chorus stressing that abstinence serves as a safeguard against temptation and a clear testimony to the transformative power of faith, a visible banner unfurled in a world too frequently shrouded in excess and moral ambiguity.

The arguments supporting strict abstinence are multifaceted and resonate both with personal experiences and collective wisdom handed down through Baptist heritage. At the heart of their case lies the belief that the Bible, far from endorsing casual drinking, issues solemn warnings that caution against the destructive consequences of wine and strong drink. Proverbs, Solomon's repository of wisdom, includes stern admonitions that "wine is a mocker" and "strong drink is raging," portraying alcohol as a deceptive substance that seduces reason, dulls judgment, and incites conflict. For advocates of abstinence, these warnings carry more than rhetorical weight; they represent divinely inspired guidelines for sustaining a holy life marked by self-control and sober-mindedness. Such voices remind their communities that Paul's exhortation to be "sober, vigilant" (1 Peter 5:8) and not given to "drunkenness" (Ephesians 5:18) are not vague recommendations but urgent imperatives. In many Baptist circles, these passages form a theological bedrock for the commitment to avoid all intoxicating substances as a way to live commendably within a fallen and fragile world.

Beyond the direct scriptural admonitions, the advocates for strict abstinence emphasize the undeniable social consequences of alcohol misuse, which impact not only individuals but entire families and communities. They argue that the wreckage left in the wake of alcoholism, broken homes, battered relationships, financial ruin, and even the tragic loss of life cannot be understated or dismissed as mere collateral damage. The call to abstinence, therefore, emerges not simply as a personal virtue but as a communitarian ethic designed to shield the church and society from these wounds. Many testimonies shared within Baptist assemblies echo stories of recovering alcoholics or families torn apart by addiction, highlighting the redemptive power of renouncing all use of alcohol. These narratives imbue the abstinence stance with pastoral urgency, transforming it from dry doctrinal assertion to lived reality wherein faith intersects with urgent, tangible human need. In this way, abstention operates not only as an antidote to sin but also as an emblem of compassionate responsibility, a deliberate choice to offer protection and healing in place of harm and despair.

Historically, the Baptist tradition's embrace of temperance and eventual advocacy of outright abstinence finds its roots in the 19th-century revivalist and reform movements that emerged amid social upheaval. In this era, Baptists often stood in the vanguard of the temperance crusade, seeing in it a necessary response to the pervasive destructiveness of alcohol in American and European society. The alignment with the Prohibition movement, while complex and ultimately contentious, underscored the denomination's theological commitment to holiness and moral rectitude, positioning abstinence not merely as a health or social issue but as a gospel imperative. This heritage, while nuanced by later reevaluations, remains a touchstone for many conservatives within the denomination. They argue that the historic stand against alcohol was not an overreach or cultural artifact but a faithful enactment of biblical principles applied to the lives of believers amid real-world challenges. Consequently, strict abstainers appeal to this lineage with a deeply felt conviction that returning to or maintaining these standards embodies fidelity to the faith and preserves the church's witness in a secularized and often permissive world.

On a practical level, those advocating for strict abstinence make the case that in an age of increasing availability of alcoholic beverages and ever-shifting cultural norms that glamorize and normalize drinking, a clear and unequivocal stance is necessary to avoid confusion and to provide a strong moral compass for believers, especially impressionable youth. They contend that moderate use is inherently fraught with risks, especially given human frailty and the ease with which "moderation" can dissolve into excess. In their view, the slippery slope from a single drink to abuse is not a hypothetical warning but a common reality that demands precautionary measures. Abstinence, therefore, is seen as the most effective and unambiguous means of practicing faith in this regard, eliminating ambiguity and temptation altogether rather than attempting to navigate nuanced and often unstable boundaries. The statisticians and counselors who accompany these advocates frequently underscore scientific findings about alcohol's addictive potential and long-term impacts on mental and physical health, bolstering the case with empirical evidence that resonates within and beyond faith communities.

The theological rationale is often buttressed by reflections on how Christlikeness is expressed through the fruit of the Spirit, especially self-control and purity. Abstinence supporters argue persuasively that alcohol impairs these qualities, softening the resolve and clouding the conscience necessary for holy living. They point to the exhortations of Paul, who urged Timothy to "use a little wine" for medicinal purposes, but who elsewhere admonished believers to maintain spiritual discipline and vigilance, framing alcohol as a potential stumbling block rather than a blessing. The discernment exercised by strict abstainers is thus less about legalistic rigidity and more about a conscious choosing of spiritual health and clarity, seeing the avoidance of alcohol as a safeguard for personal sanctity and integrity. This position resonates strongly among those who hold that engagement with the world inevitably includes struggles with temptation, and that individual believers are called to adopt whatever personal disciplines best equip them for victory over sin and fidelity to their divine calling.

Many hold firm the conviction that abstinence serves as a powerful witness in evangelism and discipleship. In a pluralistic and often skeptical cultural landscape, the decision to abstain offers a compelling counter-narrative to prevailing values and lifestyle choices. Strict abstainers within Baptist circles often express their stance as an embodiment of countercultural courage, an embodied testimony that faith entails not only belief but also tangible, daily choices that honor God. This clear distinction also fosters community cohesion, providing a shared ethical marker around which the fellowship can rally. It prevents divisiveness borne from differing attitudes toward alcohol by removing the variable entirely. For parents, youth leaders, and pastors, this unequivocal stance simplifies pastoral care and discipleship efforts, allowing them to offer crystal-clear guidance to younger believers who might otherwise be confounded by mixed messages or peer pressure. The strict abstinence position thus emerges as an anchor point within the community, reinforcing a collective identity steeped in commitment, holiness, and mutual accountability.

In the broader ecumenical landscape, the Baptist advocates for abstinence often find themselves engaged in dialogue with other traditions that permit moderate alcohol use but encourage temperance.

Yet, rather than weakening their stance, such dialogues frequently reinforce the Baptist conviction that a stricter course better reflects the call to holiness and the avoidance of cause for others' stumbling. They acknowledge, with respect, that other Christian communities interpret Scripture differently, but nonetheless hold that the Baptist emphasis on purity and precaution aligns more closely with what the gospel demands of believers who seek to live in undivided devotion to God. This perspective is often framed less as judgment of others and more as personal and communal fidelity to a higher standard, offered humbly as an invitation to consider the consequences of laxity against the clarion call of Scripture to sobriety and vigilance. This posture supports a posture of passionate conviction balanced with pastoral sensitivity, promoting unity without compromising principle.

A related concern that animates proponents of strict abstinence revolves around the unpredictable social and emotional impact of alcohol on marginalized and vulnerable populations. Recognizing that alcohol misuse disproportionately damages those with certain predispositions, histories, or emotional fragility, advocates stress that promoting abstinence protects not only the individual believer but also those in the shared community who might be negatively affected by others' drinking. This includes children of alcoholic parents, individuals recovering from addiction, and those whose faith journeys are freshly vulnerable. Such sensitivity to the collateral harm caused by alcohol underscores the Baptist commitment to love of neighbor and communal responsibility. Abstinence is thus not only a personal discipline but also a communal act of care, demonstrating how faith takes tangible shape in protecting and nurturing one another. It embodies the biblical exhortation to "bear one another's burdens" (Galatians 6:2), recognizing that the choice to forgo alcohol can be an expression of profound, practical love.

Psychological and sociological observations often accompany theological reflections within this viewpoint, highlighting the devastating patterns of family dysfunction, crime, and health crises rooted in alcohol abuse. These advocates often draw on pastoral experience or counseling expertise, attesting to the difficulty of reconciling moderation with the lived reality of addiction's ripple effects. They identify abstinence as a clear "line in the sand," a preventative measure capable of reducing community harm and advancing a kingdom-oriented ethic of compassion and sobriety. Furthermore, many propose that abstinence empowers believers to maintain clearer minds and stronger witness in social justice efforts, ministry, and leadership, unencumbered by the potential fog of alcohol's influence. In this way, abstinence aligns with a holistic vision of sanctification that encompasses mind, body, and spirit, offering a pathway toward greater spiritual maturity and effectiveness in the mission of the church.

Advocates for strict abstinence also engage with the cultural and generational shifts that have challenged traditional temperance movements. They observe that increasing secularization, commercial marketing of alcoholic beverages, and celebratory drinking embedded in social media platforms create environments particularly challenging for young believers. Abstainers express concern about the subtle normalization of alcohol consumption as a requisite for social acceptance, warning that such pressures can erode faith convictions and lead to spiritual compromise. In response, they promote abstinence as both a protective boundary and a form of protest against a culture steeped in materialism and excess, calling the church to reclaim a distinct countercultural identity marked by joy untainted by intoxication and witness unclouded by impairment. This often translates into deliberate ministry strategies, including youth education programs, sober fellowship groups, and public advocacy within local communities, emphasizing that abstinence is more than abstaining, it is actively embodying a different way of living.

Notably, some strict abstainers who embrace this stance do so after deep and often painful personal journeys with alcohol's dangers, bringing an authenticity and urgency to their advocacy that resonates powerfully within congregations. Their testimonies reveal the often-hidden struggles behind the church's public posture on drinking, underscoring why abstinence is not a mere abstract principle but a decisive, life-saving commitment. These stories bring flesh and blood to theological debates, bridging doctrine with lived experience. They invite empathy and understanding while reinforcing the theological and ethical foundations of the position. In recounting the devastation wrought by alcohol, from broken relationships to lost employment and spiritual despair, these voices illuminate why abstinence serves as both a boundary and a beacon, a tangible expression of hope and healing.

Ultimately, the call for strict abstinence within Baptist circles is not a cry of condemnation but an invitation to faithfulness expressed through discipline and love. It reflects a deeply pastoral concern to cultivate communities where holiness and health flourish side by side, where testimonies of God's grace shine unmarred by the shadow of addiction's consequences. The clarity and conviction with which abstainers stand affirm a sacred trust to bear witness in a troubled world, a trust grounded in scripture, tradition, and experience. Their advocacy challenges believers to examine not only what is permitted but what is edifying, calling the body of Christ to pursue unity not by diluting conviction, but by embracing a shared commitment to love manifested primarily through self-control and care for one another. In this way, the position of strict abstinence enriches the broader conversation within the Baptist tradition, reminding all that faith no less than fermentation requires wise stewardship, reverence, and, above all, a heart attuned to the divine call for sanctified living.

Voices for Nuanced Understanding

Within the tapestry of Baptist thought on alcohol, the voices advocating for a nuanced understanding of consumption weave a compelling narrative that calls for both reflection and reassessment. These perspectives arise not from a rejection of tradition but from a deeply rooted commitment to truth, compassion, and discernment. It is within this complex interplay between scripture, history, and lived experience that many contemporary Baptists find fertile ground to explore a middle path, one that honors the moral clarity historically championed while embracing the contextual subtleties that scripture itself presents. This emerging chorus challenges a monolithic view that categorically condemns all alcohol use, inviting believers to wrestle with the tension between liberty and limitation, joy and caution, blessing and burden.

Central to this reevaluation is the recognition that the biblical narrative itself embodies a certain ambivalence regarding alcohol. Unlike the simplistic portrayals often adopted in traditional temperance discourse, the Scriptures present alcohol as imbued with both divine blessing and human hazard. Wine, the emblematic fermented beverage of the ancient Near East, occurs frequently not merely as a symbol of excess and ruin but also as a mark of festivity, celebration, and divine generosity. The psalms sing of wine gladdening the heart, Proverbs extol its capacity to enliven spirits, and celebratory feasts rejoice in its presence. Yet alongside these affirmations lie stern warnings about drunkenness, moral decay, and the loss of self-control. It is precisely this dialectic that prompts many contemporary Baptist voices to urge a reexamination of blanket prohibitions. They argue that a mature, responsible engagement with the biblical texts requires discerning these different registers, understanding that the Scriptures advocate for temperance, not total abstinence, necessarily, but a careful stewardship of one's faculties and freedoms.

Voices for a more moderate stance often approach the subject from pastoral and practical motivations. They observe that, within Baptist communities, the historic offense to alcohol consumption has sometimes led to judgmental attitudes, social alienation, and a rigidity that stifles honest conversation. These ministers and lay leaders invite their congregants to replace fear and condemnation with education and empathy, recognizing that the misuse of alcohol is a complex issue intersecting with addiction, mental health, and personal responsibility.

Their call is not for unrestrained indulgence but for a wise and measured approach that respects individual conscience and social context. This perspective honors the long Baptist tradition of moral seriousness and self-discipline while resisting the temptation to conflate all consumption of alcohol with sin. Instead, it promotes the idea that faith communities should cultivate environments where questions can be posed openly, struggles addressed honestly, and decisions made prayerfully, rather than coerced through cultural expectations or inherited taboos.

Furthermore, this nuanced understanding is enriched by a growing awareness of the cultural and historical evolution within Baptist life. Many contemporary advocates highlight that the strong temperance stance, so woven into the fabric of Baptist identity, arose not solely from biblical mandates but also from specific social contexts, such as the 19th-century temperance movement and the cultural crises of that era. While these movements certainly reflected sincere moral convictions, they were also responses to societal problems related to alcohol abuse that shaped communal attitudes profoundly. Recognizing this historical contingency, some Baptists feel empowered to revisit traditional teachings with fresh eyes. They argue that faithful adherence to scripture includes acknowledging the ways denominational interpretations have been shaped by time-bound factors, thereby allowing room for reinterpretation in light of present realities. This does not suggest relativism but rather a dynamic faithfulness that seeks to apply timeless truths thoughtfully amidst changing circumstances.

Integral to this conversation are testimonies from within Baptist circles that reveal a rich diversity of experience and insight. Among these are narratives from individuals who have navigated the complexities of alcohol both personally and pastorally. Some share stories of liberation from harmful patterns, underscoring the necessity of strong warnings against excess and addiction. Others recount their journey towards appreciating moderate consumption as a part of cultural participation and fellowship. These voices illuminate the lived reality behind doctrinal debates and remind the community that, beyond theological abstractions, these issues touch the daily lives and spiritual growth of real people. Their stories challenge the assumption that temperance must always equate to total abstinence and illustrate how fostering grace-filled dialogue can facilitate healing, accountability, and mutual respect.

In alignment with scriptural emphasis on wisdom and discernment, many proponents advocate for a contextual hermeneutic, a method of interpreting biblical texts that takes into account the historical, cultural, and linguistic milieu of the ancient world while also considering contemporary circumstances. This approach acknowledges that the biblical texts were written in environments where wine was commonplace and socially integral, used for nourishment, ritual, and social bonding. By placing passages on alcohol within this broader frame, readers can better appreciate the intent and emphasis of biblical authors rather than imposing modern categories anachronistically. For example, the prohibitions against drunkenness are understood not as mere legalistic strictures but as warnings against behaviors that undermine community, personal integrity, and spiritual vigilance. This reading invites believers to embrace the gift of self-control rather than adopting absolute abstention as an identity marker or purity test.

Moreover, these voices highlight the theological importance of freedom in Christ as expressed in the New Testament, particularly in Pauline writings. They point to passages where liberty is affirmed, but caution is exercised, such as the admonition to avoid causing a brother or sister to stumble. This dialectic between freedom and responsibility calls for a charity that respects differing convictions within the body of Christ, thereby discouraging judgment and fostering unity. The implication for Baptist communities is profound: while temperance remains a virtue to be prized and practiced, the church should cultivate an atmosphere where disagreements over alcohol can be met not with division but with patience and understanding. By doing so, believers can demonstrate the very fruits of the Spirit, love, gentleness, and self-control, in their communal interactions.

Alongside these theological reflections is an increasing engagement with ecumenical insights. Within the wider Christian tradition, Baptists witnessing other denominations' varying approaches to alcohol, ranging from Roman Catholic liturgical use of wine to Orthodox moderation and Pentecostal prohibitions, find encouragement to hold their positions with confidence yet openness. This broader conversation enriches Baptist perspectives, inviting a humility that acknowledges the complexity of faith and practice in a pluralistic Christian world. It also challenges Baptists to articulate their convictions with clarity and charity, avoiding caricatures of other traditions while learning from their own historical and theological journeys. This exchange sustains a spirit of dialogue rather than dogmatism, advancing a collective Christian witness that models gracious engagement on contentious issues.

At the heart of these nuanced voices lies an appeal to balance, between joy and sobriety, celebration and restraint, tradition and progress. Such balance resonates beautifully with the metaphorical orchard at twilight, where ripe fruit embodies the gifts of God's creation, yet the coming night urges prudence. This image captures the essence of their message: alcohol, like many aspects of life, can be a blessing when approached with thoughtful care but a source of harm when mishandled. They call believers to embrace this tension, not as a problem to solve with simplistic rules, but as a mystery to live thoughtfully and prayerfully, guided by scripture, conscience, and communal support. This ethos encourages a faith marked by maturity and compassion, rejecting extremes of legalism or license.

Practically speaking, these perspectives encourage churches to develop resources and ministries that support individuals and families in navigating alcohol-related challenges. Education about the effects of alcohol, open forums for sharing experiences, pastoral counseling that respects diverse journeys, and community accountability measures all emerge as valuable tools. Such initiatives exemplify the integration of doctrine and practice, reflecting a holistic pastoral sensitivity that addresses both the spiritual and physical well-being of congregants. By fostering safe spaces for honest dialogue, churches can reduce stigma and build resilience rather than reinforcing division or shame.

Equally important is the emphasis on cultural sensitivity. Advocates of nuanced understanding recognize that Baptists minister in diverse contexts, urban and rural, conservative and progressive, North American and global. Attitudes toward alcohol vary widely across these settings, influenced by local customs, legal regulations, and societal norms. Therefore, a one-size-fits-all stance proves inadequate. Instead, theological principles must be applied with cultural awareness, allowing for adaptive practices that honor both Baptist convictions and the realities of particular communities. This pluralism within unity reflects a mature ecclesiology attentive to the Spirit's leading amid complexity.

Some proponents also challenge the assumption that abstinence inherently demonstrates superior spirituality. They caution against a self-righteous posture that elevates abstainers over moderate drinkers, which risks fostering judgmentalism rather than community. Instead, they encourage believers to root their identity not in consumption habits but in Christ's lordship and love. Such a posture invites humility, acknowledges human fallibility, and centers the gospel's grace as the foundation for all ethical decision-making. This subtle but profound shift in focus redirects conversations from external behavior toward interior transformation and relational harmony.

In this spirit, these voices call for renewed dialogue within the Baptist family, a conversation marked by listening, respect, and the willingness to learn from one another's experiences and convictions. They envision forums, workshops, and study groups where theological scholarship, pastoral wisdom, and personal testimonies converge. Through such engagement, believers can move beyond polarized debates toward mutual understanding, recognizing the shared commitment to holiness and community that undergirds all perspectives. This dialogical approach embodies the very humility and charity that Scripture extols, demonstrating that diversity of opinion need not fracture but can instead enrich the Body of Christ.

Ultimately, the call for nuanced understanding within Baptist circles reflects a desire to honor God's word faithfully while embodying the grace and wisdom that characterize mature faith. It resists oversimplification and invites believers to enter into the mystery of how faith informs everyday decisions about alcohol, balancing freedom with responsibility. This perspective does not discard historic temperance teachings but deepens them, discerning when total abstinence is prudent and when moderation suffices, contextualized by individual and communal discernment.

As such, this voice for balance emerges as an invitation, an opening rather than a closure, to explore the profound connections between theology, culture, and lived experience. It encourages Baptists to embrace a faith that is both robust and flexible, rooted in Scripture yet responsive to the complexities of the modern world. By doing so, it fosters a spiritual climate where respect transcends division, where joy coexists with sobriety, and where the shared mission of love and holiness is advanced amid diversity.

In weaving these thoughtful strands together, the nuanced voices in Baptist discourse offer a path forward, one informed by biblical fidelity, historical awareness, pastoral care, cultural sensitivity, and spiritual maturity. They call the community not to uniformity but to unity amidst diversity, not to rigid judgment but to compassionate discernment. Through this dynamic engagement, Baptists can better embody the harmony envisioned in theological ideal and practical reality, nurturing communities that are at once joyful, disciplined, and deeply rooted in

Christ. This vision, illuminated by wisdom and grace, invites all who hold these tensions with faithfulness to join in a shared journey toward understanding, healing, and love.

Mediating the Debate

In the labyrinth of perspectives surrounding alcohol within Baptist circles, the call for respectful dialogue and unity resonates with an urgency that cannot be overstated. The centuries-old debate, rooted deeply in theological convictions and cultural mores, has produced a kaleidoscope of opinions that often threaten to fracture the harmony of the faith community. Yet, amid the cacophony of voices either clamoring for rigid abstinence or cautiously permitting moderation, there emerges a compelling movement intent on mediating the debate, a movement characterized not by the triumph of one faction but by the grace of mutual recognition and earnest conversation. This endeavor to bridge divides is no mere academic exercise but a vital expression of faith seeking understanding, grounded in the hope that believers might navigate their differences with both honesty and charity.

At the heart of this mediation is an acknowledgment that the conversation surrounding alcohol consumption in Baptist life is far from monolithic. On one side, longstanding proponents of temperance evoke a rich heritage of moral clarity, warning of the spiritual and social perils entwined with drinking. They insist that abstinence is not only a practical safeguard but a biblical mandate, emphasizing how Scripture warns repeatedly against the snares of intoxication and the erosion of personal holiness. Their voice is emboldened by historical precedent, recalling eras when liquor was tied inexorably to personal downfall and communal decay, and when the Baptist identity was forged in the crucible of temperance advocacy. To them, maintaining an uncompromising stance preserves the integrity of both witness and doctrinal purity, offering a bulwark against the cultural currents that seem to trivialize or romanticize alcohol.

Yet, across this theological battlefield, a fresh chorus of contemporary Baptist voices calls for a re-evaluation of these traditional stances. This newer wave approaches the subject with a spirit shaped by changing social contexts, burgeoning biblical scholarship, and a desire to embody the pastoral care of nuanced scripture interpretation. They point to biblical passages that celebrate wine as a gift of God, a symbol of joy, covenant, and even spiritual blessing. They challenge the tendency to equate all consumption with sin, urging a more careful distinction between drunkenness and moderate use. These voices emphasize personal responsibility, freedom in Christ, and the avoidance of unnecessary legalism, advocating for a posture that respects individual conscience while fostering community support. Their dialogue is infused with humility and an openness that seeks not to dismiss the warnings of tradition but to weave them into a more textured understanding that can accommodate diversity without division.

The attempt to mediate between these positions requires more than mere tolerance; it demands intentionality, vulnerability, and a commitment to listening deeply. Shared theological foundations, such as a reverence for Scripture, the primacy of Christ, and the call to holiness, provide a fertile ground upon which respectful conversations can take root. Yet, the negotiations are far from simple. The deeply personal nature of alcohol as both a cultural artifact and a potential spiritual stumbling block means that discussions often touch nerves wrapped in family histories, pastoral experiences, and cherished community identities. Some remember the wreckage left by alcohol addiction in their own lives or the lives of loved ones, while others wrestle with the feeling that traditional temperance is an outdated remnant that alienates younger generations and fails to engage the complexity of contemporary life. The mediation thus becomes a dance between empathy and conviction, requiring each party to hold firm in their beliefs while simultaneously honoring the lived experiences and theological viewpoints of the other.

One crucial strategy employed by those seeking to mediate the debate is the elevation of personal testimony as a bridge-builder. Stories, more than doctrines, tend to pierce hearts and soften hardened stances. Individuals from across the spectrum share their journeys, not to coerce or convert but to illuminate the ways faith and alcohol intersect in real lives. A seasoned Baptist pastor who once embraced strict abstinence might recount a pilgrimage to a more balanced perspective, describing how a newfound understanding of biblical nuance enriched his ministry and relationships. Conversely, a longtime advocate of temperance could speak candidly about the scars left by excessive drinking, underscoring why certain standards remain indispensable safeguards. Through these exchanges, a tapestry of human experience unfolds, revealing that beneath the doctrinal differences lies a shared desire to walk faithfully with God and neighbor. Such vulnerability fosters empathy, breaking down barriers that abstract argumentation alone cannot reach.

Academic and theological forums within Baptist settings have also contributed significantly to this process of mediation. Conferences, panel discussions, and published dialogues create spaces where rigorous scholarship and heartfelt witness converge. Biblical scholars offer fresh exegeses, challenging entrenched interpretations and inviting reconsideration. Theologians explore historical contexts to clarify how Baptist positions evolved alongside cultural shifts, helping participants appreciate the contingent nature of some emphases. These scholarly insights, juxtaposed with pastoral concerns, encourage a more mature theological literacy that tempers reactionary impulses. As the theological dialogue deepens, participants begin to recognize that the tension between caution and celebration of alcohol is not an impasse but a dynamic tension akin to many areas of Christian ethics, where principles must be balanced with pastoral wisdom and cultural sensitivity.

Moreover, this movement toward dialogue often emphasizes the importance of community discernment over rigid rule-setting. Instead of issuing ultimatums, churches and Baptist associations increasingly explore models that allow for conscience-based decisions within a framework of mutual respect. This approach recognizes that faith communities are diverse ecosystems where one-size-fits-all policies may unnecessarily constrain or alienate members. The goal becomes fostering an environment where individuals can exercise freedom responsibly, supported by accountability and love. For example, some churches encourage open conversations about alcohol choices, combined with teaching on temperance virtues, thus nurturing an atmosphere where struggles and triumphs can be shared without fear of judgment. This relational approach echoes the biblical ethos of bearing one another's burdens and pursuing unity in the Spirit despite differences.

Yet, mediating this debate is not without its challenges. The ingrained associations between Baptist identity and temperance sometimes render any deviation a perceived threat to communal coherence. Traditions that have preserved the denomination's moral witness are understandably wary of compromising principles that have seemed foundational to Baptist integrity. The fear that loosening stances might lead to erosion of discipline or a slippery slope toward license is ever-present. On the other hand, youthful voices and external cultural pressures push for spaces where faith can be lived authentically without the burden of prohibitive rules that seem disconnected from lived realities. Bridging these tensions requires patience and perseverance, a refusal to resort to caricatures or dismissal, and a recognition that grace must govern both belief and behavior.

In this complex milieu, the metaphor of an orchard at twilight offers a poignant illustration. Just as the orchard contains fruits of varying ripeness, sweetness, and bitterness, so does the Baptist tradition hold within it a diversity of righteous impulses, joy, restraint, reverence, all ripening in the light of Scripture and Spirit. The aim of mediation is not to harvest only one kind of fruit but to nurture the entire grove, allowing the diversity to coexist and mature in harmony. Through dialogue, the community learns to appreciate the interplay of these dimensions, recognizing that the spiritual benefits of wine, joy, celebration, and communion do not negate the spiritual dangers of excess, but rather highlight the call to responsible stewardship of creation and self. This balanced vision offers a way forward that neither idolizes total abstinence nor glorifies permissiveness but invites a mature savoring of what faith and fermentation jointly reveal about God's good creation.

Practical initiatives born from this mediating spirit increasingly emphasize education and pastoral care as essential components in guiding congregations through the complexities of alcohol. Bible study groups examine texts with fresh eyes, pastors preach sermons that honor the tension rather than erase it, and lay leaders receive training to create supportive environments. Resources acknowledge the struggles individuals face with temptation and addiction, while also providing frameworks for those who choose moderate consumption within their faith commitments. Such pastoral attentiveness seeks to avoid the twin dangers of legalistic condemnation and moral relativism, steering the community toward a posture of grace that enacts the love of Christ in tangible ways.

The mediating dialogue also invites a reconsideration of how Baptist churches engage with broader society on alcohol-related issues. Historically, the temperance movement linked Baptists with political activism aimed at prohibition and regulation. Today's dialogue inspires a subtler engagement, where churches advocate for public health and social justice while respecting individual freedoms. This balanced stance reflects a matured ecclesiology that understands the church's role as both prophetic and pastoral, challenging harmful behaviors while extending mercy and affirmation. It acknowledges the social realities of alcohol's impact, addiction, family pain, economic consequences, without resorting to simple condemnations or ignoring the cultural significance of alcohol in celebrations and rituals. Through this lens, Baptists can contribute constructively to community well-being by fostering education, prevention, and compassionate response alongside personal faith commitments.

Importantly, this renewed conversation fosters a culture of humility within the denomination. Both conservative guardians and progressive voices come to recognize that no single interpretation holds a monopoly on truth, and that faithful discipleship involves wrestling with Scripture and tradition in living community. This humility opens space for prayerful exploration and shared learning, creating bonds where suspicion once lingered. Instead of fracturing over the issue of alcohol, Baptists may find themselves drawn into deeper relationships anchored in mutual respect and a common desire to honor God faithfully. Thus, mediation serves not only as a theological endeavor but as a spiritual discipline that nurtures unity amid diversity, embodying the biblical injunction to be "eager to maintain the unity of the Spirit in the bond of peace."

As these dialogues continue to evolve, the mediating voices often call attention to the importance of generational dialogue as well. The experiences and perspectives of older Baptists who remember the fervor of the temperance movement and younger believers who navigate a culture saturated with alcohol narratives must inform one another. Respectful intergenerational conversations mitigate misunderstandings and build empathy, ensuring that the church's response to alcohol is both rooted in wisdom and responsive to contemporary challenges. This ongoing conversation challenges assumptions from all sides, encouraging a posture of lifelong learning and adaptability that reflects the dynamic nature of the faith journey.

Ultimately, the efforts to mediate the debate about alcohol consumption within Baptist circles represent a hopeful model for addressing other contentious issues in the church. By prioritizing respect, empathy, and theological integrity, these endeavors exemplify how communities can hold differing convictions without succumbing to division. They demonstrate that faith communities are enriched, not impoverished, by nuanced conversations that honor complexity rather than demand simplistic answers. This mediating spirit invites not only Baptists but the wider Christian family to reconsider how conflict over ethical and cultural issues may be addressed: not through polarization but through the harmonizing work of dialogue grounded in love.

This path, though fraught with difficulty, holds promise for transforming a historically divisive topic into an opportunity for deepened understanding and collective growth. It encourages believers to embrace a vision of faith that can simultaneously uphold standards of holiness and extend grace for personal discernment. In so doing, it beckons the community toward a richer experience of unity, a unity that neither suppresses distinctives nor permits disarray but celebrates the manifold ways the Spirit guides believers toward responsible freedom. This is the fruit of mediation: a harvest of peace cultivated in the fertile soil of humility, insight, and enduring love.

Health, Social, and Ethical Considerations

Health Effects of Alcohol

The health effects of alcohol present a complex canvas where biology, psychology, culture, and faith intersect, inviting a layered conversation that transcends mere physicality to touch on the moral and spiritual well-being of individuals and communities. From a medical standpoint, alcohol is a substance with a dual nature, both a potential social lubricant and a risk-laden toxin, its impact woven intricately into the fibers of human health, behavior, and destiny. Modern science offers a wealth of research tracing the pathways of how alcohol is metabolized, the scope of its influence on various organ systems, and the patterns of harm it may cause when consumed irresponsibly, all while highlighting the nuanced effects of moderate intake. This scientific reality cannot be divorced from the ethical reflections that Baptist faith, with its rich tradition of temperance and moral responsibility, brings to the fore. As we navigate through these territories, it becomes clear that understanding alcohol's health effects is not merely a matter of data but a vital pursuit of holistic care that honors body, mind, and spirit alike.

Medical science identifies alcohol, or ethanol, the active component in alcoholic beverages, as a central nervous system depressant whose biochemical influence begins quickly upon consumption. The liver, tasked with the critical job of metabolizing alcohol, transforms ethanol into acetaldehyde, a toxic compound that is then further broken down before elimination. However, this metabolic pathway is far from benign, as the accumulation of acetaldehyde can cause cellular damage, oxidative stress, and inflammation, contributing to the development of liver diseases such as fatty liver, hepatitis, fibrosis, and ultimately cirrhosis.

Beyond the liver, alcohol's effects ripple outward, disrupting the digestive, cardiovascular, neurological, and immune systems. Excessive alcohol use has been linked to a heightened risk of cancers in the mouth, throat, esophagus, liver, breast, and colon, underscoring the carcinogenic potential embedded in frequent and heavy consumption. The neurological toll manifests in cognitive impairments, memory loss, and increased vulnerability to mental health disorders such as depression and anxiety, illustrating that alcohol's reach extends deeply into the architecture of both body and mind.

Yet within these sobering realities lies a more nuanced interpretation rooted in dosage and pattern of use. Research spanning decades has often suggested a paradox of alcohol's impact, notably the so-called "J-shaped curve," where moderate alcohol intake, particularly red wine, is sometimes associated with reduced risk of certain cardiovascular events. Studies attribute this effect to antioxidants like resveratrol, found in grape skins, which may contribute to improved heart health by enhancing endothelial function and increasing levels of high-density lipoprotein cholesterol. However, such findings do not endorse indiscriminate drinking; rather, they emphasize moderation, contextualized healthcare advice, and personal factors such as age, gender, genetics, and existing conditions. For instance, what might be a low-risk habit for one person could be harmful or contraindicated for another, especially for those with predispositions to addiction, liver conditions, or impaired metabolic function. Furthermore, the Atlantic Baptist and wider Christian community faces additional dimensions to the health discussion, how do these biological realities align with spiritual calls to stewardship of the body as a temple, self-control as an expression of faith, and concern for communal welfare?

The ethical reflections within the Baptist tradition amplify the focus from the individual biological consequences to the societal implications of alcohol consumption. The denomination's historical stance on temperance did not arise merely from arbitrary prohibitions but rather from a careful consideration of the detrimental impacts on families, communities, and moral integrity. Heavy or careless drinking often correlates with increased incidence of violence, accidents, broken relationships, and economic hardship, issues that ripple through the fabric of society like cracks in a communal vessel meant to hold collective peace and purpose. The World Health Organization and other global health authorities recognize alcohol as a significant contributor to global morbidity and mortality, linking its abuse to premature death and disability. For Baptists, this drives a keen awareness that physical health cannot be compartmentalized away from spiritual health or social responsibility. The health effects of alcohol thus take on a prophetic voice, calling for vigilance, compassion, and practical wisdom to protect the vulnerable and uphold the sanctity of life.

Moreover, contemporary medical research exposes the often-hidden scourge of alcohol dependency and addiction, conditions that erode autonomy and dignity, blurring lines between choice and compulsion. The biological underpinnings of alcohol use disorder (AUD) involve genetic, neurochemical, and environmental factors that collectively entrap individuals in cycles of craving and consumption despite adverse consequences. This perspective shifts the conversation from moral judgment to medical empathy, demanding that faith communities balance calls for personal discipline with the need for supportive care and rehabilitation. Baptist churches have often played integral roles in recovery movements, such as Alcoholics Anonymous and faith-based counseling, offering spaces where grace, accountability, and medical treatment intersect. The acknowledgment of addiction as a disease rather than simply a moral failing reframes how health effects of alcohol are understood and addressed within both clinical and congregational contexts. It invites inclusion rather than exclusion, healing rather than condemnation, values rooted deeply in the gospel message.

In the sphere of public health, the ripple effects of alcohol extend beyond the immediate drinker, affecting families through domestic violence, impacting children through neglect, and burdening healthcare systems with preventable injury and illness. The ethical mandate for Baptists, therefore, extends toward proactive community engagement and responsible leadership. Advocating for policies such as education on alcohol's risks, supporting legislation that limits unsafe access, and fostering environments where healthy choices flourish aligns with the broader call to love one's neighbor as oneself. The church's prophetic voice in this arena models a holistic concern where physical health is inseparable from spiritual and social well-being, demonstrating that faith-informed responses to health challenges can offer strength in public discourse and service.

It is also important to reflect on the cultural lens through which alcohol is often viewed in Baptist contexts. For many, alcohol symbolizes more than a beverage; it is linked with celebration, fellowship, and sometimes spiritual ritual, as witnessed in the biblical references to wine used in joyous occasions and sacred sacraments. However, within certain Baptist circles, cultural memory is strongly marked by the awareness of alcohol's potential to fracture communities and lives, a legacy entwined with experiences of addiction and loss. This cultural memory shapes medical perspectives and ethical responses alike, cautioning against dismissing alcohol's health risks lightly. It invites a posture of humility and openness within the faith community, acknowledging that what might be medically benign or even beneficial for some could carry spiritual and cultural hazards for others. Such sensitivity enriches the dialogue around alcohol's health effects, encouraging mutual respect and empathetic listening even in disagreement.

From a pastoral care perspective, the health effects of alcohol extend into the emotional and spiritual domains, where clergy and lay leaders are often front-line responders to crises triggered by drinking-related harm. Addressing the multifaceted impact on individuals requires not only theological knowledge but also psychological insight and practical resources. The interplay between physical health and spiritual vitality is evident when alcohol misuse strains faith, engenders guilt or shame, and challenges commitments to personal holiness and communal witness. Baptist pastoral counselors and chaplains are tasked with walking alongside those who struggle, offering guidance that integrates medical understanding with scriptural hope. This integration models a compassionate approach that honors the whole person, recognizing that healing involves restoration of body, mind, and spirit in concert. In this way, the health effects of alcohol become a profound locus where faith and science collaborate in the shared pursuit of human flourishing.

Reflecting on pregnancy and family health reveals additional layers of medical concern and ethical responsibility. Alcohol consumption during pregnancy is a well-established cause of fetal alcohol spectrum disorders (FASD), conditions that permanently impair the cognitive, behavioral, and physical development of children. The awareness of these dangers underscores the Baptist conviction to protect life at all stages and fortifies public health messages advocating abstinence from alcohol in expectant mothers. The ripple effect continues as family health is jeopardized, with alcohol misuse contributing to unstable homes, impaired parenting, and increased risk of neglect or abuse. These realities demand compassionate yet firm teaching on responsible stewardship of the body and care for the vulnerable, reinforcing the Baptist ethos that love must manifest in tangible care and protection for the least and the weakest. The intersection of medical data with faith convictions here prompts ongoing education and outreach within the community.

Turning toward the emerging field of alcohol's influence on mental health, recent decades have unveiled intricate connections between drinking and psychiatric conditions. Alcohol can directly exacerbate symptoms of depression, anxiety, bipolar disorder, and psychosis, sometimes triggering their onset or worsening their course. Conversely, some individuals use alcohol as a form of maladaptive self-medication, entangling themselves in a dangerous feedback loop of relief and deterioration. From the medical viewpoint, integrated treatment approaches that address both substance use and mental health disorders simultaneously offer the best chance for recovery, a model that faith communities are increasingly inclined to support. This holistic concern aligns closely with Baptist understandings of the unity of soul and body, highlighting that health effects of alcohol reach beyond the physical into the realms of emotional and spiritual vitality. The church's role in destigmatizing mental health challenges related to alcohol and providing resources for integrated care marks a progressive step in Christian compassion and communal wellness.

In summary, the health effects of alcohol, when viewed through the combined lenses of medicine and Baptist faith, offer a compelling narrative of intricate balance between healing and harm, freedom and constraint, joy and responsibility. Medical science unmasks the physiological realities and consequences of alcohol use, emphasizing the dangers of abuse and the potential moderated risks or benefits, while theology and ethics enrich understanding by framing these realities within the broader context of human dignity, community welfare, and spiritual obedience. The Baptist tradition's emphasis on temperance emerges as a wise response to the challenges posed by alcohol, advocating prudence and care that reflect reverence for God's gift of life. At the same time, the acknowledgment of addiction's complexity and the need for grace-filled support systems speaks to a faith that embraces compassion alongside conviction. This holistic approach invites believers and seekers to engage with alcohol's health effects not as isolated facts but as an invitation to deeper reflection on how faith informs moral choices about the body and community. It is within this sacred dialogue between science and spirit that a balanced, thoughtful pathway emerges, one that honors restraint without judgment, joy without excess, and reverence that nurtures both individual and collective thriving in the orchard of life.

Social Impact and Responsibility

In the vast vineyard of human interaction, where faith and daily living intertwine, the topic of alcohol consumption stretches beyond the personal palate into the very fabric of community and relational dynamics. It is within this complex terrain, the fertile ground of social impact and responsibility, that the Baptist tradition wrestles thoughtfully with the implications of alcohol not merely as a beverage but as a powerful social force. The conversation here extends far beyond admonitions or approvals. It touches on the heart of collective well-being, ethical stewardship, and the call to love one's neighbor in tangible, often challenging ways. This subchapter seeks to illuminate the nuances involved, weaving in scientific insights alongside the rich moral tapestry of Baptist thought, striving to provide a holistic understanding that honors both truth and grace.

To begin with, alcohol is unique in human society, unlike many other consumables. Its social presence is ubiquitous, woven into celebrations, rituals, and moments of deep communal bonding. Yet, paradoxically, it also carries with it a shadow of harm and hardship. Scientific research has demonstrated time and again that alcohol, when misused or abused, can be a source of devastating social consequences. From impaired judgment leading to accidents and violence, to the gradual erosion of familial stability, the ripple effects of irresponsible drinking penetrate the very bedrock of community life. Within many Baptist communities, this reality is not theoretical but lived experience; the scars of addiction and broken relationships testify to the destructive potential of alcohol when freed from restraint.

The ethical dimensions come sharply into focus when we consider the Baptist commitment to moral clarity and personal holiness as part of corporate witness. Temperance emerges not as a mere personal preference but as an act that safeguards the vulnerable and honors the communal good. When an individual steps beyond measured consumption into excess, the consequences extend beyond their own body, spilling into the lives of spouses, children, friends, and neighbors. Consider the tragic stories of families fractured by the unseen hand of addiction, children growing up in environments of neglect or abuse, spouses burdened with emotional and financial strain, communities facing increased demands on social services and law enforcement. The call to responsible stewardship is therefore not a mere doctrinal abstraction but a pastoral imperative rooted in love and the tangible realities of suffering.

Within the Baptist tradition, this communal aspect of responsibility is historically underscored by a rejection of anything that would enslave or diminish one's full devotion to God and neighbor. Alcohol, viewed through this lens, poses a potential barrier to spiritual and social flourishing. It is therefore not surprising that Baptist churches have historically championed temperance movements and actively engaged in community efforts to reduce alcohol-related harms. Yet, what is crucial in this contemporary reflection is the recognition that a posture of love must also leave room for compassion and understanding. The binary of prohibition or indulgence oversimplifies a nuanced reality where individuals' experiences with alcohol vary widely. Some may navigate social drinking without harm, while others face serious struggles. Responsible community care demands both protecting against harm and supporting those caught in its grip without stigma or judgment.

Modern scientific insights provide additional layers to this ethical conversation. Neuroscience, for instance, reveals the intricate ways alcohol interacts with the brain's chemistry, how it can dull inhibitions and impair decision-making without immediate awareness, setting the stage for risky behaviors. Epidemiological studies link alcohol misuse to a higher prevalence of domestic violence, mental health challenges, and chronic diseases, all of which strain communal resources and weaken social cohesion. Yet, paradoxically, moderate alcohol consumption, within safe limits, has been associated in some studies with certain cardiovascular benefits and social bonding effects. For Baptist communities, these scientific nuances invite a posture of discernment, a careful weighing of potential harms against any perceived benefits, always through the prism of scripture and witness.

Importantly, the ripple effects of alcohol consumption extend into the economic and societal realms. Increased alcohol-related healthcare costs, loss of productivity due to intoxication or hangovers, and the social fallout from alcohol-induced violence bear heavily on community development and well-being. In many Baptist congregations, whose members often exhibit keen awareness of social justice and service, these broader impacts are cause for sober reflection. The stewardship of resources, both financial and human, is an essential dimension of responsible faith living. Here, the challenge lies in fostering environments that cultivate healthy habits and provide support for addiction recovery, placing community welfare above personal preference or cultural norms.

This sense of social responsibility also prompts vital questions about pastoral care and church leadership. How does a congregation embody grace toward those struggling with alcoholism while upholding standards of temperance? The tension can be significant, for the church is called simultaneously to be a refuge for broken lives and a beacon of moral integrity. Baptists have developed varied approaches, some foster tightly knit support groups, others advocate for strict abstinence. Yet, underlying these different strategies is a common heart: the desire for restorative healing rooted in spiritual transformation and communal accountability. The challenge is to hold these values in tension without alienating those who wrestle with dependence and guilt. This delicate balancing act involves deep listening, patient teaching, and persistent prayer, recognizing that the journey toward freedom from addiction is often arduous and nonlinear.

Moreover, the relational effects of alcohol touch on the very core of communal worship and fellowship. Celebrations that include alcohol can both unite and divide, depending on personal convictions and experiences. For some, a shared cup symbolizes fellowship and joy; for others, it risks triggering past wounds or causing spiritual stumbling. The Baptist emphasis on congregational unity and mutual edification thus prompts thoughtful dialogue about how to navigate these sensitivities.

Some churches adopt alcohol-free fellowship events to ensure inclusivity, while others encourage responsible sharing of wine during communion with caveats for those who abstain. Such decisions highlight an ethic of love and respect, prioritizing the spiritual and emotional welfare of all members over individual preferences.

The metaphor of the twilight orchard is particularly evocative here, just as twilight casts a mingling of shadow and light over ripened fruit, so too does alcohol occupy a space that is neither purely good nor purely evil but complex and nuanced. The fruit offers joy through its sweetness yet demands restraint to avoid spoilage. Likewise, alcohol in community life can foster joy, celebration, and connection, but without careful stewardship, it risks sowing division, pain, and loss. The Baptist principle of loving one's neighbor calls for vigilance and care in this delicate balance, recognizing that the well-being of the whole community often depends on the choices of the individual.

In the broader cultural context, the Baptist approach to alcohol also grapples with societal messages that glamorize drinking or downplay its risks. Popular media and advertising frequently depict alcohol as synonymous with fun, success, and social acceptance. Such images challenge Baptist values of sobriety and moral discipline, especially among youth and vulnerable populations. Churches and faith communities thus bear a crucial responsibility to offer counter-narratives that emphasize holistic health, spiritual wellness, and the dignity of self-control. Educational programs, youth mentorship, and open conversations around peer pressure and addiction become vital tools in equipping members to resist cultural currents that may undermine faith and community health.

The social impact of alcohol within Baptist life also intersects with pressing issues of social justice and community outreach. In many urban and rural contexts, alcohol-related problems disproportionately affect marginalized populations, exacerbating cycles of poverty, violence, and health disparities. Baptist churches frequently engage in ministries aimed at addressing these systemic challenges, **providing** compassion through recovery programs, counseling services, and advocacy for policy changes. These efforts embody the call to be "salt and light" in a world where alcohol's consequences often deepen human suffering. They also invite believers to reflect on societal structures that contribute to addiction and to advocate for holistic solutions that extend beyond personal morality to communal transformation.

An essential dimension of this social responsibility extends to families, often the frontline arenas where the consequences of alcohol consumption unfold most visibly. The Baptist tradition's emphasis on strong, nurturing families means that safeguarding domestic environments is paramount. Alcohol misuse can fracture familial bonds, sow mistrust, and introduce unpredictability that destabilizes children's emotional and spiritual development. Conversely, families that model healthy attitudes toward alcohol, practicing moderation or abstinence as a shared value, offer fertile ground for faith formation and mutual support. The church's role in equipping parents with wisdom and resources to navigate these challenges cannot be overstated. Pastoral counseling, family-oriented education, and community support mechanisms serve to strengthen these foundational units of faith and society alike.

Further, the relational dimension of alcohol's social impact touches on friendships, work relationships, and civic engagement. In small-town Baptist churches or urban congregations alike, the fabric of social life is finely woven with threads of trust, encouragement, and mutual accountability. Alcohol consumption patterns invariably influence these relationships. Responsible drinking can enhance fellowship and relaxation, yet overindulgence risks alienation and conflict. The integrity of one's witness and the health of the church community hinge on discerning choices that foster harmony rather than discord. This relational responsibility resonates deeply with the Baptist emphasis on believer's baptism and regenerated membership, underscoring the freedom and accountability inherent in faith commitments.

Within contemporary Baptist dialogues, there is a growing awareness of the need to foster environments that are inclusive and compassionate toward those wrestling with alcohol-related issues, while still upholding scriptural calls to holiness and self-control. This nuanced perspective marks a subtle evolution from historical rigidity toward a more pastoral sensitivity, one that embraces individuals with empathy without diluting core convictions. Stories from within Baptist circles tell of congregations embracing members who once struggled with alcoholism, offering grace-centered recovery ministries that restore dignity and belonging. These personal testimonies challenge stereotypes and motivate communities to adopt a posture that is simultaneously firm and tender.

The social impact and responsibility surrounding alcohol in Baptist life therefore invite ongoing reflection and dialogue. It is neither a subject to be dismissed as trivial nor a debate to be hardened into division. Rather, it remains a sacred conversation, a shared stewardship of God's vineyard where each cluster of grapes, each human life, is precious and vulnerable. Here, faith serves as a guiding light, illuminating paths toward joy that do not sacrifice sobriety, calling for joy tempered by wisdom, celebration balanced by restraint, and freedom harmonized with responsibility. Through such balanced stewardship, the Baptist community can model a faithful response to alcohol's social realities, promoting both individual flourishing and collective well-being.

Ultimately, engaging with alcohol's social impact in the Baptist context calls believers beyond mere avoidance or indulgence into a richer embrace of communal care. It challenges repeated refrains of "it's a personal choice" by uncovering how every act of consumption sends ripples across relationships and communities. It invites believers to picture themselves as gardeners within the twilight orchard, tenderly pruning and nurturing, ever-watchful for overripe fruit that might cause injury, while also celebrating the sweetness that responsible enjoyment can bring. In this, the social impact of alcohol becomes a mirror reflecting larger truths about faith, love, and the intricate web of human interdependence that God calls his people to cherish and uphold with unwavering responsibility.

Ethical Reflections from a Baptist Lens

Within the rich tapestry of Baptist faith, the question of alcohol consumption is never merely about personal preference or social custom; it is inextricably woven into a broader fabric of ethical reflection, community responsibility, and spiritual integrity. To engage thoughtfully with the ethics of drinking from a Baptist perspective is to embark on a journey that transcends simple prohibition or permissiveness and instead ventures into the nuanced terrain where faith principles encounter real, lived human experience. At the heart of this exploration lies the principle of love, love for God, love for one's neighbor, and self-love rooted in stewardship of the body and soul. The Baptist tradition, with its emphasis on personal holiness, scriptural obedience, and communal accountability, invites adherents not only to consider what is lawful or **unlawful** but what is beneficial, edifying, and life-giving in the context of alcohol use.

Ethics in the Baptist tradition often springs from a twofold foundation: the primacy of Scripture as the ultimate authority and the lived expression of faith within a communal setting that values both individual conscience and collective well-being. This biblical framework advocates for sobriety, not only in the narrow sense of abstaining from drunkenness but as a broader call to vigilance, self-control, and discernment. The Apostle Paul, in his pastoral epistles, underscores the importance of being "sober-minded" (1 Timothy 3:2, Titus 2:2), a sobriety that encompasses mental clarity and spiritual alertness essential for sustaining a vibrant Christian witness. Drinking alcohol, therefore, from this viewpoint, is not dismissed outright as forbidden; rather, it is subject to ethical scrutiny that weighs the motive, manner, and consequences of its use. The ethical imperative is not simply to avoid sin but to cultivate virtues, prudence, temperance, and love that orient behavior toward **a flourishing life** both personally and communally.

Integral to this ethical reflection is the recognition of alcohol's dual character as both a gift and a potential snare. Biblically, wine is portrayed in celebratory and sacramental contexts as a symbol of joy, blessing, and covenantal relationship, a signifier of God's goodness in creation and communal fellowship. Yet, equally present in Scripture are strong admonitions against excess, drunkenness, and the social harms wrought by intemperance (Proverbs 20:1, Ephesians 5:18). This duality requires Baptists to avoid simplistic moral absolutism and instead to exercise a balanced discernment informed by both theology and practical wisdom. The ethical question thus becomes: How does one honor the good gift of fermentation without falling into patterns that damage body, soul, or community?

Science offers crucial insight into this ethical evaluation, reminding the believer that choices surrounding alcohol carry consequences measurable in physical health, mental well-being, and social cohesion. Empirical data reveal that while moderate alcohol consumption has sometimes been linked to certain health benefits, the risks of misuse, including addiction, impaired judgment, and chronic disease, are profound. Importantly, these risks are not equally dispersed; vulnerable populations, including youth, recovering addicts, and those predisposed to alcoholism, face disproportionate harm. Within the Baptist ethos, steeped in a theology of care for the marginalized and the call to bear one another's burdens, these realities command a heightened sense of ethical responsibility. To drink without conscience is to ignore the potential collateral damage **to** family, church, and society.

Moreover, the ethical deliberation within Baptist circles frequently wrestles with the principle of "community above self." Unlike certain theological perspectives that emphasize purely individual freedom,

Baptist ethics cherishes the communal dimension of faith life, where personal choices ripple outward affecting others. This dynamic engenders a collective duty to foster environments that support health, sobriety, and sustained spiritual growth. Practical applications of this principle can be seen in Baptist churches' historical advocacy for temperance movements and the ongoing promotion of accountability structures, small groups, pastoral care, and teaching that prioritize sobriety as a form of discipleship. The ethical stance here is preventative and proactive: to cultivate habits and cultures that minimize temptation, encourage mutual care, and safeguard the vulnerable, recognizing that the welfare of the community strengthens the individual.

Another vital theme in Baptist ethical reflection on drinking is the call to authenticity and integrity before God. Baptists insist that faith is a lived reality, one that requires congruence between belief and behavior. Drinking, then, is scrutinized not just for its outward legality or social acceptability but for how it affects one's testimony and witness. Does the use of alcohol clarify or cloud the believer's spiritual vision? Does it build up the church or lead to stumbling blocks? Baptists often wrestle with the challenge of maintaining personal freedom in Christ while avoiding causing others to fall (Romans 14:13-23). This ethical tension reflects a sobering awareness that spiritual liberty coexists with responsibility, calling for a careful assessment of how drinking may influence not only personal holiness but also the faith journeys of others within the community.

The ethical conversation further recognizes that the Baptist impulse toward temperance derives not from legalistic zealotry but from a profoundly pastoral heart, striving to guard souls from the perils of excess that distort the image of God's redeeming work. Temperance, understood as moderation and prudence, honors the principle that the body is the temple of the Holy Spirit (1 Corinthians 6:19-20) and that the mind must remain alert to spiritual realities. This understanding resists simplistic notions of abstinence as the only righteous path and instead embraces a nuanced ethic attentive to context, intention, and outcomes. The challenge lies in discerning when drinking ceases to be a harmless pleasure and becomes a stumbling block or a gateway to bondage. Here, Baptist ethics embrace a dialectic of freedom and discipline, a call to enjoy God's gifts responsibly while recognizing the fragility of human nature marked by inclination to sin.

Contemporary scientific insights enrich this ethical discernment, particularly as addiction studies have elucidated the neurological mechanisms underlying alcohol dependence and relapse. Such knowledge fosters compassion over condemnation, transforming ethical judgments from mere moralizing into pastoral care attuned to human frailty. Recognizing addiction as a disease rather than a moral failure aligns with Baptist theology's affirmation of grace, redemption, and restoration. It invites believers to respond with empathy, support, and accountability rather than judgment alone, embodying Christlike compassion that heals and empowers. Ethical reflection here extends into the realm of social responsibility, advocating for prevention programs, supporting rehabilitation, and creating church cultures that welcome and restore those struggling with addiction.

In addition, the intersection of faith and ethics in Baptist thought acknowledges the broader societal implications of alcohol use. The detrimental effects of alcohol-related violence, accidents, and family disintegration are of grave concern to any community invested in holistic well-being. This awareness prompts Baptists to consider their role not only in private morality but also in public witness. Baptists have historically engaged in activism for social reform, including temperance campaigns, motivated by a vision of a just and holy society. Within this trajectory, ethical reflection encompasses the promotion of policies that protect the vulnerable while respecting personal dignity, a challenging balance requiring wisdom, humility, and dialogical engagement with the wider culture.

Yet, amid concerns and caution, the Baptist lens does not reduce alcohol ethics to fear or prohibition. Rather, it emphasizes responsible enjoyment within the bounds of Christian liberty, fostering joy and fellowship that reflect the goodness of God's creation. This perspective affirms that the ethical use of alcohol is possible and even beneficial when it nurtures relationships, celebrates life's blessings, and supports spiritual rest and renewal. The orchard dusk metaphor, wherein each fruit tells a tale of rejoicing tempered by restraint, is particularly fitting here, encapsulating the Baptist ideal of living fully in the freedom of the Spirit while holding fast to discipline. Such an approach resists extremes, neither legalistic denial nor reckless indulgence, but seeks the "golden mean" that honors God and enriches community.

The Baptist ethical discourse also wrestles poignantly with the power of example. Pastors, leaders, and laypersons alike are mindful that their behavior around alcohol can either strengthen or weaken the faith of others. The biblical injunction to avoid causing anyone to stumble is a guiding principle that informs a cautious pastoral stance on alcohol. Leaders, therefore, often adopt sobriety or moderate abstinence not only for personal holiness but to model integrity and protect the flock. This ethical concern is especially salient in culturally diverse Baptist communities where varying backgrounds and convictions exist. Ethical reflection in this context calls for sensitivity, respect, and unity amid diversity, a synergy that strengthens the Body of Christ.

At the intersection of such theological and ethical considerations lies the imperative for ongoing dialogue, an openness to listen, learn, and adapt within Baptist communities. Ethical judgments about drinking should not be static or isolated but dynamic and communal, crafted through prayerful discernment, scriptural study, and empathetic conversation. This posture echoes the Baptist value of the priesthood of all believers, affirming that ethical wisdom emerges not from top-down decrees but from the collective seeking of God's will. Such openness creates a space where opposing views are met with respect rather than division, where convictions are held firmly yet kindly, and where unity is prized above uniformity.

In this light, the ethical reflections from a Baptist lens recognize the multiplicity of factors shaping attitudes and practices around alcohol. Historical experiences, cultural contexts, personal narratives, and theological convictions all interplay to form a mosaic of beliefs and behaviors. The Baptist ethical task is to navigate this complexity with humility and grace, ever mindful that the ultimate goal is faithfulness to Christ and love for neighbor. This demands not only self-discipline but also a posture of mercy, embracing those who choose abstinence alongside those who, with conscience intact, may partake moderately. The ethic of love, therefore, contextualizes all rules and prohibitions, underscoring that morality within the Baptist faith is relational rather than solely prescriptive.

When scientific data and theological principles converge, they illuminate a path forward for Baptist communities contending ethically with alcohol. Public health statistics invite sober reflection on the implications of drinking patterns, compelling churches to balance personal liberties with gospel mandates of care and witness. The theological ethos calls believers to embody the fruit of the Spirit, self-control, goodness, faithfulness, in every aspect of life, including their relationship with fermented beverages. That relationship, when approached with wisdom and grace, can symbolize a harmonious unity of joy and restraint, celebration and sobriety, freedom and responsibility. Such a balance enriches not only individual believers but also the broader faith community as it navigates the perennial complexities of moral living in a fallen yet redeemable world.

Thus, to engage ethically with alcohol from a Baptist perspective is ultimately to participate in a sacred dialogue between Scripture and science, individual conscience and communal good, freedom and covenantal obligation. It is a call to wisdom that is both ancient and ever-new, inviting believers to steward their bodies and spirits with reverence, to extend compassion to those ensnared by addiction, and to foster a fellowship marked by unity amid diversity. In doing so, Baptists can embody a faith that honors God's creation, respects the depth of human experience, and resonates with grace, imbuing the seemingly ordinary act of drinking with profound spiritual significance. In this sacred orchard, under the twilight sky, each choice bears witness to a journey of faithfulness, a dance of temperance and joy that reflects the very heart of the gospel itself.

Ecumenical Perspectives: How Other Christian Traditions View Alcohol

Catholic and Orthodox Views

In the venerable traditions of the Catholic and Orthodox churches, the role of alcohol assumes a dimension far more sacramental and culturally embedded than what one might commonly encounter in many Baptist communities. These ancient branches of Christianity approach wine not merely as a beverage but as a profound symbol, intricately woven into the fabric of their liturgical life and spiritual expression. Here, fermentation transcends its earthly properties and ascends into the realm of divine mystery, where wine's transformation mirrors the believer's surrender and renewal in Christ.

Within the Catholic Church, the Eucharist stands as the quintessential encounter with the sacred, where bread and wine are consecrated to become, in the doctrine of transubstantiation, the actual body and blood of Christ. The very act of offering wine during Mass is laden with theological weight, reverence, and an acknowledgment of its sanctified purpose. This sacramental use, ancient in its origin, finds its roots in the Last Supper narratives, where Jesus took the cup of wine and invited His disciples to "drink from it, all of you." The Catholic liturgy does not treat the wine as a mere symbol alone but as a real participation in the mystery of Christ's sacrifice and resurrection. This theological stance inherently shapes Catholic cultural attitudes towards alcohol. Unlike the Baptist emphasis on temperance and often an avoidance or outright abstention from alcohol, most Catholic communities embrace moderate and reverent consumption as part of both religious life and social custom.

The reverence for wine extends beyond the sanctuary and into daily life, where festivals, rituals, and communal meals commonly incorporate wine as a symbol of joy, blessing, and communal fellowship. The rich Italian, Spanish, and French Mediterranean traditions, among others, showcase wine as a gift of the earth, a fruit of God's creation to be enjoyed responsibly and gratefully. Such cultural inheritances reinforce the theological openness to alcohol, presuming moderation and respect rather than abstinence. Indeed, the Catholic Church does caution against the misuse and excess of alcohol, recognizing the dangers of drunkenness and addiction, yet it simultaneously affirms the goodness of creation when embraced with temperance and thanksgiving. This balance between reverence and realistic acknowledgment of human frailty permeates Catholic teachings, fostering a nuanced understanding that values both divine grace and human responsibility.

Parallel to this, the Eastern Orthodox tradition maintains a deeply sacramental view of wine that is both ancient and imbued with mysticism. The Divine Liturgy, central to Orthodox worship, solemnly consecrates bread and wine into the actual body and blood of Christ, a mystery preserved with profound awe and solemnity. Orthodox theology often emphasizes the transformational aspect of sacraments, where earthly elements like wine are imbued with divine grace and power. This mystical approach engages with wine not only as a liturgical necessity but as a symbol of the transformation expected of the believer, of death to sin and resurrection in the Spirit. The Orthodox Church's reverence for wine is thus inseparable from its understanding of salvation and sanctification.

Culturally, Orthodox Christianity appears across diverse regions, from the vineyards of Greece and the wine-rich valleys of Georgia to the steppes of Russia and the Cappadocian hills. In these lands, wine is as much an expression of spiritual life as it is of cultural identity. Shared meals after the Liturgy, emblematic feasts, and traditional practices surrounding marriage, baptism, and other sacraments frequently call for the presence of wine as a tangible sign of divine blessing and human joy. Unlike some

Christian groups that adopt a more restrained or negative stance on alcohol, many Orthodox believers grow up within a milieu where wine functions as a natural part of religious and communal celebrations, symbolizing abundance, healing, and sacred covenant.

Yet, this embrace of wine does not come without caution. Both Catholic and Orthodox traditions, deeply mindful of the potential for alcohol to cause harm, stress the virtue of moderation and the perils of excess. Scriptural admonitions and patristic wisdom echo through generations, reminding the faithful that wine, while good, can also lead to moral and spiritual downfall if abused. Early Church Fathers, such as St. John Chrysostom and St. Augustine, provide nuanced commentary that upholds the goodness of wine in moderation but sternly warns against intemperance. This dual recognition ensures that the sacramental and cultural love for wine is balanced by pastoral care and moral guidance.

This duality of wine as both a sacred symbol and a common earthly pleasure can be vividly encountered in the rituals surrounding Holy Communion. The Orthodox practice of intinction, dipping the consecrated bread into the consecrated wine, epitomizes a tangible joining of elements, reinforcing the unity of body and blood, humanity and divinity. The blending of these elements becomes a profound mystery of union, hospitality, and covenant. In Catholic Mass, the priest's precise prayers during consecration elevate the wine to a sanctified state, a sacred bridge between heaven and earth. These ecclesial actions underscore a theological acceptance of alcohol's place within divine worship, distinctively different from Baptist practices that often avoid alcohol in all forms or substitute grape juice during Communion to sidestep controversy or temptation.

The cultural impact of these theological positions reaches far beyond the sanctuary doors. In many Catholic and Orthodox societies, wine production and enjoyment have become hallmarks of identity, economy, and social cohesion. Monastic communities, for example, have long been centers of viticulture, blending prayerful devotion with agricultural mastery. The monks' labor in vineyards represents more than mere work; it manifests a spirituality that honors creation's fruits and labor's dignity. This intertwining of faith and fermentation crafts a legacy whereby vineyards become sacred spaces, blessings upon the land, and tangible expressions of God's providence.

In contrast, the Baptist tradition, often arising from revivalist roots and emphasizing personal holiness and community purity, tends toward caution or abstinence concerning alcohol. This divergence highlights the theological and cultural contrast: where Catholic and Orthodox sensibilities view alcohol as a blessed part of cultural and sacramental life, Baptists frequently prioritize moral clarity and social consequence over symbolic richness. The Baptist wariness of alcohol springs from historical contexts, temperance movements, social reform, and concern for vulnerable individuals, which press for a stringent ethic aimed at preventing sin and sustaining communal witness. This difference, however, need not be cause for division but rather an invitation to appreciate diverse ways the Christian faith wrestles with living faithfully amidst the blessings and challenges of creation.

Ecumenically, recognizing these differing perspectives invites deeper understanding of how Christians interpret the symbolism and use of alcohol within their traditions. It also prompts reflection on how cultural history shapes theology and practice, reminding believers that drinking wine, abstaining from it, or discerning its role in worship is never a mere individual choice but one informed by centuries of narrative, doctrine, and lived faith. Like the twilight orchard where different fruit trees grow and mature at varied paces and yields, the Catholic and Orthodox traditions reveal a harvest rich with sacramental meaning, cultural heritage, and spiritual caution, offering a textured and generous vision of how faith engages fermentation.

Above all, these traditions remind us that alcohol, when engaged with reverence, moderation, and gratitude, can be a conduit of grace and joy rather than merely a cause for concern. Their embrace of wine as an emblem of divine mystery invites all Christians to contemplate not just the moral dimensions of drinking but the spiritual possibilities contained in creation's gifts. This vision challenges narrower views and opens doors to hospitality, celebration, and solemn remembrance. It urges contemporary believers often shaped by sharp polarization to consider the wisdom passed down through generations that finds in wine a symbol of covenant, communion, and the sweetness of God's enduring presence.

Thus, the Catholic and Orthodox perspectives on alcohol invite a profound meditation on the role of material substances in spiritual life. They teach that creation itself, including the humble grape, is called to participate in divine glory, transformed through sanctification and human cooperation into a foretaste of heavenly banquet. This sacramental outlook serves as a gentle corrective to dichotomies that separate the sacred from the secular, reminding the faithful that everyday acts, sharing a glass of wine in joy or solemnity, can be infused with holiness when approached with the right heart. As readers journey through the varied Christian landscapes of faith and fermentation, they encounter in these ancient eyes a call to recognize the sacred potential in all of life's gifts, to drink deeply from grace itself, and to savor the complex interplay of joy, restraint, and reverence that the vineyard of faith continually offers.

Mainline Protestant Approaches

Within the diverse tapestry of American and global Christianity, mainline Protestant traditions such as Methodism, Lutheranism, and Anglicanism offer a rich spectrum of attitudes toward alcohol, attitudes that both converge with and diverge from those held within the Baptist tradition. Exploring these varied approaches provides vital context for understanding the distinctive Baptist stance on temperance and offers a broader ecumenical perspective that fosters dialogue and mutual respect among Christian communities. In the Methodist tradition, for instance, the conversation about alcohol consumption has long been shaped by a strong emphasis on holiness, personal piety, and social responsibility, tempered over the centuries by shifting cultural norms and theological reflections. Historically, Methodism emerged during the 18th-century revivalist movement with John Wesley at its helm, who advocated for prudent moderation if not outright abstinence, particularly given the social ills alcohol often engendered. Wesley's own sermons and writings did not condemn moderate drinking unequivocally but rather called for serious caution, warning that even lawful pleasures could become spiritual obstacles if abused. Over time, the Methodist Church institutionalized temperance efforts, particularly as the 19th-century's fervor for social reform gripped American Methodism, aligning strongly with the broader temperance and later prohibition movements. Yet, in more recent decades, many strands of Methodism have shifted toward a nuanced recognition of alcohol as a gift of God to be enjoyed responsibly, celebrating moderation and warning against excess with pastoral sensitivity rather than rigid prohibition.

This evolving Methodist posture illustrates a willingness to embrace complexity: alcohol is neither inherently evil nor beyond **redemption's** reach when approached with wisdom and respect for one's neighbor. Lutheranism presents another fascinating facet of Protestant engagement with alcohol, rooted in the theological reflections of Martin Luther himself, who famously transformed the sacramental use of wine during the Reformation. Luther's theology embraced wine as part of God's good creation, a divine blessing intended for joy and community rather than shame or ruin. Unlike the more restrictive currents within Baptist circles, Lutheranism has historically held a more permissive and even celebratory view of alcohol, seeing it as woven into the fabric of human fellowship and liturgical life. Lutheran worship, for example, retains wine as a central element of Holy Communion, a practice that both reflects and reinforces a theology of grace and embodiment. The Lutheran standpoint often emphasizes the "means of grace," wherein the physical elements of bread and wine symbolize the fullness of Christ's presence; to diminish or substitute these elements risks spiritual diminishment.

Beyond sacramental theology, the practical pastoral approach in Lutheran communities typically espouses moderation and responsibility rather than abstinence, recognizing the dangers of misuse but upholding the legitimacy of moderate consumption as a matter of Christian liberty. This orientation has generated a cultural ethos where social drinking is commonly accepted, provided it is exercised with self-control and regard for one's neighbor, a balance that resonates with Luther's broader doctrine of vocation and ethical stewardship in everyday life. Anglicanism, straddling a unique intersection of Catholic and Protestant heritage, adds yet another dimension to the discourse on alcohol within mainline Protestantism. The Anglican tradition, marked by its *via media* or "middle way" ethos, historically embodies a nuanced, almost ambivalent stance toward alcohol, one that honors tradition, scripture, and reason in equal harmony. Anglican liturgy, much like Lutheran worship, retains wine as the sacramental element in the Eucharist, underscoring a sacramental worldview that imbues ordinary creation with sacred significance. Historically, the Church of England did not promote outright prohibition but rather emphasized temperance and the responsible use of alcohol, recognizing both its role in Christian life and its potential for harm.

Anglican pastoral practice often privileges discernment, communal accountability, and pastoral care, rather than blanket moral judgments. This approach reflects a broader theological maturity within Anglicanism that embraces paradox and wrestles with moral complexity, offering space for both those who choose abstinence for personal or spiritual reasons and those who enjoy wine with moderation. This balanced lens has allowed Anglicanism to engage meaningfully with issues such as addiction, social justice, and health, encouraging compassionate support and education while respecting individual conscience. Comparing these three traditions to the Baptist viewpoint illuminates not only differences but also unexpected convergences. Baptists historically have emphasized personal holiness, accountability, and clear moral stances, often resulting in an unequivocal temperance ethic grounded in scriptural interpretations warning against drunkenness as a sin and a social evil. Methodists share this moral sensitivity but often temper it with a stronger social advocacy impulse, while Lutherans bring a sacramental and theological embrace of alcohol's goodness under grace's umbrella. Anglicans, bridging Catholic and Protestant worlds, offer the widest latitude for conscience and pastoral discretion.

Together, these varied mainline Protestant perspectives form a valuable backdrop against which Baptist convictions stand both distinct and yet dialogically enriched. This ecumenical context reminds readers that Christian engagement with alcohol is never monolithic but shaped by historical trajectories, theological convictions, pastoral concerns, and cultural realities, all of which invite ongoing reflection and mutual respect. It is worth noting that within each of these traditions, contemporary shifts reflect the influence of social changes, scientific research on alcohol's effects, and renewed theological emphasis on mercy and inclusion. While older generations may have adhered firmly to temperance or moderation, younger clergy and laity often seek more open conversations, recognizing addiction's complex realities and the pastoral need for grace in judgment. Thus, Methodists, Lutherans, and Anglicans today often emphasize education, pastoral care, and community responsibility alongside spiritual discipline and moral formation. This evolving landscape is not without its tensions and controversies, as voices within each tradition debate the boundaries between liberty and license, joy and excess, tradition and innovation. For Baptists who have long fostered a strict temperance ethic, understanding these dynamics proves crucial for respectful dialogue and integrating biblical faith with contemporary pastoral realities.

Beyond the purely theological and ecclesiastical, mainline Protestant approaches also carry significant cultural and social implications that illuminate the complex interplay between faith and alcohol. Methodism's historic leadership in temperance movements often linked faith to social reform, combating poverty, domestic violence, and public health crises associated with alcohol abuse. This activism reflects a faith deeply engaged with societal wellbeing, framing moderation not merely as personal virtue but as communal necessity. The Lutheran embrace of alcohol as a blessing aligns with a cultural ethos that often treats wine and beer as integral to social gatherings and celebrations, fostering community through conviviality without moralizing consumption itself excessively. Anglicanism, especially in its British and global contexts, sits at the crossroads of religious identity and cultural tradition, frequently engaging alcohol as part of national and regional customs, from pub life to festive toasts, while advocating pastoral sensitivity to addiction and abuse. These cultural inflections remind us that Christian attitudes toward alcohol are embedded in lived realities, shaped by economic, historical, and social factors as much as by scripture or doctrine.

This recognition further enriches Baptist self-understanding by highlighting how faith communities wrestle with alcohol's blessings and burdens in varied settings. Viewed through this wider lens, Baptist sobriety is both a principled stance and a pragmatic response to particular historical and cultural conditions. Yet, the presence of other Protestant traditions that embrace responsible consumption challenges rigid dichotomies and invites deeper theological and pastoral reflection. Thus, Baptists might consider how their call to holiness coexists with mercy, how their moral clarity might engage dialogue without alienation, and how scriptural fidelity might incorporate cultural sensitivity. Mainline Protestant approaches offer a critical mirror reflecting both the strengths and limits of any single doctrinal position on alcohol. In encouraging believers to approach this topic with humility and openness, these perspectives model a faith that embraces complexity in pursuit of grace, justice, and communal flourishing.

Finally, these Protestant traditions exemplify a spirit of ecumenism that may inspire Baptists and others to cultivate spaces for honest conversation and shared learning, particularly in contexts where alcohol's role generates tension or misunderstanding. Recognizing the diversity within the body of Christ concerning alcohol use fosters humility and compassion, reminding believers that the ultimate measure lies not in uniform practice but in mutual love, respect, and spiritual unity. Through understanding the rich **methodologies** and lived experiences across Methodism, Lutheranism, and Anglicanism, readers are invited to envision a broader orchard at twilight, where the fruits of joy, restraint, and reverence grow side by side, nurtured by faith's light and communal care. This ecumenical awareness positions "Faith and Fermentation" not merely as a Baptist discourse but as a bridge toward greater harmony among Christian traditions grappling earnestly and prayerfully with one of faith's most enduring challenges: how to embrace God's gifts in a fallen world with wisdom, grace, and hope.

Evangelical and Pentecostal Perspectives

Among the diverse landscape of American Christianity, the evangelical and Pentecostal traditions occupy prominent spaces, their voices vibrant and often passionate concerning matters of faith and practice. When contemplating their perspectives on alcohol, particularly through the lens of contemporary conservatism and charismatic vitality, one enters a realm both distinct from and, in some ways, consonant with Baptist understandings. These theological families wrestle with the subject not merely as an ethical question but as a spiritual battleground where holiness, witness, and cultural engagement intertwine. Exploring their views illuminates the rich tapestry of belief about alcohol within broader Christian discourse and offers fertile ground for dialogue alongside Baptist convictions.

Evangelicalism, with its roots in a commitment to Scripture's authority and the transformative power of personal conversion, often exhibits a range of attitudes toward alcohol that can appear both nuanced and sharply delineated by denominational boundaries and local context. At its core, evangelicalism prizes moral clarity and the pursuit of sanctification, shaping a cautious stance toward anything that might imperil spiritual integrity or public witness. For many conservative evangelicals, abstinence from alcohol is not merely a personal choice but a communal standard, a means of safeguarding the vulnerable and upholding the distinctiveness of a holy life set apart from worldly excess. This abstinence is frequently grounded in concerns for temptation and the potential for drunkenness, with an eye toward scriptures that warn against the perils of overindulgence and degradation. "Do not get drunk on wine, which leads to debauchery," Paul advises in Ephesians, a verse that evangelical preachers often invoke as a sentinel against the slippery slope of alcohol's misuse.

Simultaneously, evangelical thought does not universally condemn moderate consumption; indeed, certain evangelical circles recognize the biblical precedent for wine's enjoyable and sacred role, especially in the context of the Lord's Supper and celebratory rejoicing. However, the cultural expressions within evangelicalism, shaped by waves of revivalism and the legacy of the temperance movement, have tended to emphasize abstinence as a practical outworking of scriptural caution, especially within youth ministries and pastoral guidance. Here arises a tension: the theology sings paeans to freedom in Christ, yet the social-cultural ethos calls for restraint, often tilting communities toward total avoidance to prevent scandal or stumbling. This tension reflects a broader evangelical principle: liberty must always walk hand in hand with love and wisdom, prioritizing the spiritual health of the community over individual indulgence.

Pentecostalism, as a vibrant and expressive branch of evangelicalism, shares much of this ethos but carries it further into a realm deeply saturated with expectations of spiritual empowerment and distinctiveness. The Pentecostal movement, emerging in the early 20th century as both a revival and a radical reawakening to the charismatic gifts of the Holy Spirit, often adopts even more rigorous prohibitions against alcohol use. For many Pentecostals, the consumption of alcoholic beverages is not simply unwise but often viewed as incompatible with the baptism and filling of the Spirit. The spiritual lens here interprets sobriety as a visible fruit of holiness and a supernatural sanctification that demands separation from what is perceived as worldly or potentially defiling practice. This sacramental sobriety is tightly interwoven with the expectation that the believer's body is a temple of the Holy Spirit, consecrated for God's purposes and impervious to substances that might cloud judgment or weaken spiritual alertness.

The Pentecostal emphasis on walking in the Spirit inherently involves an experiential dimension not often foregrounded in broader evangelical circles. It is not merely about following biblical rules but embracing a transformative power that changes appetites and inclinations. Within Pentecostal preaching and practice, the avoidance of alcohol often symbolizes a triumphant victory over the fleshly desires that once held sway, a signpost on the journey toward perfect holiness and anticipation of Christ's return. This approach reverberates in the vibrant worship settings that Pentecostalism is known for, where sobriety fuels ecstatic praise, prophetic utterance, and healing. To consume alcohol would be to dull the sharpness of spiritual awareness, thus hindering the believer's readiness to serve and bear witness.

Yet Pentecostal perspectives are not monolithic. Some Pentecostal groups hold to more moderate views, allowing limited consumption of alcohol, especially in cultural contexts where wine and beer are embedded in social rituals or familial heritage. This latitude, however, is tempered by ever-present calls for self-control and vigilance against addiction. The charismatic dimension, with its emphasis on the Spirit's guidance, allows room for individual discernment, but within frameworks that elevate the community's testimony and the sanctity of the believer's walk. The discussions within Pentecostalism often reflect a dynamic tension between cultural accommodation and spiritual distinctiveness, echoing the broader tension in evangelicalism but with arguably more fervent weight placed on the Spirit's immediate empowerment.

What sets both evangelical and Pentecostal perspectives apart in this discussion is the vibrant interplay between doctrine and experience. The biblical texts serve as powerful anchors, but the lived reality of conversion, empowerment, and holiness communities shape the contours of alcohol attitudes profoundly. For many in these traditions, alcohol is not simply a matter of cultural preference but a spiritual symbol, a test of faithfulness, and an index of one's commitment to God's sanctifying grace. Therefore, conversations about alcohol in these circles often transcend mere behavioral ethics and move into the terrain of spiritual formation. The call to sobriety becomes a call to spiritual vigilance, a concrete expression of a heart consecrated to God, beating to the rhythm of the Spirit's leading.

Interestingly, these perspectives carry both points of convergence and divergence with Baptist beliefs. Like conservative Baptists, evangelicals and Pentecostals emphasize temperance, the need to avoid drunkenness, and the value of moral clarity. However, Pentecostalism's more pronounced emphasis on the indwelling Spirit's power as a direct influence on lifestyle choices adds a layer of experiential theology that can elevate sobriety to a charismatic hallmark. Meanwhile, evangelicals tend toward a reasoned approach that blends scriptural obedience with communal wisdom, sometimes foregrounding social concerns like the protection of youth and the maintenance of a Christian witness in predominantly non-Christian societies. Baptists, depending on their historical and cultural pedigree, often balance between evangelical caution and charismatic zeal, embracing sobriety while wrestling with the complexities of witness and personal liberty.

In these broader evangelical and Pentecostal contexts, the conversation around alcohol also resonates with cultural and ethical concerns that transcend theology. Many evangelicals lament the pervasive influence of alcohol-related social ills, addiction, family breakdown, and moral compromise, which they see as calls to redouble commitment to abstinence or sobriety as a witness to a redeemed life. Pentecostals, likewise, often frame sobriety as part of a holistic holiness that confronts personal and societal brokenness with divine intervention and communal accountability. In both spheres, contemporary conservative voices frequently align alcohol abstinence with spiritual warfare language, portraying the journey away from alcohol as a battle against fleshly desires and demonic strongholds. The stakes are depicted as high, interwoven with eternal destinies and earthly testimonies.

Yet, amidst these rigorous stands, contemporary evangelical and Pentecostal communities are not devoid of debate or diversity. The growing influence of cultural pluralism and increased engagement with broader Christian scholarship have fostered nuanced conversations that wrestle openly with biblical texts that extol wine as a gift of creation and a symbol of divine blessing. Some contemporary evangelical theologians have urged a reevaluation of perennial abstinence norms, arguing for a biblically informed moderation that respects freedom in Christ while maintaining a wary guard against excess. Likewise, within Pentecostalism, younger voices have begun questioning whether strict prohibitionist stances inadvertently sow division or alienate those who struggle with legalism, advocating instead for a gospel-centered approach rooted in grace and pastoral sensitivity.

Moreover, charismatic circles increasingly recognize the complexity of alcohol-related ethics, acknowledging that cultural backgrounds, personal histories, and pastoral contexts shape how individuals navigate the terrain of drinking. The Spirit's leading, they suggest, may call some to abstain entirely, while guiding others toward responsible and joyful participation in social customs involving wine or beer. This perspective reframes sobriety not as a hard line but as a living journey of faithfulness, sanctification, and discernment. It also echoes the fruit of the Spirit's gentleness and self-control, inviting believers into a grace-imbued dialogue marked by compassion and mutual respect rather than rigid condemnation.

This emerging dialogue within evangelical and Pentecostal circles acts as both a bridge and a challenge to Baptist conversations. It invites Baptists, many of whom carry temperance deeply rooted in denominational history, to consider the multifaceted nature of faith and fermentation in their own midst. It encourages a posture that is at once faithful to scriptural admonitions and open to the Spirit's nuance in personal conscience. It also recognizes the importance of unified witness in a fractured world, where the message of Christ's redeeming love transcends disputes over beverages but flourishes in shared commitment to holiness and community.

In the twilight orchard of faith across evangelical and Pentecostal traditions, just as in Baptist groves, the fruit of alcohol issues is rich and complex. It is a fruit that tells stories of joy and caution, liberty and discipline, tradition and innovation. In the glow of spiritual reflection, it reveals not only the challenges of making moral decisions in a fallen world but also the splendid possibility of grace-filled community, where believers, guided by scripture, illuminated by history, and empowered by the Holy Spirit, savor the delicate balance of faith and fermentation. This balance calls for humility and boldness, for the courage to uphold convictions and the grace to honor the convictions of others, all in pursuit of a faith that is vibrant, united, and ever growing in love.

Gary E. Risenhoover

Toward a Faithful Dialogue: Tools for Conversation

Principles for Respectful Dialogue

Navigating conversations around faith and alcohol, especially within Baptist communities, requires more than knowledge; it demands a heart attuned to empathy, a mind open to understanding, and a spirit committed to unity. The challenge lies not merely in what is said but in how it is said, the posture from which dialogue begins, and the intention that guides each exchange. This delicate terrain, rich in personal convictions and sacred values, calls for principles of respectful dialogue that not only foster clarity and insight but also safeguard relationships, inviting a community of believers and seekers alike into meaningful, constructive conversations.

At the core of respectful dialogue is the profound commitment to listen deeply, not simply to respond, but to hear the story beneath the words, the fears veiled by certainty, the hopes nestled within caution. Listening in this context is an act of love, requiring one to set aside preconceived judgments and the defensive posture that conversations about alcohol, with its moral and spiritual ramifications, often trigger. When a daughter shares her struggle with navigating the church's teaching on temperance, or an elder expresses concern for the younger generation's perceived laxity, the real dialogue opens when each participant feels genuinely heard and understood. This empathetic listening creates a sacred space where vulnerability is met with grace, not condemnation, allowing the conversation to breathe and grow beyond mere argumentation.

Equally vital is the posture of humility, acknowledging, even joyfully embracing, the reality that none of us holds the full picture. Within Baptist communities, firmly grounded in scriptural authority, it is a temptation to enter discussions with a posture of certainty, rigidly guarding doctrinal positions as immutable truths. Yet, the spirit of the gospel invites an openness that recognizes the diverse ways God's wisdom might be revealed through the Holy Spirit's working in each believer's heart. Humility invites us to say, even silently, "I may not fully understand your perspective, but I seek to grasp it honestly and respectfully." This stance does not diminish doctrinal conviction but rather enriches it, confirming that faith and intellect thrive best not in isolation, but in communal discernment marked by affection and respect.

In addition to listening and humility, clarity of intention must arise as a cornerstone of respectful dialogue. Drifting into conversations with the sole aim of "winning" or proving a point inevitably erects barriers. Instead, dialogue should flow from the desire to learn, to bridge gaps, and to foster mutual flourishing in faith. This entails a conscious decision to prioritize relationships over rhetoric, people over positions. Within families, this principle recalibrates discussions that could otherwise fracture bonds; in church settings, it tempers debates that too easily veer into divisions; within wider communities, it transforms potential conflicts into opportunities for witness and reconciliation. When the intention is to build up rather than tear down, even difficult topics surrounding alcohol become gateways to deeper trust and shared growth.

The words we choose in these conversations also wield immense power. Language, ideally, molds dialogue towards graciousness and clarity rather than accusation or ambiguity. Practicing kindness in speech means avoiding inflammatory terms, refraining from assumptions about motives, and steering clear of absolute declarations that leave no room for differing experiences or understandings. For example, instead of asserting, "You are wrong about drinking," one might say, "I see things differently because of my experience, and I'm eager to hear yours." This shift not only softens the tone but also invites collaboration in discovering common ground. Through illustrations, personal anecdotes, and metaphors, complex theological concepts become accessible bridges rather than walls of abstruse doctrine, enabling hearts to connect despite differing journeys.

Another essential principle is the mutual recognition of the sacred personhood behind each viewpoint. Every participant in these dialogues carries a unique tapestry of life experiences, theological reflections, cultural contexts, and personal struggles. To reduce someone's stance to a caricature or stereotype, such as "the legalist," "the liberal," or "the uninformed", is to deny their dignity and obscure the genuine reasons that shape their beliefs. Faithful conversations flourish when we remember that behind passionate statements are real men and women wrestling with the same divine questions, often seeking, like us, the will of God amid the complexities of life. Acknowledging this shared humanity creates fertile soil where difficult discussions transform into joint journeys of spiritual discovery rather than confrontational battlegrounds.

Mindful awareness of timing and setting also profoundly shapes the quality of dialogue. Some conversations require the privacy of a quiet room and unhurried time to unpack layers of emotion and theology; others benefit from the wider stage of church forums designed for communal learning. Recognizing when the heart or spirit is too burdened or distracted to engage effectively is a form of respect both to oneself and to others. Rushing into debates amid fatigue or heightened emotion can harden stances and close hearts. Instead, patience often proves a sacred gift, offering a pause that invites reflection and prayer, preparing all parties to return with renewed openness. This pacing honors the unfolding of understanding as a process rather than a race to a conclusion.

In tandem with emotional and spiritual readiness, the commitment to seek common points of agreement, even if seemingly small or tangential, is a vital lifeline in preserving dialogue. The landscape of discussions about alcohol within faith communities is often strewn with polarized viewpoints, yet beneath these divides often lie shared commitments: love for God, desire for holiness, concern for community welfare, and the pursuit of wisdom. Highlighting and affirming these shared values becomes a bridge that eases tension. For instance, both those advocating abstinence and those endorsing moderate drinking may deeply agree about the dangers of drunkenness, the call to self-control, and the need to protect vulnerable individuals. Building upon these foundations fosters a tone of unity and shared mission, even amidst diverse applications of faith.

A related but challenging principle is the willingness to acknowledge the legitimacy of differing interpretations without compromising one's own convictions. Scriptural passages on wine and alcohol have long invited variegated understandings, from metaphorical to literal, from culturally specific to universal application. Recognizing this hermeneutical diversity, especially within the broader Christian tradition and among Baptist voices themselves, invites a posture of respectful disagreement. This doesn't dilute theological integrity but rather exemplifies maturity, maturity that can say, "While I hold firmly to my understanding, I honor your sincerely held perspective as part of our rich and humble wrestling with God's Word." Such a stance fosters resilience in faith communities, enabling space for varied convictions to coexist without fracturing fellowship.

Equipped with these principles, participants also benefit immensely from cultivating what might be called a "dialogical grace", an openness to being changed by the conversation itself. When both speaker and listener anticipate growth rather than confrontation, the exchange takes on a sacred dimension, becoming a mutual gift. The dialogue then reflects the relational nature of faith itself, where transformation and sanctification occur in community through love and truth. This grace does not guarantee ease, but it does promise a deeper connection to one another and to God's unfolding truth, allowing humility and charity to temper the sharp edges of disagreement.

Practical strategies further embody these principles. Paraphrasing or reflecting back what one hears ensures accuracy and shows respect, demonstrating that the speaker's words are valued. Asking open-ended questions invites exploration rather than shutting down conversation. Avoiding "you" statements that might feel accusatory and instead expressing feelings or thoughts through "I" statements softens potential defensiveness. These communication techniques, though seemingly simple, underpin a transformative dialogue climate, subtly shifting interactions from discord to discovery.

In family contexts, respectful dialogue can mean balancing generational wisdom with youthful perspectives, recognizing that each generation wrestles differently with cultural shifts and scriptural application. Elders might share with patience, avoiding undue pressure, while younger members express their struggles candidly yet respectfully. Churches face their own challenges, where communal identity intertwines with doctrinal stances; in such settings, creating forums for honest yet loving conversation models the grace of Christ's community and prepares congregations to engage the world with authentic faith.

Beyond immediate circles, respectful dialogue on faith and fermentation carries wider social implications. Alcohol's role in society, tied to celebrations, struggles with addiction, and cultural identities, means that how faith communities converse internally reverberates outward. When church members argue without grace, the message to outsiders can be one of judgment, exclusion, or irrelevance. Conversely, when believers embody respect, humility, and love in their discussions, they testify not just to their position but to the transformative power of the gospel to unite on difficult topics, modeling a faith that embodies restoration and hope even amid complexity. This witness becomes a beacon in a fractured world seeking bridges over boundaries.

In closing, perhaps the most profound source of power for respectful dialogue resides not in techniques or principles but in prayer and dependence on the Holy Spirit. Recognizing that human wisdom alone falters in matters touching the heart of faith invites a posture of reliance on divine guidance. Prayer fosters inner peace, tempers pride, and opens hearts to God's ongoing work in each participant's life. It reorients the motivation of dialogue from self-assertion to God-glorification, weaving conversations into the broader tapestry of God's redemptive narrative. When we approach dialogue on faith and alcohol with this spiritual awareness, every exchange becomes an opportunity for grace to flow, for understanding to deepen, and for community to be strengthened, an orchard at twilight where every fruit, ripe with Christian charity, tells a story of joy, restraint, and reverent love.

Thus, engaging respectfully and thoughtfully in discussions about alcohol within families, churches, and communities is not merely a skill but a sacred discipline. It requires intentionality, courage, and a heart attuned to the nuances of faith and human relationships. By embracing empathetic listening, humility, clear intention, gracious language, acknowledgment of shared humanity, patience, seeking common ground, honoring diverse convictions, dialogical grace, practical communication strategies, and prayerful dependence on God's Spirit, we craft conversations that mirror the very character of Christ, patient, kind, and unifying amid diversity. In this way, the complex and oft-contentious topic of faith and fermentation becomes not a source of division but a fertile ground for spiritual growth, communal love, and lasting harmony.

Navigating Differences with Grace

In the delicate dance of differing opinions, especially on a topic as interwoven with personal conviction and spiritual identity as alcohol consumption within the faith community, navigating differences calls for an artistry of grace that transcends mere tolerance. It requires a profound embrace of empathy, humility, and patient listening, qualities that are as much marks of spiritual maturity as they are practical tools for peaceful discourse. When disagreements arise within families, churches, and broader communities, the potential for tension can quickly escalate, coloring interactions with defensiveness or judgment. Yet, with intentional strategies rooted in respect and understanding, these moments of conflict can transform into opportunities for deepened relationships and enriched faith. The first, and perhaps most foundational, element of navigating difference with grace is cultivating a posture of listening that seeks to genuinely understand rather than merely to respond or refute. This means entering conversations with open ears and an open heart, willing to acknowledge the validity of others' experiences and convictions even when they diverge sharply from one's own. In the context of alcohol and faith, such listening involves recognizing the complexity of personal histories, cultural backgrounds, and theological interpretations that shape each person's stance. For example, a family member who holds a strict abstinence position may be driven by a painful past entwined with addiction or loss, while another advocating moderate drinking may see it as an expression of cultural joy and biblical symbolism of celebration. Approaching such differences with curiosity rather than suspicion invites a space where honest stories can be shared without fear of dismissal or attack.

Building on this foundation of attentive listening, the practice of humility emerges as a vital counterbalance to the human impulse to assert certainty. No single believer or community possesses a monopoly on divine wisdom; rather, each perspective is a lens refracted through the kaleidoscope of Scripture, tradition, and personal experience. Acknowledging this reality is not a concession of weakness but a courageous act of faith that honors the mystery and depth of God's truth. It allows room for the possibility that one's own interpretation, however deeply held, might be enriched, challenged, or even corrected by engaging honestly with differing viewpoints. In practical terms, humility manifests as starting conversations with statements that affirm one's respect for the other's beliefs, phrases such as "I want to hear more about your perspective" or "You make a good point, and I want to understand it better." This approach softens defenses and encourages reciprocal openness, essential for meaningful dialogue.

Navigating tension also demands a keen awareness of boundaries, both personal and communal. Recognizing where to draw the line in discussions about alcohol is crucial, as these conversations can unearth raw wounds or evoke deeply ingrained fears. Establishing clear boundaries about what topics are open for discussion, the tone and timing of conversations, and the willingness to pause or disengage when emotions run high preserves the integrity of relationships. Within families, this might mean agreeing to table certain discussions where past experiences have caused pain, or within churches, it might involve creating forums where respectful dialogue is facilitated under the guidance of skilled moderators. Boundaries protect the sacredness of community and guard against the corrosive effects of prolonged conflict.

Equally important is fostering an attitude of patience, recognizing that reconciliation of differing beliefs will rarely occur in a single conversation or confrontation. Graceful navigation of differences is an ongoing journey, not a one-time event. Patience allows space for the slow unfolding of understanding, the softening of hardened positions, and the gradual building of trust. It invites a long view of relationships where moments of disagreement are not endpoints but steps along a pathway toward greater unity. This patience often calls for stepping back from the heat of debate to allow emotions to settle, reflecting individually and prayerfully before re-engaging in dialogue.

Another crucial strategy is cultivating a vocabulary of respect that replaces inflammatory or judgmental language with words that affirm the dignity of all participants. Language shapes perception, and in discussions about alcohol within faith communities, words can either build bridges or erect walls. Avoiding terms that imply moral superiority or shame, and instead using language that conveys empathy and shared commitment to spiritual well-being, fosters an environment of mutual respect. For example, instead of saying, "You shouldn't drink because it's sinful," one might say, "I understand why you choose to abstain, and I respect the convictions that lead you there." Such reframing does not dilute one's beliefs but honors the relational context in which they are expressed.

Integrating scriptural insights as a common touchstone can also guide conversations by reminding all parties of the shared faith foundation that undergirds differing viewpoints. Scripture offers numerous exhortations toward love, gentleness, and bearing with one another in Christ, which, when foregrounded, shift the focus from winning arguments to preserving fellowship. Recalling passages such as Ephesians 4:2–3, which call believers to humility, gentleness, and patience, or Romans 14, which addresses disputes over disputable matters with a call to mutual acceptance, can temper conversations with theological grace. These texts underscore the priority of unity and love over doctrinal rigidity, inviting interlocutors to view each other through the lens of Christlike compassion rather than as adversaries.

Equipping communities with structures for dialogue can transform individual efforts into collective movements toward understanding. Churches, for example, can facilitate small-group discussions, workshops, or study series that explore alcohol and faith in a manner that encourages honest confession, shared learning, and collective prayer. Creating spaces where diverse voices are heard and valued diminishes the sense of isolation that often accompanies dissenting views. These forums can be led by trained facilitators who help navigate tough questions, manage emotions, and keep conversations constructive. By positioning such dialogue as part of the spiritual formation process, communities model how faith engages real-life complexities with both conviction and compassion.

An often-overlooked but powerful method for handling disagreement is storytelling. When individuals share their narratives, their struggles, their blessings, their wrestling with Scripture and conscience, they offer windows into the lived realities behind theological positions. Stories humanize abstract debates, cultivating empathy and breaking down stereotypes. For instance, hearing a young couple's cautious approach to alcohol because of family history, or an elder's joyous memories of communion involving wine, can enrich understanding far more than theological treatises alone. Stories invite listeners not just to hear words but to feel the hearts behind them, creating relational bonds that soften the hardness of division.

In family contexts, where conversations about alcohol and faith may intersect with long-standing dynamics and deep emotional stakes, grace-filled navigation additionally calls for a balance between honesty and tenderness. Transparency about one's convictions is necessary for authenticity, but coupling that honesty with a spirit of love and a willingness to prioritize the relationship over winning the argument keeps communication healthy. Families might find it helpful to establish shared goals for their discussions, such as mutual respect, maintaining peace, and honoring each person's journey, to guide interactions and remind all involved of the higher purpose behind their words.

Psychological insights into conflict resolution can also illuminate pathways to grace. Recognizing cognitive biases, emotional triggers, and the role of identity in shaping responses enables participants to respond not reactively but with deliberate awareness. For example, understanding that a strong reaction to alcohol discussions may stem from a wounded sense of identity or fear of moral compromise helps detach personal offense from the core of the disagreement. Embracing this awareness fosters compassion, as one perceives the other not as an enemy but as a fellow traveler bearing burdens and hopes.

Importantly, grace does not equate with passivity or the avoidance of truth. Navigating differences with grace involves a courageous commitment to truth spoken in love. It invites believers to articulate their convictions clearly while doing so with gentleness that welcomes dialogue rather than defensiveness. This balance nurtures an environment where honesty and respect coexist, allowing theological differences to be aired without fracturing fellowship. It also models a mature Christian witness to both insiders and outsiders, exemplifying how faith can engage complex issues in ways that honor God and neighbor alike.

Another nuanced dimension is the willingness to embrace ambiguity and uncertainty. Recognizing that some questions about alcohol and faith resist easy answers or neat categories invites humility and patience. Embracing this mystery can relieve the pressure to force consensus and open space for diversity within unity. It acknowledges that faith communities can hold differing convictions not as signs of division but as reflections of the multifaceted nature of God's kingdom. This posture allows for a richness of experience and understanding that transcends rigid boundaries.

Cultivating prayer as a communal and individual practice is a vital element in navigating differences. Prayer centers the heart, aligns intentions with God's will, and invites divine guidance in moments of tension and confusion. It fosters reliance on the Holy Spirit to soften hearts, illuminate minds, and unite believers in love despite disagreement. Incorporating prayer into conversations about alcohol and faith frames them as spiritual journeys, not mere debates, infusing discussions with reverence and hope.

Moreover, embodying forgiveness when offenses arise is indispensable. Even with the best intentions, words can wound and hearts harden. Extending grace through forgiving one another preserves the possibility of restoration and healing, reinforcing the bonds that transcend specific disputes. Forgiveness is a practical outworking of the theological truths about God's mercy and Christ's reconciling work, reminding believers that relationships matter more than positions.

Finally, approaching schools of thought and individual persons within the Baptist tradition, and beyond, with curiosity rather than condescension enriches the collective faith experience. Recognizing the

Baptist heritage's emphasis on conscience, Scripture, and local autonomy invites respectful engagement with varying interpretations rather than imposed uniformity. It honors the dynamic tension between shared faith foundations and individual conviction, allowing for a vibrant and living tradition.

In closing, navigating differences about alcohol within faith communities is a microcosm of the broader Christian call to love amidst diversity. By embracing empathetic listening, humility, clear boundaries, patience, respectful language, scriptural grounding, structured dialogue, storytelling, psychological insight, truth spoken in love, acceptance of ambiguity, prayer, forgiveness, and curiosity, believers can turn potential conflict into avenues of grace. This not only preserves unity but also enriches the spiritual journey, allowing faith and fermentation to coexist in a way that reflects the beauty and complexity of God's creation. Such grace-filled navigation becomes a witness to the transforming power of the gospel, inspiring communities to savor a deeper understanding of divine guidance, fostering harmony, and strengthening bonds of love that hold fragile tensions in hopeful embrace.

Building Community Amid Diverse Views

In the gentle unfolding of a shared faith journey, one of the most delicate yet essential tasks is building and sustaining community amid diverse views, especially on topics as nuanced and deeply personal as alcohol consumption. As believers traverse the intersection where biblical instruction meets contemporary practice, they often find themselves navigating a labyrinth of convictions, interpretations, and cultural backdrops that shape their understanding. It is within this intricate web of differing perspectives that the true challenge, and opportunity, of Christian fellowship arises: fostering unity not by uniformity, but through mutual respect and compassion that honors the heart behind each stance. This endeavor demands a spirit of humility that acknowledges the limitations of personal wisdom and the expansive mystery of divine truth, inviting every member of the community to engage not as adversaries defending rigid boundaries, but as pilgrims walking alongside one another toward deeper grace and understanding.

When approaching discussions within families, where generational beliefs and emotional investments in tradition intermingle, it is vital to nurture an environment where conversations about alcohol and faith are framed by love rather than contention. Families often carry the weight of inherited convictions that can make candid dialogue feel like walking on fragile glass. Here, the practice of listening becomes an art form, attentive and patient, free from the urgency to correct or persuade. In these sacred spaces, inviting questions rather than asserting answers opens pathways for empathy and discovery. For instance, a grandparent's caution rooted in stories of past hardship can be met with curiosity rather than dismissal, while younger family members' calls for a fresh understanding may be received with gentle acknowledgment instead of skepticism. This mutual exchange honors the tapestry of faith woven across generations and reminds all that the core of Christian kinship lies not in agreement on every issue but in shared devotion to Christ and one another.

Within the broader church community, the task becomes even more intricate, as a mosaic of cultural, theological, and experiential backgrounds gathers under the common banner of faith. Congregations are microcosms of the wider body of Christ, reflecting a spectrum of convictions about alcohol that range from strict abstinence to moderate enjoyment, all grounded in a sincere desire to live faithfully. Here, leaders play an indispensable role in setting a tone that champions dialogue over dogma. When pastors and elders openly acknowledge the complexity of the subject and encourage congregants to wrestle with Scripture thoughtfully and respectfully, they carve out a space where diverse viewpoints can coexist without fracturing community bonds. Teaching that emphasizes the Christian principles of love, grace, and responsibility rather than rigid prohibition fosters an ethos where individuals feel valued even if their perspective differs from the majority.

Moreover, churches that intertwine their community life with opportunities for shared experiences, meals, fellowship events, and service projects create natural contexts where relationships deepen beyond theological positions. These lived interactions cultivate trust and reveal the multifaceted humanity behind each viewpoint, softening the edges of disagreement. When a member who abstains from alcohol is known not just for their stance but for their kindness and generosity, and when one who enjoys a glass of fermented grape is recognized for their integrity and faithfulness, the community becomes a living example of unity amid diversity. This dynamic illustrates the profound truth that the Spirit's work in building the body transcends human divisions and calls forth a love that "keeps no record of wrongs," instead **weaves** together a fabric of acceptance.

Outside of family and church, the sphere of community encompasses friends, neighbors, and fellow citizens whose beliefs about alcohol may be colored by cultural background, personal history, or moral philosophy distinct from the Baptist tradition. Engaging in these broader conversations requires both cultural sensitivity and clarity of conviction. It beckons a posture of listening that seeks to understand the fears, hopes, and values that inform others' views, whether they champion strict temperance as a safeguard against societal harm or embrace moderate use as part of celebratory life. In these exchanges, faith becomes a lens not only for declaring doctrinal truths but for exemplifying Christ-like patience and gentleness. The apostle Paul's admonition to "be completely humble and gentle; be patient, bearing with one another in love" (Ephesians 4:2) rings especially true, urging believers to prioritize relationship and witness over victory in debate.

One of the greatest barriers to constructive dialogue is the tendency for convictions about alcohol to become entangled with personal identity, making opposition feel like an attack rather than a difference of perspective. To move beyond this impasse, it helps to employ the practice of speaking from personal experience, using "I" statements and storytelling to convey the nuances of one's journey with faith and fermentation without imposing judgment. For example, a member of a Baptist congregation might share how their commitment to abstinence grows from a desire to honor the struggles of those harmed by alcohol, framing it as a personal act of love rather than a moralistic mandate. Conversely, another might recount the joy and fellowship experienced through moderate consumption, emphasizing discernment and self-control as expressions of spiritual maturity. These narratives humanize abstract debates and invite empathy, fostering a climate where differing views are not merely tolerated but genuinely received.

Equally crucial is the discipline of approaching Scripture with a posture of charity and openness, recognizing that even within the Bible's complex anthology, passages regarding alcohol span a spectrum from celebration to caution. Encouraging Bible study groups and small communities to examine these texts together, rather than defaulting to pre-set conclusions, allows the Holy Spirit room to illuminate and guide understanding in fresh ways. Such shared exegetical journeys can reveal the weight of cultural context, the symbolic resonance of wine in biblical imagery, and the consistent call to wisdom and self-control. Participants emerge with richer insight and a collective humility that tempers certainty and strengthens communal bonds. This approach guards against the pitfalls of selective proof-texting that often entrench division and instead models a faith that wrestles honestly with nuance.

In promoting such dialogue, communication styles shape the tenor of engagement as much as content. Embracing a language of curiosity, inquiry, and acknowledgment rather than accusation and absolutism invites hearts to soften and minds to remain open. When disagreement is met with statements like, "I see your point," or "That perspective challenges me to think deeper," it signals respect and paves the way for constructive discourse. Conversely, language that brands viewpoints as foolish or sinful erects walls that harden into estrangement. Building community thus thrives on an ethos of respect that permeates speech and action alike, that holds fast to truth without resorting to pride or dismissiveness.

Another intricate layer to fostering unity resides in addressing the fears and concerns often at the heart of conflicting viewpoints. For many Baptists who champion abstinence, the rationale stems from a profound desire to protect loved ones, particularly vulnerable youth, from the dangers of addiction and moral compromise. Understanding this motivation as an expression of care rather than legalism reframes the conversation, inviting dialogue about how communities can collectively support healthy boundaries while honoring individual conscience. Solutions such as establishing clear church policies that respect members' convictions without alienation, providing education about addiction and responsible behavior, and offering safe spaces for candid discussion contribute to a culture where fears are acknowledged and addressed constructively.

At the same time, advocates of moderate, responsible consumption within the Baptist fold often emphasize the biblical affirmations of wine as a creation of God meant for joy and refreshment. They invite reflection on how exuberance and celebration can be forms of worship and thanksgiving, so long as they are marked by sobriety and reverence. This perspective challenges communities to reconsider assumptions that associate all alcohol use with moral compromise, encouraging spaces that practice inclusion without compromising ethical standards. When these voices are heard with sincerity, they enrich the community's understanding of grace as expansive and dialogic, not constrictive.

It is within such a delicate balancing act of honoring conviction and extending grace that the imagined twilight orchard metaphor calms the heart. Each fruit hanging from the branches, each belief and practice concerning alcohol, tells a unique tale of joy, restraint, and reverence. Some fruits gleam with the vibrant red of abstinence, reminding us of strength and deliberate choice; others shimmer in the golden hue of moderation, echoing celebration and wisdom. The orchard invites pilgrims to gather beneath its canopy, sharing stories and sustenance, aware that no single fruit encompasses the fullness of God's provision. Together, they create a tableau rich in diversity and resplendent with shared faith.

This orchard is more than a poetic vision; it is a blueprint for community. It calls for leaders to cultivate soil conditions, spaces of trust and openness, where each fruit can ripen without fear of judgment or exclusion. It beckons participants to water relationships with kindness and prune discourse with patience, recognizing that growth takes time and caregiving. Ultimately, the orchard flourishes not through enforced uniformity but through the steady interweaving of differing branches, whose varied fruits together testify to the abundance of God's grace.

In practical terms, fostering such a community requires intentionality. Developing educational programs that offer balanced insights into biblical texts about alcohol, Baptist doctrinal positions, and cultural considerations equips members to engage the subject thoughtfully rather than reactively. Encouraging small groups to share personal stories fosters vulnerability and connection, while intergenerational conversations bridge divides often widened by age and experience. Hosting forums where contemporary Baptist voices who hold varying views can speak with mutual respect models constructive dialogue and reduces polarization. Additionally, embracing ecumenical perspectives broadens understanding and reminds communities that they are part of a larger body wrestling with these questions.

Even beyond structured settings, everyday acts of kindness and respect lay the foundation for unity. Choosing to refrain from criticism when observing others' practices regarding alcohol, offering hospitality without stipulations, and seeking common ground around shared faith priorities demonstrate that commitment to Christ supersedes all secondary matters. When members witness such grace embodied in their communities, barriers dissolve, suspicion wanes, and bridges strengthen, creating a resilient fellowship capable of weathering contentious discussions with love intact.

Indeed, the journey toward unity amid diverse views on alcohol is not a linear progression but a dynamic dance marked by occasional missteps, repentance, and renewed commitment. It calls all participants to lean into the tension with courage, recognizing that unity does not erase difference but welcomes it into a harmonized chorus where multiple voices contribute to a richer melody. This posture demands trust, not only in one another but in the Spirit's ability to knit hearts together beyond human capacity. It requires patience as individuals grow in understanding and humility as convictions evolve.

In the end, the measure of community is less about consensus on every detail and more about the quality of love prevailing despite differences. When believers cultivate spaces where questions about faith and alcohol can be raised without fear, where stories are heard with open hearts, and where grace cushions disagreements, they embody the church as Jesus envisioned: a family bound not by uniform thought but by sacrificial love. It is within this family that faith and fermentation find not opposition but a sacred relationship, where both joy and discipline coexist, revealing the depth and breadth of God's kingdom.

Thus, building community amid diverse views is a sacred art of weaving together varied threads into a tapestry vibrant with faith, hope, and love. It means embracing the inevitable tensions of human perspective while holding fast to the unshakable foundation of Christ's unity. As the dusk settles across the orchard of belief, those gathered beneath its branches can rest in the knowing that their differences do not diminish their fellowship but enrich it, turning conversation into communion, disagreement into dialogue, and diverse fruits into a feast of grace shared abundantly.

Synthesis and Reflection: Embracing Complexity with Faith

Revisiting the Orchard at Twilight

As the sun gently dips beneath the horizon, casting a soft amber glow across the orchard, there stands a quiet invitation, not merely to witness the twilight hour, but to step within a living metaphor woven from every branch, leaf, and fruit that the land generously yields. This orchard, an emblem of faith and fermentation intertwined, beckons us to linger in its twilight, where shadows temper the brilliance of daylight, and both coexist in a harmony that defies simple definition. To revisit this orchard at twilight is to embrace the paradoxes that have surfaced throughout our exploration, the blessings and burdens of alcohol in biblical teaching, the tensions and triumphs in Baptist thought, and the deeply human dance between restraint and rejoicing. It prompts us to reconsider the idea that faith and fermentation are locked in conflict, challenging us instead to discover a sacred balance where reverence, discipline, and joy cultivate a fruitful life.

In this stillness, the orchard reveals itself not as a place of stark dualities but as a landscape rich with subtle hues, where every vine tells a story of growth nurtured by both sun and shade. The grapes hanging heavy with promise are not unlike the complexities within scripture, sometimes golden with blessing, other times shadowed with caution. The twilight whispers that to hold fast to faith is not to deny the realities embodied by fermented wine, but to engage them thoughtfully, acknowledging the gift and the gravity that coexist in one glass. There is a sacred tension here that resists simplification; it is the very essence of what it means to live a faith that is both grounded and expansive. To revisit the orchard is to affirm that spiritual maturity arises precisely when we can hold contradictions in a single embrace, honoring the depth of divine truth and the nuanced culture in which we sip and share.

As we journey deeper into this metaphorical orchard, the twilight hour becomes a symbol not of uncertainty but of illuminated complexity, a moment saturated with possibility before night unfurls its veil of mystery. Here, the stories of scripture intertwine with the lived experiences of those within the Baptist tradition and beyond, weaving a tapestry rich with texture. It is in the half-light that we glimpse how wine has been portrayed as both a symbol of God's blessing and a cautionary emblem of human frailty; the fermenting fruit embodies joy and danger in equal measure. This twilight reminds us that the spiritual journey is rarely about absolute abstinence or unfettered indulgence but rather about the delicate art of discernment. Every season in the orchard calls for a different kind of tending, and the wisdom to know when to reap, when to refrain, and when to celebrate becomes our gift and responsibility as faithful stewards.

There is profound beauty in recognizing that fermenting grapes, much like the moral and theological nuances surrounding alcohol, require patience, care, and the interplay of many elements, heat, cold, time, and touch, all contributing to a final product whose quality reflects the harmony of these forces. So too does the faith journey involve balancing joy and discipline, freedom and restraint. To embrace fermentation is to invite transformation, a process that involves vulnerability and trust as much as it does the assertion of personal and communal values. It asks us to acknowledge the gifts of conviviality, celebration, and even sacred ritual, all of which hold a place alongside the sober call to holiness and responsibility. In the orchard at twilight, judgment softens into reflection, and division gives way to dialogue. We are reminded that within the Baptist community and the broader Christian fellowship, there can be spaces of understanding where different practices regarding alcohol do not fracture unity but deepen it.

The twilight orchard also offers a fertile ground for reconciling historical Baptist convictions with the richly textured biblical witness. The denomination's strong emphasis on temperance and ethical clarity has served as a vital beacon, guiding communities away from harm and into the clarity of moral integrity. Yet, as we stand among the orchard's whispering leaves, we see how scripture itself is neither monolithic nor simplistic but invites a dynamic engagement that can accommodate a range of convictions and expressions. The Baptist theologian's voice contrasts rigor with grace, insisting on clarity even as it acknowledges the complexity of lived experience and textual interpretation. The biblical scholar enriches this dialogue by illuminating ancient cultural contexts that shift our understanding of wine from a singular symbol of indulgence to a multifaceted sign of God's providential care. Together, these voices blend like the mixed leaves and folded shadows of the orchard, offering a panoramic view that encourages thoughtful consideration rather than reductionist certainty.

Among the fruit-laden branches, personal stories emerge, like glowing fireflies in the growing dusk, testimonies of believers who have wrestled with the issue of alcohol in their faith journeys and found surprising paths toward peace and understanding. These narratives breathe life into theoretical discourse, revealing how the orchard is not just a metaphor but a living reality in the hearts and homes of many. From those who choose complete abstinence out of conviction to those who embrace moderate drinking as a form of fellowship, the orchard welcomes all, reminding us that the vineyard is vast and varied. Its boundaries are not defined by rigid lines but by the shared commitment to honor God in every choice made, every habit examined, and every community nurtured. These stories challenge us to move beyond stereotypes and assumptions, opening us to empathy and renewed respect for one another's journeys through the interplay of faith and fermentation.

In these concluding moments under the twilight sky, the orchard invites us to reconsider what it means to live a life marked by reverence and joy, discipline and grace. Fermentation itself becomes a profound metaphor for spiritual formation, an ongoing, sometimes messy process that yields something unexpectedly beautiful when attended with care and intention. Just as the seasons govern the growth and ripening of the fruit, so do the rhythms of prayer, study, fellowship, and self-examination guide our moral choices and shape our communities. The twilight allows us to glimpse the horizon where faith's clarity meets the complex realities of human life, where joy is not reckless abandon but a fruit of the Spirit cultivated through wisdom and love. Through this lens, alcohol ceases to be a mere substance fraught with divisiveness; it becomes an emblem of God's capacity to transform ordinary elements into vessels of blessing, teaching us humility and trust along the way.

Moreover, the orchard at twilight gently presses against the boundaries of individual belief and communal identity, inviting dialogue that transcends division. It encourages readers, whether skeptic or believer, teetotaler or moderate drinker, to enter conversations not as battlegrounds but as shared spaces of discovery. The metaphor insists that no single perspective holds the full truth; rather, truth unfolds as we listen with open hearts to the diverse experiences and convictions that animate our faith communities. It models an embrace of tension as fertile ground, where unity is not uniformity but the harmony of distinct voices singing together in a complex yet beautiful chorus. In this way, the twilight orchard becomes not an endpoint but a beginning, a sacred space where thoughtful reflection on faith and fermentation takes root and grows, offering hope for reconciliation and spiritual depth.

As we prepare to leave this orchard, the imagery lingers, grapes still clinging to their vines, leaves catching the last flickers of light, the air sweet with the scent of earth and promise. This is an invitation to carry forth a renewed mindset into our daily lives, to sip thoughtfully and live intentionally, to engage our faith with openness to complexity, and to cultivate communities that honor both conviction and compassion. The orchard at twilight teaches us that faith need not fear the fermenting processes within and around us; rather, it can draw strength from them, learning that transformation is often wrought in the balance of restraint and release, of solemnity and celebration. To revisit the orchard is ultimately to acknowledge the sacred potential in all aspects of life that touch our spirit, inviting us to wrestle with questions, celebrate blessings, and walk forward with hope, humility, and joy. Herein lies the heart of the journey: a faith that drinks deeply from the wells of tradition and scripture, rising to meet new understanding with the grace of twilight's embrace.

Faith as Compass and Conversation

In the twilight orchard where faith and fermentation meet, we find ourselves standing at a crossroads that calls not for simple answers but for deep, ongoing conversation. This conversation, much like the intricate dance of flavors in a finely aged wine, demands patience, subtlety, and a willingness to savor complexity. At its heart, faith acts as both a compass and a catalyst, guiding us with spiritual wisdom while inviting us into a community of dialogue, reflection, and humility. It is in this delicate balance of reverence and reason, discipline and delight, that we discover not a rigid mandate but a living journey, one that honors the sacred mystery intertwined with every pour, every shared moment, and every heart seeking understanding.

Faith, in its richest expression, is never a solitary endeavor; it is the vibrant pulse of a community voluntarily bound by shared convictions yet open to difference. When we approach the topic of fermentation, alcohol in all its biblical, cultural, and moral dimensions, through this lens, we step beyond the confines of individual preference or fear. We enter a space where scriptural teachings serve not as walls but as windows, inviting fresh light and new perspectives to illuminate our understanding. Here, faith acts as a compass, not dictating a fixed trajectory, but orienting our hearts and minds toward wisdom that is both ancient and profoundly relevant. It reminds us to hold fast to reverence for God's provision, discipline in moral choices, and joy in the gift of life's fullness, avoiding the twin pitfalls of legalistic restraint and reckless abandon.

The scriptures, rich with imagery and counsel on the use of wine and fermented drink, reflect the nuanced reality of human experience, one where blessing and caution dance together in perpetual tension. Wine is at once a symbol of divine blessing, a means of celebration, and a test of self-control. These dimensions cannot be compressed into a single, simplistic rule without losing their vitality. Hence, faith invites us to hold this complexity with both hands, not shying away from difficult questions but embracing them as part of a vibrant spiritual journey. This means listening attentively to the wisdom woven through biblical text, appreciating the historical and cultural contexts that shaped those texts, and honoring the interpretative tradition that Baptist communities have cultivated with avid care.

Yet, faith also guides us toward conversation, not merely internal reflection, but active, ongoing dialogue with others whose journeys may differ. This dialogue is not always comfortable; it probes the tensions between conviction and compassion, between individual freedom and communal responsibility. It requires humility, acknowledging that our understanding is always partial and contingent on the limits of human insight. In this respectful exchange, faith neither demands uniformity nor excuses irrelevance; rather, it sets the tone for discourse that is both candid and caring, a pursuit of truth conducted with love. It is this dynamic conversation where growth flourishes, transforming personal belief into communal wisdom enriched by diverse voices and lived realities.

Within Baptist traditions, this conversation takes on a distinctive shape. Baptists possess a robust heritage of moral clarity and social concern, often emphasizing temperance as a reflection of holiness and public witness. Yet, the lived expressions within the denomination are far from monolithic, encompassing voices that advocate for varying degrees of personal freedom around alcohol use. Recognizing this diversity is essential to moving beyond polarizing debates toward a shared commitment to understanding. Faith, as a guiding compass, calls each believer to weigh scriptural principles alongside personal conscience, cultural context, and the well-being of the church body. It prompts questions not only about whether to drink but how the manner and motives of drinking reflect the character of Christ in us.

This deepened perspective invites a more comprehensive exploration of what it means to live faithfully in a world imbued with both blessing and vulnerability. The biblical admonitions against drunkenness, for example, gain new urgency; they remind us that discipline is not an end but a means, one that secures our freedom in Christ rather than enslaving us to any external regulation. In this sense, faith's compass points not toward abstinence as a legalistic achievement but toward a kingdom ethic of self-control, love for neighbor, and the pursuit of holiness. It challenges us to consider how our actions impact others, how choices about alcohol are not isolated personal matters but threads in the fabric of community health, witness, and hospitality.

Faith also opens space for joy, a vibrant joy that is neither careless nor constrained. The biblical narrative celebrates wine as part of God's creation meant to enliven the heart and bless fellowship. This joyful dimension reminds us that faith does not demand somberness or deny the pleasures of life; instead, it sanctifies them by inviting us to receive them gratefully, responsibly, and in ways that draw us closer to God and one another. It is a joy marked by reverence, a joyful sobriety that perceives the sacred in life's ordinary gifts, including the fruit of the vine. Approaching alcohol with such reverence turns simple drinking into an act of worship, a sacrament of creation's goodness, and a celebration of God's abundant provision.

But what does it look like to live into this vision, faith as compass and conversation, in the flesh and blood reality of Baptist communities today? It means fostering environments where questions about alcohol are met not with judgment but with a patient's listening ear. It means pastors, families, and congregations cultivating spaces where stories can be shared honestly, including struggles with temptation, failures in self-control, and moments of joy and moderation. It means recognizing that the journey toward wisdom regarding alcohol is rarely linear; it is marked by setbacks and renewed commitments, by grace extended and boundaries respected. Within these lived experiences, the ancient texts come alive, not as static dictums but as guiding stars that orient believers toward love, mercy, and truth.

Moreover, embracing this faithful conversation requires humility to face uncomfortable questions that challenge long-held assumptions. What might it mean for Baptist churches to dialogue openly about the biblical passages that seem to sanction wine drinking as a good gift, even as they historically advocate for abstinence? How might acknowledging cultural shifts and scientific understandings about alcohol influence pastoral care and communal expectations? What pastoral approaches best balance calling for holiness with recognizing human frailty? Answering such questions is not about capitulation or abandoning doctrine but about embodying a faith robust enough to hold tension without fracture, generous enough to listen without dismissiveness, and wise enough to discern faithfulness amid complexity.

In addition, this dialogue must extend beyond denominational boundaries, inviting ecumenical engagement that enriches Baptist conversations with perspectives from other Christian traditions. Such exchange exposes us to the breadth of Christian thought on alcohol, from the wine rituals of liturgical churches to the sobriety movements in evangelical circles, providing a wider lens through which to view our own convictions. Faith's compass is broadened by this diversity, pointing not toward uniformity but toward a shared pursuit of holiness and truth grounded in the gospel's spirit. In this widened fellowship, we find encouragement to relinquish rigid stances that alienate, replacing them with grace-filled approaches that seek unity without sacrificing integrity.

Ultimately, embracing faith as both compass and conversation means recognizing that the question of alcohol use is emblematic of broader spiritual dynamics: how we balance freedom and restraint, celebration and sobriety, personal conscience and communal responsibility. It reminds us that the Christian life is a pilgrimage marked by continual learning, repentance, and grace. No single answer can encapsulate the fullness of this journey, but faith equips us to navigate it with courage, openness, and love. It teaches us that the vineyard of our spiritual lives requires careful tending, an attentive hand, and an open heart willing to learn from vineyard workers old and new.

To step into this sacred dialogue is to acknowledge that faith calls us not away from the complexities of life but into their heart. It challenges us to move beyond polarized debates and into a space where we might hold apparent contradictions in creative tension, treasuring the command to abstain from excess, while celebrating the gift of wine; respecting diverse convictions, yet striving for communal harmony; practicing discipline without losing sight of joy. In doing so, we allow faith to be our compass, steady, sure, and luminous, even when the path winds through the shadows of uncertainty.

As the twilight deepens over the orchard, we see that every cluster of grapes bears its own story, stories of ancient blessings and modern struggles, of covenant and community, of love restrained and love expressed. To journey in faith with fermentation is to become part of a conversation that spans centuries, cultures, and convictions, a conversation that invites us to listen with humility, speak with grace, and walk together in spirit. May this ongoing dialogue inspire us to savor both the mystery and the clarity that faith reveals, equipping us not only to drink deeply of scripture and tradition but to pour out lives marked by wisdom, compassion, and joy. In this sacred dance, faith is not a quiet spectator but a lively partner, guiding us step by step, word by word, glass by glass, into the fullness of abundant life.

Looking Ahead with Hope and Clarity

As we stand at the threshold of the future, gazing beyond the intricate landscapes of scriptural wisdom and Baptist tradition, it is neither simplicity nor certainty that offers the warmest comfort but the deliberate embrace of complexity itself. To look ahead with hope and clarity is to accept that faith and fermentation, those intertwined threads weaving through millennia of human experience, cannot be unraveled into neat binaries or pat answers. There is an enduring beauty in this nuanced intersection, a sacred space where reverence for God's Word, the discipline of moral self-examination, and the joy of communal celebration converge like the sweet tang of well-aged wine, rich with layers of flavor born from time, patience, and tender stewardship. This is the horizon toward which we now turn our gaze, inviting each reader to see not division but harmony, not restriction but liberation through understanding.

In this unfolding vision, hope blossoms from the soil of honest dialogue and humble listening. We acknowledge the tension that has long existed between biblical affirmation of wine as a gift and the Baptist tradition's earnest call for temperance. These are not irreconcilable positions but facets of a joint heritage that calls for wisdom, empathy, and balance. Much like tending a vineyard, where both the tender leaves and the robust clusters must be carefully nurtured, the relationship between faith and fermentation requires thoughtful care, neither casting aside joy momentarily glimpsed at the feast of Cana nor ignoring the sobering warnings nestled within Proverbs, Psalms, and the Epistles.

To look ahead with clarity is also to recognize that the text of Scripture is alive, engaging us anew with every encounter. It invites us into a dynamic conversation, one where questions are more telling than answers and where interpretation seeks to honor divine mystery alongside human responsibility. The biblical references to alcohol are woven into stories of hospitality, blessing, and celebration, yet they carry veiled cautions against excess and the spiritual dangers of addiction. The Baptist tradition, shaped by history's passionate debates and revivalist fervor, brings to this dialogue a profound concern for holiness and a desire to shield the community from harm. Rather than viewing these emphases as contradictory, they can be understood as complementary, a balance of grace and truth where the spirit leads us to neither reckless indulgence nor compulsive abstinence but to sober joy grounded in self-control and mutual care.

Throughout this book, we have walked through the shaded orchard at twilight, a metaphor for the complex, multifaceted relationship between faith and fermented beverages. Each tree and fruit reflects stories of restraint, joy, reverence, and sometimes struggle. To walk forward now is to carry this orchard within us, as a testimony that moral clarity does not mean rigidity, and that embracing the worthiness of wine, along with the call to temperance, can coexist in a responsible, spiritually fulfilling lifestyle. This vision does not seek to erase uncomfortable conversations but to deepen them, reminding us that a mature faith holds tensions and paradoxes without fracturing.

When we speak of temperance in the Baptist tradition, we acknowledge the earnest desire not only to obey commands but to foster environments where the sacredness of life is upheld and loved ones are protected from the ravages of excess. Temperance here is not cold austerity but a vibrant discipline rooted in love and respect for the body and soul. It is an invitation to view the consumption of alcohol not as an end in itself but as a theological reflection of stewardship, over ourselves, our communities, and the gifts bestowed by the Creator. This stewardship challenges believers to be mindful of the weight carried by daily choices, to recognize the potent symbolism encoded in every shared cup, and to approach drinking with humility and accountability.

This future perspective also opens space for the stories and voices that have long been marginalized or misunderstood within our faith communities. Contemporary Baptist voices, often rooted in personal testimony, demonstrate the spectrum of experiences surrounding alcohol, from those who find moderation in wine as a source of fellowship and joy, to those who abstain as an expression of sanctification or as protection from past wounds. These narratives remind us that the theological discourse is not purely academic but profoundly personal, touching on human fragility, cultural identity, and spiritual formation. By embracing this diversity, the community grows resilient, learning to listen deeply and respond with compassion. The future beckons us to cultivate a broader empathy that transcends inherited divisions and fosters profound unity.

Furthermore, looking ahead with clarity involves recognizing the cultural shifts permeating our world, where social attitudes toward alcohol are as variable and complex as scriptural interpretations themselves. Faith communities must navigate these changes not by retreating into dogma but by engaging culture critically and charitably, acknowledging both the dangers of alcohol abuse and the cultural contexts in which wine and beer have rich ritual and social significance. Baptist churches and believers are called to become bridges between the ancient vineyard of Scripture and the contemporary banquet of human experience, crafting spaces where sobriety and celebration, reverence and joy, discipline and grace meet in holy harmony.

This balanced future also demands a renewed theological humility that resists simplistic answers or moral absolutism. It calls us to recognize that no single individual or group holds all the insights necessary for perfect discernment. Instead, the collective body of Christ, with its manifold traditions and perspectives, must journey together, bearing one another's burdens and learning from each other's strengths and struggles. This ecclesial humility leads to respectful conversation rather than judgment, building relationships not on division but on shared commitment to God's kingdom values. Looking ahead is not merely about resolving disputes over alcohol consumption but about modeling the gospel's radical love that breaks down walls and welcomes all seekers into community.

Moreover, this horizon is illuminated by a renewed appreciation of the spiritual disciplines that undergird temperance, prayer, fasting, reflection, and accountability. These practices empower believers to navigate the complexities of daily life with wisdom and grace, helping to discern when to embrace joy and when to exercise restraint. They remind us that boundaries around alcohol are ultimately about loving God and neighbor, not imposing arbitrary rules. Keeping faith at the center nurtures a posture of gratitude for God's creation, including the gift of fermentation, and fosters a mindful presence in every moment, mindful of how each choice impacts body, mind, and spirit.

At this crossroads, joy emerges not as a fleeting indulgence but as a holistic experience that celebrates life's abundant blessings in all their forms. The Bible's rich imagery of vineyards and festal tables invites believers into a joyful spirituality that does not shun earthly pleasures but rejoices in God's good gifts when received with thankful hearts and disciplined minds. This joy is a sacred fruit of faith, blossoming in those who live balanced lives, rooted in divine grace, nourished by community, and seasoned with sober celebration. It is this deeper joy that holds the promise of a future where faith and fermentation coexist without fear or shame but with hope and peace.

Finally, to move forward with hope and clarity is to embrace a call to witness. In a world often marred by addiction, polarization, and misunderstanding, believers who embody this balanced approach become beacons of light, testifying to the possibility of living faithfully amid complexity. Their lives become fresh parables echoing with biblical themes but lived in contemporary contexts, bringing healing to those struggling with alcohol-related challenges and offering wisdom to those seeking joyous fellowship. By modeling temperance infused with grace, by sharing stories that transcend stereotypes, and by fostering dialogue that bridges divides, the church fulfills its mission to be a witness to God's reconciling love in all spheres of life.

Embracing the future in this way invites every reader into an ongoing journey where faith guides the heart's choices around alcohol with both discipline and delight. It challenges us to attend carefully to the fruits of the Spirit, self-control, love, patience, and to perceive, in the everyday act of sharing a drink or abstaining, a sacred opportunity to reflect God's holiness and grace. May we walk forward not in fear or judgment but with reverent hearts, discerning minds, and joyful spirits, ever mindful that faith and fermentation, held in harmonious balance, can enrich our lives, our communities, and our testimonies to God's enduring goodness.